D0148674

TOWN AND COUNTRY UNDER FASCISM

Town and Country under Fascism

The Transformation of Brescia 1915–1926

ALICE A. KELIKIAN

CLARENDON PRESS · OXFORD
1986

Oxford University Press, Walton Street, Oxford OX2 6DP

Oxford New York Toronto
Delhi Bombay Calcutta Madras Karachi
Kuala Lumpur Singapore Hong Kong Tokyo
Nairobi Dar es Salaam Cape Town
Melbourne Auckland
and associated companies in
Beirut Berlin Ibadan Nicosia

Oxford is a trade mark of Oxford University Press

Published in the United States
by Oxford University Press, New York

British Library Cataloguing in Publication Data

Kelikian, Alice A.
Town and country under Fascism: the
transformation of Brescia 1915–1926.
1. Fascism—Italy—Brescia—History
I. Title
320.5'33'094526   DG571
ISBN 0-19-821970-9

Library of Congress Cataloging in Publication Data

Kelikian, Alice A.
Town and country under fascism.
Bibliography: p.
Includes index.
1. Brescia (Italy)—Politics and government.
2. Fascism—Italy—Brescia.   3. Italy—Politics and
government—1915–1922.   4. Italy—Politics and
government—1922–1945   I. Title.
DG975.B85K44 1986   945'.26   86-808
ISBN 0-19-821970-9

Set by Joshua Associates Ltd, Oxford
Printed in Great Britain
at the University Printing House, Oxford
by David Stanford
Printer to the University

TO MY MOTHER
AND TO THE MEMORY OF
MY FATHER

Acknowledgements

MANY people have lent a hand in the course of completing this work. Adrian Lyttelton, my teacher and friend, deserves special mention. He directed my studies at Oxford and cheered on my researches from Bologna. Senator Noberto Bobbio gave invaluable advice and encouragement during the initial stages of the project. I also owe thanks to Stefano Merli, who offered scholarly support and warm hospitality during my stay in Milan. At Brescia, Sandro Fontana, Don Antonio Fappani, and Luigi Micheletti helped locate sources and hunt down clues. In addition, I received some useful information from an interview with the late Alfredo Giarratana. The manuscript benefited from careful readings by Rudolph Binion, Anthony Cardoza, Paul Corner, Alexander De Grand, Steven Hahn, Arno Mayer, Roland Sarti, Stephen Schuker, and David Wasserstein.

I gratefully acknowledge the assistance of Mario Missori and Giovanna Tossati at the Archivio Centrale dello Stato in Rome, and the welcome of Gian Paolo Gandolfo at Italsider in Genoa. Many thanks as well to the staffs of the other splendid institutions, listed in the bibliography, whose documents I have consulted. Gianni Bonardi of Brescia took the time and trouble to place at my disposal his family's papers. The Fondazione Luigi Einaudi, the Istituto Italiano per gli Studi Storici, the National Endowment for the Humanities, and Smith College helped finance research. A grant of leave from Brandeis University allowed me to prepare this book in its final form.

Contents

Abbreviations

UCL	Unione Cattolica del Lavoro
	(Catholic Union of Labour)
UIL	Unione Italiana del Lavoro
	(Italian Union of Labour)
USI	Unione Sindacale Italiana
	(Italian Syndicalist Union)
Confindustria	Confederazione Generale dell'Industria Italiana
	(CGII, General Confederation of Italian Industry)
Federterra	Federazione Nazionale di Lavoratori della Terra
	(National Federation of Agricultural Labourers)

Introduction

'How the country came to be so well irrigated is a question', ruminated Arthur Young as he travelled through Brescia on 18 October 1789 in a dung cart with two local merchants, who never stopped muttering paternosters and counting beads.[1] Such compulsive worship perplexed the English apostle of *la grande culture*, for prayers could 'neither dig canals nor make cheese'. Incantation and innovation, antithetical though they might seem to the foreign eye, in fact created an active mercantile civilization embracing all varieties of productive activity and social life. The mixing of old ways and new, of order and change, gave development a special dynamic in the Lombard province. A century later, growth there still reflected an uneasy equilibrium between progress and tradition. By the eve of World War I, this precarious balance characterized the Italian economy as a whole.

Christian belief did not preclude commercial prosperity. The Brescians adapted to new economic conditions over the course of the nineteenth century, but they did so in ways that protected their vested interests. Local conditions bore witness to striking variations in patterns of settlement and quality of life. In the foothills, where the church taught co-operative farming techniques, subsistence producers became involved in cash exchange through archaic patronage networks. Basin dairy and grain estates, both early outposts of specialized commodity culture, showed signs of class antagonism in the capitalist mould. Gunsmiths, who had long produced their wares for export, stayed isolated in the uplands, while silk manufacturers proliferated on the high ground. Artisans, schoolmasters, and traders crowded the capital city.

National unification changed this provincial panorama, primarily in political terms. The church-state conflict made civic life more acrimonious, and ideologies imported from abroad gained currency among local élites. Those urban democrats who had little enthusiasm for the new monarch nevertheless delighted in defying the papacy.

[1] A. Young, *Travels in France and Italy During the Years 1787, 1788 and 1789* (London, 1915), p. 245.

Progressive landlords, on the other hand, might have used the name of the Vatican to strengthen the prerogatives of property in the secular sphere. The Holy Penitentiary's *non expedit*, in any case, kept obedient Catholics away from the polls and hid the numerical weakness of liberalism in the hinterland. Agrarian support of the new government hinged upon a rather limited construction of central power in the rural backwaters, and that arrangement continued as an administrative reality until World War I. So long as suffrage remained limited and mass participation inhibited, private claimants from both town and country turned public authority to their own advantage.

While the loose integration of local notables and central government persisted throughout the Giolittian period, the rural regions of Northern Italy did not remain insulated from the incursion of capitalist values into agricultural enterprise. A growing commercial community on the periphery laid the basis for economic development. Rural manufacture, specialized farming, and demographic pressure spurred the dynamism of entrepreneurship in Lombardy and in Piedmont. Though public investment and protective tariffs stimulated and sustained activity in the producer goods sector, expansion of both domestic and export markets took place generally outside the sphere of official intervention. The regime in Rome may have distorted the pattern of industrialization on the peninsula, but it could not claim credit for the surge of optimism at the turn of the century.

Despite government ambitions to support those industrial sectors which would complement the drive for national self-assertion, the function of state stimulation in the market-place remained unclear until 1915. During the war mobilization, public and private domains overlapped: the state moved from passive compliance with the old power bloc to more active intervention by regulating output, distributing resources, and mediating social conflict. Moreover, the rapid and disorderly expansion in capital goods production gave birth to a military-industrial compact free from democratic controls. The centralized bureaucracy that emerged habitually circumvented parliament, taxing the tenuous structures of liberal governance after the armistice.

The Great War also displaced the broad network of agricultural and manufacturing interests upon which the liberal state had rested. Collective bargaining during the industrial mobilization represented a breakthrough for trade union organization and social legislation. Labour in the cities and throughout the farmlands united under the banner of socialism; the Italian working class transcended the realm of traditional community to awaken to mass party politics. And although at first some conservative stalwarts seemed unwilling to forsake their earlier independence, both urban and rural élites abandoned outdated strategies with a view to maintaining social privilege and economic position. In the resulting impasse of post-war government, fascism provided the popular basis for political consensus without democratization. By playing town against country in the seizure of power, the blackshirts managed to exploit parliamentary frailty in the capital and civic fragmentation in the provinces. Mussolini redefined the contours of the old equilibrium between industry and agriculture by imposing a hierarchical reordering.

This book examines the relationship between an economy geared towards military procurement and the flight to fascism after the cessation of hostilities. It focuses upon the gradual evolutions and the radical changes in government and society which reached a peak on the peninsula during the decade following intervention. The study seeks to explain the political consequences of industrial development under the impact of war in a key manufacturing centre of Lombardy. In 1915, Brescia typified an infant commercial community shifting the locus of productive activity from a rural to an urban environment. The province proved no cradle for business reaction, nor did it generate a sophisticated workers' movement. But the intrigues of the socialist party, the tenacity of popular Catholicism, and the growing pains of native enterprise belie our traditional assumptions about the post-war crisis. The account here describes much more than a simple struggle between terrified capitalists and the rebellious masses. A fundamental hypothesis underlying my research is that World War I changed the role and the domain of the administrative state while it mobilized a previously divided labour force. Both developments placed demands on government that liberalism failed to fulfil.

Not only did the terms of social conflict change dramatically, but transformed élites emerged from traditional sectors to dominate the modified relationship between state and society. Certain businessmen survived the wartime overhaul and helped erode the autarky of the provincial economy, while other entrepreneurs fell victim to concentration and the growth of cartels. My work examines how initiatives from Rome affected producers in the provinces. Even in a major manufacturing zone like Brescia, fascism gained electoral strength by exploiting the reaction of employers in the countryside. The expansion

of an acquisitive commercial community in farming led to social instability during the immediate post-war period. This book studies the
ways in which dictatorship altered the developmental rhythms of agriculture and industry by the imposition of political controls.

The social heterogeneity, geographic dispersion, and political
allegiances of the Brescian population made the seizure of power by
the blackshirts a slow and intermittent process. The vitality of the
Catholic lay movement, the strength of socialism among the urban
working class, and the broad appeal of the veterans' association in the
hill country circumscribed attempts to consolidate a mass following.
Augusto Turati, the local fascist boss, took on an imposing task when
he set out to convert the industrial proletariat. The presence of strong
neighbouring chieftains complicated the story. With Gabriele
D'Annunzio residing at Gardone, Pietro Capoferri in Bergamo,
Antonio Arrivabene in Mantua, and Roberto Farinacci in Cremona,
Turati had to carve his own niche. And he did so using the convenient
cachet of the party corporations in engineering and steel. Tensions
distancing Rome from the provinces, which were translated into
conflict between the government and the paramilitary arm of the
movement, muddled the objectives of the future PNF secretary right
up to the fascist metallurgical strike of 1925.

This microhistorical study of one province draws attention to the
persisting complexity of social conflicts on the peninsula during the
1920s. It underscores the inadequacy of simple models, whether
formulated by those who point to a 'Prussian road' to capitalism, or
those who see in the fascists the progenitors of 'developmental
dictatorship'. The 1887 tariff alliance between the industrialists of the
North and the landowners of the South did not, as Antonio Gramsci
and Emilio Sereni have suggested, anticipate the class configuration
of Mussolini's regime.[2] Nor could totalitarian rule deliver a 'messianic
belief system' comparable to Leninism and Maoism, in the interests of
modernization and technology.[3] The structure of Lombard society,

---

[2] On the parallelism between industrial expansion and parliamentary decay in liberal
Italy, see A. Gramsci, *Selections from the Prison Notebooks* (London, 1971), pp. 55-102;
E. Sereni, *Il capitalismo nelle campagne (1860-1900)* (Turin, 1968); N. Tranfaglia, *Dallo
stato liberale al regime fascista: Problemi e ricerche* (Milan, 1975), pp. 15-17; G. Are, 'Alla
ricerca di una filosofia dell'industrializzazione nella cultura economica e nei
programmi politici in Italia dopo l'unità', in G. Mori (ed.), *L'industrializzazione in Italia
(1861-1900)* (Bologna, 1977), pp. 171-86.

[3] A. J. Gregor, *Italian Fascism and Developmental Dictatorship* (Princeton, 1979), pp. 306,
319-34.

and indeed that of Italy as a whole, derives more from traditional divisions and the particular character of the national polity than from any imported ideology. The legacy of old governing coalitions, the limits on growth placed by nature, and the stratification of peasant society impeded progress along the lines of foreign examples. In the eighteenth century, Oliver Goldsmith acutely observed: 'Had Caesar or Cromwell exchanged countries, the one might have been a sergeant, and the other an exciseman'.[4]

[4] O. Goldsmith, *Essays* (London, 1766), pp. 3-4.

I

Silk, Steel, and Society

GEOGRAPHY, wrote the young lawyer Giuseppe Zanardelli in 1857, inclined his native Brescia to an idyllic self-sufficiency.[1] With the economic and the physical contrasts of the peninsula compressed into some 4,700 square kilometres, local folk could limit their horizons and markets to the natural boundaries of their home ground. Hemmed in by the Alps to the north and by Lakes Garda and Iseo on either side, the Brescian panorama did indeed encompass the foremost landscapes of upper Italy. Its mountain range, though less spectacular than the heights of the Swiss or the Tyrolean frontier, stored the industrial treasure of the eastern Lombard community, iron ore. In the rugged country an impoverished peasantry toiled in closed proximity to forges, foundries, and furnaces. Workshops nestled along the numerous waterways of this broken terrain, and pastoral activity included animal husbandry and subsistence farming. Below the sub-alpine zone stretched the hill region, where garden cultivation and consumer manufacture reinforced each other. Despite the great want of water and the intense demographic pressure, growers in this mulberry district prospered so long as the silk trade stayed alive. The agricultural riches of the province, however, lay in the lowlands bordering the Po basin zones of Mantua and Cremona. Industry figured very little in the economic life of the plains, since the vast expanse of fertile fields was devoted to the production of commercial crops on large holdings.

Against the geographic diversity of its environs stood the apparent uniformity of the provincial capital. Streets intersected at right angles in the rectilinear city, and visitors encountered small piazzas and few porticoes. Zanardelli celebrated the austere harmony of stone and slate, for it reflected a civic identity not rooted in a worn-out past but tied to a promising future. Unlike the tradition-bound façades of the

---

[1] G. Zanardelli, *Notizie naturali, industriali ed artistiche della provincia di Brescia (Lettere pubblicate nel 1857 sul Giornale 'Il Crepuscolo')* (Brescia, 1904), pp. 25-8.

great Italian cities, Brescia's clean buildings, tidy shop-fronts, and orderly business centre looked decidedly modern and bourgeois.[2]

While the linear regularity of the cityscape dated back to Roman times, Brescia did have a middle-class tone about it. The administrative and market town had not yet, to be sure, grown into an industrial metropolis. In 1862 little over 40,000 residents, almost one-tenth of the provincial number, could be counted within its limits.[3] An 1867 survey estimated the manufacturing population at about a quarter of the inhabitants, a proportion second only to Milan.[4] These operatives were hardly proletarians. Half produced consumer goods on a small scale, especially clothes and leather, and the metal trades remained completely artisan. Brescia also boasted the highest per capita concentration of professionals on the peninsula, with Turin trailing close behind. And most of the educators in the province were urban dwellers, making the municipality the largest cluster of schoolteachers in the nation. Farming contributed to the Brescian economy by stimulating commerce, but it did not affect the occupational structure of the community. Apart from some absentee landowners residing near Piazza della Loggia, few townspeople earned their livelihood from the land, and the processing of foodstuffs accounted for only a fraction of those employed in manufacturing concerns. Social geography thus mirrored the physical contrasts between the provincial capital and its hinterland: the sleepy centre became a *petit-bourgeois* enclave with major industrial and agricultural activity dispersed on the periphery.

Topography and Economy in Nineteenth-Century Brescia

Economic opportunity lay outside the city limits. Access to ore and timber brought Brescia's renowned mining and metallurgical concerns to the mountains that cover half the province. Dispersed throughout the Trompia, Camonica, and Sabbia valleys, the upland ironworks had their heyday in the eighteenth century, when there were ninety-seven mines and whole forests could be felled for fuel. But the local forges consumed wood voraciously until supplies declined. The severity of the shortage, coupled with the emergence of Carinthian competition, hampered charcoal-burning enterprises and related industries. During the years of Napoleonic domination, only

---

[2] Ibid., p. 321.
[3] Camera di Commercio e Industria di Brescia, *L'economia bresciana (Struttura economica della provincia di Brescia)*, vol. i, fasc. 1 (Brescia, 1927), pp. 139-41.
[4] *L'Italia economica nel 1873* (Rome, 1874), pp. 139-42.

five mines stayed in operation, of which four disappeared after the Restoration. With a labour force of 1,830, iron manufacture had been reduced to six blast furnaces, ninety-four workshops, and two foundries by 1825.[5] Even so, on the eve of national unification, the Brescians still managed to turn out a yearly average of 5,200 tons of cast iron, over 40 per cent of Lombardy's total output.[6]

Producing some 40,000 rifles a year for the military and for customers in the Levant, the mountain gunsmiths enjoyed their zenith during the days of French rule.[7] Located in the Val Trompia, seventy-six workshops with 546 operatives continued manufacture after Napoleon's collapse despite barriers placed on their export business, thanks to a standing order from Franz I and a thriving home market.[8] When war came in 1848, 5,000 gun barrels left the province each month, most of them for Vienna. But when peace returned, Franz Joseph clamped down on the production of firearms in Lombardy-Venetia.[9] The new emperor's policy forced the age-old industry into decline. From 1853 to 1855 the gunsmiths made a few hundred barrels. Even after the Austrians relaxed controls yearly output peaked at only 12,000.[10] Small wonder that manufacturers in the area so staunchly supported the nationalist cause.

Yet the Brescians fared no better under the tricolour. The gun-shops prepared to produce firearms again but had trouble finding a clientele. The government in Turin snubbed the Lombards, distributing most of its contracts to Piedmontese firms instead. A few operators, though, did do business with the Italian state. Francesco Glisenti, the only steel-founder on the peninsula, furnished rifles for the national guard.[11] He also exported weaponry to the French army, unlike the majority of Val Trompia owners, who lost their competitive

[5] K. R. Greenfield, *Economics and Liberalism in the Risorgimento: A Study of Nationalism in Lombardy, 1814–1848* (Baltimore, 1934), pp. 106–7.

[6] F. Facchini, *Alle origini di Brescia industriale: Insediamenti produttivi e composizione di classe dall'Unità al 1911* (Brescia, 1980), p. 30; B. Caizzi, *L'economia lombarda durante la Restaurazione (1814–1859)* (Milan, 1972), p 154.

[7] C. Cocchetti, 'Brescia e sua provincia', in C. Cantù (ed.), *Grande illustrazione del Lombardo-Veneto*, vol. iii (Milan, 1858), p. 228.

[8] K. R. Greenfield, *Economics and Liberalism in the Risorgimento*, p. 107; 230 of these worked in the foundries. For Austrian restrictions on Brescian exports see B. Caizzi, *L'economia lombarda durante la Restaurazione*, p. 172.

[9] G. Zanardelli, *Notizie naturali, industriali ed artistiche*, p. 104.

[10] B. Caizzi, *Storia dell'industria italiana dal XVIII secolo ai giorni nostri* (Turin, 1965), p. 254; C. Cocchetti, 'Brescia e sua provincia', p. 229.

[11] P. Maestri, *L'Italia economica nel 1868* (Florence, 1868), p. 254.

edge on the continental market to Belgian industry. The first decades of national unity found charcoal-burning enterprise hard hit too. The appearance of coal as a fuel replacing wood ended the locational advantage of the upland ironworks.[12] With chemical and hydraulic resources yet to be tapped, proximity to transport rather than isolation near a forest was at a premium. The move of Italian metallurgy from the mountains in the second half of the nineteenth century coincided with the expansion of the capital goods sector in steel. Cast-iron production in Brescia slumped, dropping from 4,400 tons in 1881 to 2,150 five years later. Crude iron and steel output, by contrast, increased by 38 per cent over the same period, as industrial activity began to descend towards the city.[13]

But more than just administrative partiality, foreign competition, and new fuel destroyed the prospects for time-honoured industry in the province. The entrepreneurs of Brescia had a bad reputation. One contemporary complained that poor commercial spirit, limited outlook, and timid capital bore the chief responsibility for the erratic nature of economic development in the area.[14] Apart from a few pioneers such as Glisenti, Beretta, and Gnutti, the bulk of manufacturers were strictly small-time. Some preferred to survive on the brink rather than expand their family-based operations. Other companies proved no match for bigger outfits near Milan producing milder steels and they shut up shop once improved transport ended their commercial seclusion. The antediluvian methods used at the mountain ironworks appalled Zanardelli. He also deplored conditions at the archaic refineries and primitive mines. A number of workers looked only seven or eight years of age, 'embodiments of impotence and illness'.[15] Most came from homesteads nearby and returned there late in the day to cultivate crops.

This double life does not appear to have bothered management much. Indeed, the prudent employer preferred the rural recruit. Efficiency perhaps suffered, one local booster conceded, but in relative terms the moonlighter gave better value: the hardy peasant, who grew his own food and had a household to fall back on, could

---

[12] B. Caizzi, *L'economia lombarda durante la Restaurazione*, pp. 153-8.

[13] F. Facchini, *Alle origini di Brescia industriale*, pp. 9-10; M. Bonardi, *Il ferro bresciano* (Brescia, 1889); G. Scagnetti, *La siderurgia in Italia* (Rome, 1923), pp. 166-70.

[14] *Atti della Giunta per l'Inchiesta agraria e sulle condizioni della classe agricola*, vol. vi, fasc. 2 (Rome, 1882), p. 295.

[15] G. Zanardelli, *Notizie naturali, industriali ed artistiche*, pp. 89-90.

afford to accept lower wages.[16] One arms manufacturer, ignorant about economies of scale, pointed to the simple formula of hard work and government protection to stimulate business.[17] The pistol magnate Pietro Beretta, known for his modernity, installed his fifteen-year-old Giuseppe in the factory as a junior apprentice and made the boy climb the ladder to the top. The vast majority of Val Trompia's fifty-odd gunsmiths employed no more than six operatives each, and the family firms maintained high labour-fixed capital ratios even in larger shops.[18] The iron and steel establishments ranged from small to middling in size as well.[19] More than half the metallurgical concerns in the country were concentrated in the province during 1887, but local production accounted for merely 7 per cent of Italy's total output.[20] Triggered by tariff war, credit-inspired inflation, and agricultural crisis, the slump of the late 1880s hit heavy industry in Brescia with particular severity.

Like mining and metallurgy, sericulture and silk manufacture shared a geographical propinquity. Although Brescian foothills occupied only one-fifth of the provincial landscape, the green belt surrounding the city became the most active district of indigenous entrepreneurship over the course of the nineteenth century. As mulberry cultivation pushed south to the high ground during the last years of Napoleonic rule, reeling mills began to cram the hilly terrain. Averaging six open-fire heaters each, 942 of these tiny silk-winding shops dotted the countryside in 1845.[21] Mulberry plantations abounded by the middle of the century, since peasants added the trees to their mixture of crops and sold cocoons for cash exchange. Starting in the 1850s, however, pebrine and flaccidity ravaged the silkworms of the North. Disease decimated silk culture and commerce throughout the province. In 1856 there were 687 filature mills and by 1876 just 400 had managed to stay afloat.[22] Yet the crisis that nearly obliterated the industry from local economic life also transformed it by encouraging

---

[16] G. Robecchi, *L'industria del ferro in Italia e l'officina Glisenti a Carcina* (Milan, 1868), pp. 8-9.

[17] *Atti del Comitato dell'inchiesta industriale*, Categoria 15/4, Armi (Rome, 1874), pp. 1-3.

[18] P. Maestri, *L'Italia economica nel 1870* (Florence, 1871), pp. 205-6; M. Cominazzi, *Cenni sulla fabbrica d'armi di Gardone di Valtrompia* (Brescia, 1861).

[19] G. Luscia, 'Sulla proposta di una Società Anonima Bresciana per l'industria del ferro in Valtrompia', in *Commentari dell'Ateneo di Brescia*, 1865-1868, pp. 69-72.

[20] A. Frumento, *Imprese lombarde nella storia della siderurgia italiana: Il contributo dei Falck*, vol. i (Milan, 1952), p. 192; F. Facchini, *Alle origini di Brescia industriale*, p. 41.

[21] C. Cocchetti, 'Brescia e sua provincia', p. 233.

[22] B. Benedini, 'Industria e commerci', in *Brixia* (Brescia, 1882), p. 437.

concentration, and the importation of Japanese eggs helped breeders in the area to recover from the catastrophe by 1881. A decade later steam-powered factories had replaced backward reeling enterprises. Employing over 4,500 women and children, the mills had been reduced to a seventh of their 1876 number, but units of production increased fivefold. Silk-twisting for the export of warps and wefts underwent a notable expansion after those difficult years. The eighty-seven throwing mills in business during 1856 shrank to twenty-eight by 1890, while the number of spindles jumped from 12,291 to 55,336. Almost 3,000 operatives worked in the yarn branch of manufacture.[23]

Based on imported raw material, cotton-spinning was slow to take hold in Brescia. Local entrepreneurs, preferring to invest in home-grown silk, stayed away from the young field of manufacture, so both stimulus and capital for the industry came from outside. A Swiss financier opened the first cotton manufactory in 1837 with no fewer than 1,500 spindles, and a decade later another plant appeared on the edge of the city with triple that number. Finally, during the first years of protective tariffs, real progress could be seen when eight more firms, largely from Milan and Switzerland, set up shop in the hills. By 1890 the sector claimed 43,300 spindles and 477 looms as well as a work-force of 1,171.[24] The wool trade predated cotton and silk in the province but lagged behind both at the time of unification. The ninety blanket firms that used to provide winter employment for some 2,200 peasants until 1848 had swindled to a mere fifteen by 1856.[25] Specializing in luxury linens, the Bellandi textile company in the basin village of Pralboino also dabbled in woollen bedcovers and carpets; its employees worked outside their own homes, apart from the weavers stationed in the plant.[26] In 1890 a Swiss-owned factory opened in the low foothills, and the Lanificio di Gavardo's success was extraordinary. Starting out with 12,000 spindles, it doubled them by the turn of the century to become the third largest spinner of wool in Italy.[27]

[23] Ministero di Agricoltura, Industria, e Commercio, Direzione Generale della Statistica, *Notizie sulle condizione industriali della provincia di Brescia* (Rome, 1892), pp. 52-3.

[24] Ibid., p. 77; A. Giarratana, 'L'industria nei secoli XIX e XX', in *Storia di Brescia*, vol. iv (Brescia, 1964), pp. 1018-19; T. Spini, *Niggeler e Kupfer S.p.A.: Filatura e tessitura di cotone (1876-1963)* (Bergamo, 1963).

[25] C. Cocchetti, 'Brescia e sua provincia', p. 233.

[26] K. R. Greenfield, *Economics and Liberalism in the Risorgimento*, pp. 125-6.

[27] A. Giarratana, *L'industria bresciana ed i suoi uomini negli ultimi 50 anni* (Brescia, 1957), p. 90; Camera di Commercio e Industria di Brescia, *L'economia bresciana*, vol. ii, fasc. 1, pp. 121-8.

Despite this expansive atmosphere in textiles, small and medium-sized businesses continued to populate most other branches of consumer manufacture. Traditional handicrafts held on to their markets and resisted stagnation. The tanning of Alpine hides occupied 268 men in twenty-three shops during the last years of the Restoration, and by 1890 the tanners numbered 388, divided among thirty-eight firms with unchanged methods of production. The old paper works continued to operate along time-worn lines for decades. The thirty-five mills that employed about 650 labourers in 1856 grew to include forty-one shops and a work-force of 1,480 by 1881. Yet manual technique still dominated the industry: only two continuous paper machines existed in the province. Nearly 2,000 workers held jobs at 760 local grain mills, and 527 outfits in other areas of food processing engaged 1,190 more. Two new industries stood apart from this preponderance of petty enterprise. Backed by a staff of 342 women, four modern factories prospered in 1890 to make the hillside town of Palazzolo on the Oglio river the peninsula's button capital.[28] And by 1900 Brescia's three hosiery plants with 330 female workers gave way to mechanization.[29]

Industrialization slowly proceeded along rural lines. A 1903 survey showed 25,370 people, less than 5 per cent of the provincial population, in employment at the 3,103 manufacturing concerns of Brescia.[30] Most of these shops were not based in the metropolis but scattered throughout the lower mountain and foothill valleys. Though demographic pressure from the 1880s on brought the aggregation of new people in the city suburbs, urban opportunity remained slight for the recent migrants.[31] In 1900 even the capital goods sector drew the bulk of its manpower from the countryside. Peasant women and children toiled in textile mills, while small farmers sought industrial employment to supplement meagre returns from the land. The overlap of the agricultural and manufacturing labour supply kept the divide

[28] F. Ghidotti, *Palazzolo 1890: Notizie sull'agricoltura, l'industria e il commercio e sulle condizioni fisiche, morali, intellettuali, economiche della popolazione* (Palazzolo sull'Oglio, 1969).

[29] A. De Maddalena, 'L'economia bresciana nei secoli XIX e XX', in *Storia di Brescia*, vol. iv (Brescia, 1964), pp. 570-4; F. Facchini, *Alle origini di Brescia industriale*, pp. 62, 74-6.

[30] Ministero di Agricoltura, Industria e Commercio, Direzione Generale della Statistica, *Statistica industriale: Riassunto delle notizie sulle condizioni industriali del Regno*, vol. ii (Rome, 1905), pp. 60-7.

[31] A. Bettoni, 'Condizioni demografico-sanitarie del comune di Brescia in rapporto all'abitato urbano', in *Commentari dell'Ateneo di Brescia*, 1911, pp. 48-50; between 1881 and 1911, the inner city grew from 40,121 inhabitants to 46,131, while the suburban population increased from 17,015 to 36,514.

between cultivator, artisan, and worker hazy well into the twentieth century.

Agriculture somehow sustained the population. The soil, by and large, was ungenerous. Bordering the provinces of Sondrio and Trent, the mountainous zone extended over 2,514 square kilometres of barren forest, summer pasture, and marginal farmland. The foothills accounted for just 903 square kilometres but claimed the densest population. There, pressure on the land was immense and the over-worked plots, subject to severe erosion, produced inadequate yields. The plains alone, measuring 1,304 square kilometres near the confines of Mantua and Cremona, presented a more promising picture.

With woodlands occupying over 40 per cent of the steep slopes, physical features militated against farming activity in the mountains. Timber and cattle represented important sources of income, but a tendency towards self-sufficiency limited the output and marketing of other goods. As in most systems of open-field agriculture, technique remained primitive and centred around the hoe and sickle. Living conditions in the stone huts were precarious at best. Cereals, chest-nuts, potatoes, pigs, and sheep formed the basis of the subsistence economy. Maize constituted the main food of all rural dwellers, and one investigator estimated that peasant consumption of corn-meal porridge added up to about two kilograms daily for the average adult male.[32]

Peasant proprietorship prevailed in the provincial uplands. Small-holders owned and operated four-fifths of the arable surface, though their farms averaged under two hectares. Due to the almost uniform size of these miniscule lots, homestead advocates hailed the subalpine settlement as a stable and egalitarian agrarian community. The social conservatism and Catholic piety of its self-reliant farmers struck Christian reformers, who marvelled at the extraordinary labour spent on terrace cultivation. But land ownership and economic independence were far from being associated, and survival came to depend upon municipal control of ever-contracting wilderness. Escape from poverty during a bad season proved difficult for even the most enter-prising peasant. Many hill people had to work on the valley estates of others in order to get by. After the 1870s agricultural distress accentuated the plight of the highlander who scratched a living from a marginal plot, for the tiny allotments could no longer feed a rising

---

[32] O. Cavalleri, *Il movimento operaio e contadino nel Bresciano (1878–1903)* (Rome, 1973), p. 41; *Atti della Giunta per l'Inchiesta agraria*, pp. 257-60.

population. With declining local industry unable to absorb the growing surplus of hands, seasonal and permanent migration appeared the only alternatives to the miserable simplicity of the mountain commonwealth.[33]

A more variegated portrait emerged of the foothills and high ground which linked the provinces of Verona and Bergamo. The diversity of terrain and climate in the green tier below the mountains led to chequered patterns of tenure and considerable gradations of wealth. Farms ranged from one to 150 hectares, but half the cultivated surface was divided into holdings of less than ten hectares. Size did not necessarily reflect the quality of the soil. In the lakeside district of Salò alone, 1880 real-estate values ran from 500 to 2,000 lire per hectare, and both the cheapest and most expensive plots measured under five hectares.[34] Extreme poverty coexisted with landed affluence in the crowded zone.

Spared much of the woods and most of the pasture that circumscribed agriculture in the back country, the hill region retained a larger share of land for cultivation. While summer hailstorms and droughts took their toll of harvests, the extensive use of the spade in place of the plough doubled yields to bring forth an array of products. Silkworms and wine grapes made up the main cash crops, but the soil also nourished cereals, lemons, olives, vegetables, and livestock. Direct management accounted for over a third of the arable surface, though the richest estates were entrusted to farm agents supervising a permanent staff of employees.[35] Sharecroppers bulked large throughout the foothills, and in the rocky country surrounding the provincial capital small leaseholders could be found.[36]

The terms of *mezzadria* differed from valley to valley in the disseminated hillside settlements, according to local custom and soil quality, but the landlord in this share tenancy arrangement always provided living quarters, an integrated farm, and half the seed. He also paid taxes, reimbursed the sharecroppers for improvements,

[33] G. Rosa, *Le condizioni economiche-morali dell'agricoltura bresciana* (Milan, 1878), pp. 19-20; W. H. Beauclerk, *Rural Italy* (London, 1888), pp. 166-75; see also D. Brentano, *La vita di un comune montano* (Brescia, 1934).

[34] *Atti della Giunta per l'Inchiesta agraria*, pp. 458-9, 673-6.

[35] Camera di Commercio e Industria di Brescia, *L'economia bresciana*, vol. i, fasc. 2, p. 235.

[36] B. Benedini, *Terra e agricoltori nel circondario di Brescia* (Brescia, 1881), pp. 151-7; G. Medici, *Rapporti fra proprietà, impresa e mano d'opera nell'agricoltura italiana: Lombardia* (Rome, 1932). pp. 70-1; C. Bonato, *L'economia agraria della Lombardia* (Milan, 1952), pp. 152-3.

sometimes furnished the oxen, and reserved the right to charge rent should male tenants peddle their labour elsewhere. Proprietors retained control over farming operations and could enforce an annual amortization of accounts. The peasant household comprised the primary productive unit with all members engaged in cultivation, so family size and solidarity assumed a special significance. The intense cohesion of these patriarchal circles limited activities off the farm but ensured subsistence on it. In addition to the services of his kin, the *mezzadro* supplied the tools, the remaining seed, and usually the draught animals. Most contracts divided the crops down the middle, but exceptions to equal distribution were frequent in the more prosperous zones. One popular variation left the peasant with a third of the take. Some wine growers near the Garda lake received half the goods only during bad years, landlords keeping two-thirds of a bountiful harvest.[37] And involvement in staple production did not usually entail market contact for the cultivator. Silk and grapes went straight to the master who, serving as a middleman, would later return a portion of the profits in cash.[38]

All this tenant isolation and landlord control indubitably made for social stability, but agricultural reformers questioned the economic logic of the *mezzadria* contract. Advocating specialized cultivation under direct management, critics attributed low productivity and a poor mixture of crops to self-sufficient farming on subdivided holdings. Concern for subsistence, however, did not prevent progress. The existing agrarian structure could adapt itself to new demands, as it did when the proliferation of mulberry trees during the first half of the nineteenth century placed the sharecropper somewhere between commercial and household enterprise. Far from eliminating the customary form of tenure, the advance of staple agriculture bolstered sharecropping by increasing the profitability of the arrangement. Sericulture allowed foothill proprietors to assume a market orientation without their resorting to wage labour and left age-old notions of hierarchy and authority unchallenged. Peasants still focused on satisfying their own needs, but exchange supplemented home consumption. Providing an additional source of income, the silk trade invigorated the family economy. Not only did farmers produce the commodity in the form of cocoons, but women reeled thread in the evenings and

---

[37] *Atti della Giunta per l'Inchiesta agraria*, p. 465.
[38] W. H. Beauclerk, *Rural Italy*, p. 179; S. Jacini, *La proprietà fondiaria e le popolazioni agricole in Lombardia* (Milan, 1856), p. 262.

girls looked for opportunities in the mills. Cheap rural help kept local textiles competitive. As long as it lasted, the silk boom brought an unusual degree of harmony to traditional property relations. Landlords made money with little risk of compromising their role as peasant patrons, and tenants could share in manufacturing activity while keeping their ties to the land intact.[39]

Sound reason, not peasant routine, steered the farming population away from monoculture. Mulberry and vine cultivation may have brought new life to rural communities, yet they also made farmers vulnerable to an economic downturn. Blight struck these two sources of agricultural wealth in the middle of the century. When it lifted, silk-growers had to contend with oriental competition while local viticulture never recaptured the initiative. Retreat from the market-place, more than the spread of commercial relations as such, first strained share tenancy after unification. Croppers viewed staple production as a means to acquire material comfort and money for land purchase, but they relied upon the security of diversified yields to feed the family. Owners showed greater interest in economic gain, and the search for profit led them to pursue a tougher line. With debts no longer settled through the sale of cocoons and grapes, proprietors felt less disposed to part with working capital or to give cash advances, and many tried to shift the expense of improvement to the cultivator. But peasants most often held the plots on yearly leases, so threats of eviction made them conservative. The onset of depression in the 1880s, coupled with increased state taxation, heightened antagonism between the two contracting parties. As the *mezzadria* system began to unravel, conflict and coercion came to replace partnership and paternalism.[40]

On the wane in the provincial basin, sharecropping represented only 6 per cent of the cultivated surface there. Leaseholders populated two-thirds of the arable land, half of them on plots measuring over fifty hectares. The fecundity of the plain depended upon a web of canals, ditches, and sluices fed by the Alpine rivers and lakes. Scarcity of water predisposed the vast level of monotonous landscape to large holdings, for the maintenance of the widely spaced farms required considerable outlays of capital. Artificial irrigation and elaborate crop

[39] E. M. Cesaresco, *Lombard Studies* (New York, 1902), pp. 193, 196-7; see also L. Cafagna, 'La "rivoluzione agraria" in Lombardia', in *Annali dell'Istituto Giangiacomo Feltrinelli* (Milan, 1959), pp. 425-6.

[40] A. Lyttelton, 'Landlords, Peasants and the Limits of Liberalism', in John Davis (ed.), *Gramsci and Italy's Passive Revolution* (London, 1979), pp. 116-20.

rotations, ranging from four- to eight-year cycles, combined to produce forage, maize, wheat, flax, and mulberries in the western and central zones, and the manure of dairy cattle replenished the clover fields. Such intense cultivation of varied crops did not extend to the drier tracts of the eastern plain near Mantua, where the commercial production of grain prevailed.[41]

Some proprietors in the basin lived in the countryside, but left the business of farm administration to an overseer. During the latter half of the nineteenth century, however, the prosperity of lowland agriculture increasingly came to rest in the hands of substantial tenants. The practice of letting an estate as a single unit to a rural entrepreneur created a small yet powerful class of renters in the zone. Most of these market-orientated farmers came from peasant stock, many of them starting out as modest stewards in the plains of Cremona, Milan, and Pavia. Despite their humble origins, the outsiders grew to command a good deal of money and expertise, which they applied to the land. Secure tenures allowed the ambitious leaseholders to manage the property as their own. Contracts were long, running from nine to eighteen years, with twelve years as the most common duration. The landlord appointed an engineer or agent to regulate all ground and hydraulic improvements and would reimburse the tenant for betterment at the end of the term. Annual rent oscillated from 120 to 200 lire per hectare, depending on the extent of irrigation, but the lessee required working capital three times that amount to realize a profit.[42]

In the basin the estate agent became the most privileged member of the farm staff, superintending field operations and labour relations in his employer's absence. The flock of peasant specialists who cared for livestock also exercised considerable authority over unskilled help. The trained foremen lived well. A share of the harvest supplemented their wages. The master, moreover, fed, quartered, and clothed them. Others in permanent employment processed dry crops and moved from one task to another as the seasonal demand for manual labour required. While these fixed-salary workers got paid in cash and kind too, they received no rations and instead cultivated the marginal plots allotted to them.

[41] Camera di Commercio e Industria di Brescia, *L'economia bresciana*, vol. ii, fasc. 2, pp. 22-3, 239; G. Medici, *Rapporti fra proprietà, impresa e mano d'opera*, p. 102.

[42] G. Rosa, *Le condizioni economiche-morali*, pp. 21-2; ACS, Min. Agricoltura, Inchiesta parlamentare, b. 11, fasc. 123, D. Codignola, *Memoria sull'organismo agrario del circondario di Verolanuova* (manuscript source for the Jacini inquiry, 1879), p. 126.

Both categories of dependent labour enjoyed the security of year-round occupation, but not all those engaged in agriculture could find permanent employment. With hordes of rural workers descending from the highlands seasonally, farmers relied on casual help during the peak months. The migrant circuit was the lowest a peasant might sink short of begging. Hungry mountaineers, petty holders, and evicted tenants, driven by the pressure of need from one field to the next, had little affection for the land they cropped. The duration of work was brief, usually lasting through the summer, and the pay poor. Living conditions bordered on the threshold of survival. Trying to subsist on as little as possible, the harvesters camped out in squat, earthen-floored huts or huddled alongside cattle in a stable. The unhygienic dwellings even made a local doctor squeamish when he saw 'the young, the ragged, the naked, and the snotty' sleeping on stacks of damp hay and piles of dried manure.[43] Disease, parasites, and excrement suffused the foul shelters. Almost every meal consisted of polenta cooked from cheap, mildewed autumn maize. While this frugal diet may have staved off starvation, it brought on another scourge. Pellagra, a symptom of extreme poverty, was rampant throughout the plains: in the central basin district of Verolanuova, it afflicted 6 per cent of the inhabitants.[44] Leading to madness and death, pellagra became the perennial malady of the landless.

During the winter not all migrants headed for home. Between 1861 and 1901 the provincial population rose from 433,236 to 538,427, but the overcrowded countryside could not accommodate the expanding human surplus.[45] Four communes in the eastern plains doubled in density once reclamation work got under way, and forgotten lowland hamlets turned into shanty towns as the reservoir of casual labour continued to expand. The superfluity of unemployed hands kept agricultural pay scales down. The 1895 daily wage of field workers, for example, averaged almost 10 per cent below the going rate in 1881, which had been a crisis period for all of Italy.[46] Some peasants simply left the continent to escape the harshness of rural life; after 1875 transatlantic emigration began to increase steadily. Others fled to the

[43] Ibid., p. 138.

[44] W. H. Beauclerk, *Rural Italy*, pp. 190-1.

[45] Istituto Centrale di Statistica, *Comuni e loro popolazione ai censimenti dal 1861 al 1951* (Rome, 1960), pp. 98-106; Camera di Commercio e Industria di Brescia, *L'economia bresciana*, vol. ii, fasc. 2, pp. 153-8.

[46] P. Albertario, *I salari agricoli nelle zone ad economia capitalistica della Bassa Lombarda nel cinquantennio 1880-1930* (Pavia, 1930), p. 227.

provincial capital in search of jobs. During the economic trials of the
1880s, thousands departed for the city, which grew to 70,614 inhabitants in 1901 and 83,338 a decade later. The rush to town, however, brought little security to the wandering poor. Urbanization
preceded industrialization by a good many years, and Brescia
attracted more transients than it could absorb. Floating from construction sites in the spring to farms in the basin at harvest, the rustics
continued to lead a nomadic existence. Even those in permanent
employment stayed on the fringes of the local economy. Women
sought positions as domestics, while men looked to unskilled service
and building trades. Housing patterns accentuated their occupational
segregation. Concentrated in the suburbs, where food and lodging
cost less, the newcomers lived outside the old walls, and the civic
world remained a mystery to them. Notwithstanding the massive
influx of people from the hinterland, the impact of the alien numbers
on the social composition of the inner city was slight. As the nineteenth century drew to a close, the urban community appeared as
impenetrable as ever to the impoverished residents of its outskirts.[47]

A Political Profile of the Old Order

Under the old Austrian regime, the provincial aristocracy and the
church hierarchy dominated the proprietary class of Brescia, but the
French occupation of 1796 brought with it a host of reforms that transformed the complexion of the rural élite. As elsewhere in Napoleonic
Italy, the sale of ecclesiastical domains and the abolition of entails,
trusts, and primogeniture activated the local land market, allowing
men of substance if not title to acquire holdings. During the first
decades of the nineteenth century, country merchants and urban
entrepreneurs sought to consecrate their movable wealth through the
purchase of real estate. While a few of the large fiefs in the plain
managed to retain their juridical autonomy until unification, the
proliferation of smaller holdings in place of the great demesnes
accompanied the final suppression of feudal rights for most of the
province.[48] This land transfer proved difficult to abrogate after the
defeat of Bonaparte. The slow alienation of the commons to private
owners continued under the Restoration governments. In the wine-

[47] Istituto Centrale di Statistica, *Comuni e loro popolazione*, pp. 98-101; A. Bettoni,
'Condizioni demografico-sanitarie', pp. 48-82.
[48] C. Magni, *Il tramonto del feudo lombardo* (Milan, 1937), pp. 234-9; L. Ostiani, 'I
feudatari e i buli', in *Commentari dell'Ateneo di Brescia*, 1887, pp. 8-9.

growing districts of the hills and high ground about a third of the property again changed hands when phylloxera forced many a farmer to sell out to buyers from the city.[49]

Though the advance of bourgeois ownership seemed to betoken an end to traditional patterns of power and prestige, the titled keepers of the agrarian order did not stand in the way of land redistribution during French rule. A small clique of feudatories, most of whom belonged to the Venetian patriciate, resented the loss of seigneurial rights and remained loyal to the Habsburg monarchy. But the majority of lesser notables applauded Napoleon and embraced his reforms. Anxious to break the monopoly of office enjoyed by their rarefied brethren, progressive blue-bloods and scions of secondary families gained political sway under the kingdom of Italy and found investment opportunities in the sale of state property. Together with the old aristocrats and the large freeholders of the third estate, the intermediate noblemen made up the rural élite of the modern period.[50]

When it ceased to be a caste of feudal office-holders indifferent to country life, the landed establishment broadened its social base and developed a new cohesion. As property instead of privilege came to represent the foundation of rural authority, the lower ranges of the provincial ruling class acquired the local influence once exercised by a handful of inbred clans. Unlike the absentee grandees with little interest in their vast holdings, the younger breed was a working nobility that stayed close to the land. Active in community affairs and concerned about farming techniques, these agrarians sought to restore aristocratic legitimacy through enlightened proprietorship. At the Athenaeum of Brescia they would discuss the latest methods of production. Some took their message to a wider audience. Count Lodovico Bettoni opened an institute of horticulture to promote the growing of garden crops; another inspired gentleman at Orzivecchi set up a school to teach stewards efficient management. The fortunes of silk during the Restoration gave landlords the confidence to step out of the confines of agriculture and into the world of manufacture. Not only did they extend the area of cultivation devoted to the staple on their estates, but many built reeling mills alongside mulberry groves to

[49] E. M. Cesaresco, *Lombard Studies*, pp. 220-1; see also F. Della Peruta, *Democrazia e socialismo nel Risorgimento* (Rome, 1965), p. 43.

[50] U. Da Como, *La repubblica bresciana* (Bologna, 1926), pp. 41-9, 355-63; C. Cocchetti, 'Brescia e sua provincia', pp. 159-67.

process fibre for export. No longer purveyors of a patrician past, the landowning élite took their wares to the market.[51]

The improving proprietors ventured into public pursuits as well. They supported the Piedmontese Count Camillo Cavour in his campaign for national unification under a constitutional monarchy. Self-interest informed their creed of unity and liberation. With the defence of private property as the doctrinal foundation of the moderate programme, their vision of the common good had its limitations. Like other rural notables in the upper half of the peninsula, the Brescian landlords saw in the Risorgimento a movement that would ensure their continued preponderance in government while at the same time eliminating all obstacles to free trade and commercial expansion. Eager to create a modern economy unencumbered by regional jurisdiction, they none the less refused to abandon the recognized hierarchy of traditional society. During the first decade and a half of independence, prominent agrarians went on to play a guiding role in the political life of the new nation. Their leadership carried the penalty of a legal system based on status and standing. Property requirements restricted suffrage to 2.7 per cent of the provincial population. The new oligarchs dominated the electoral lists; the leverage possessed by these men over the land and labour markets prolonged the persistence of local liberties.[52]

Safe constituencies may have permitted agrarian moderates to pose in parliament as the representatives of the people, but the true spokesmen for the rural masses at home remained the clergy. The Risorgimento tested popular piety in the countryside only to reveal its strength. Papal intransigence became a thorn in the side of Italy's liberal architects, and the hostile presence of Catholicism after unification loosened the hegemony of the landowning élite. Superior in social influence to secular authority, the church did more than keep the faith. Besides administering the rites of passage, it touched the everyday concerns of the village community through pastoral, educational, and welfare work. The values preached by the clerics reflected the mores of the landed upper classes: the peasant learned the virtues of obedience at the altar as well as on the estate. The priest taught deference and professed paternalism just like the proprietor, but political circumstances and material conditions brought him

[51] E. M. Cesaresco, *Lombard Studies*, pp. 220-1; *Atti del Comitato dell'inchiesta industriale*, Categoria 6/1, Trattura della seta (Rome, 1873), p. 4.
[52] R. Chiarini, *Politica e società nella Brescia zanardelliana* (Milan, 1973), pp. 258, 285-7.

closer to the congregation. Estranged from officialdom after 1860, he could side with the impoverished cultivator against government exactions. And in contrast to the urban ecclesiastics recruited from the minor nobility, he was normally a man of modest means whose low standard of living, like that of his parishioners, offered no protection against pellagra. As traditional property relations became increasingly depersonalized during the late nineteenth century, the country curate more than the liberal landlord sheltered the flock from the alien forces of the market and the state.[53]

The church-state conflict weakened the internal cohesion of the agrarian leadership, since not all men of property so easily abandoned their friends at the Vatican. Count Luigi Martinengo, a papal loyalist from the oldest patrician family of Brescia, worked with ecclesiastical authority to establish a clerical party through lay associations. Andrea Maj, another rural notable who also presided over the board of the Banca San Paolo, sought to reunite the priest and the proprietor in their roles as peasant patrons. In 1878 he began to give financial support to a Catholic mutual aid society in the basin commune of Travagliato, where he served as mayor for many years. Subsidizing the organization's pension and sickness programmes, this socially conscious grandee wanted to rescue the helpless cultivator from the clutches of 'certain large landlords ... who use agents and managers to drain every last drop of peasant blood'.[54] Maj himself never used impersonal middlemen on his demesne, and he urged fellow employers to put their Christian principles into practice and treat hired hands like part of the family. With Luigi Cottinelli, board member of the Credito Agrario Bresciano bank, he founded an agricultural school at Bornato to educate the small farmer. A few estate owners even looked to Leo XIII's encyclical *Rerum Novarum* for illumination. They introduced collective leaseholding to discourage the rack-renting of marginal plots. Securities from sympathetic credit institutions allowed teams of tenants to work large units for private profit and to pool marketing facilities. By the turn of the century, the provincial clergy administered some forty-six co-operative banks to aid active parishioners in land purchase. The political and economic power represented by such important financial connections made the

[53] O. Cavalleri, *Il movimento operaio e contadino*, pp. 241-56; E. M. Cesaresco, *Lombard Studies*, pp. 211-12; M. Rossi, *Le origini del partito cattolico* (Rome, 1977), pp. 8-12.
[54] For Maj's letter to Professor Toniolo see O. Cavalleri, *Il movimento operaio e contadino*, pp. 668-9.

clerical cause a force to be reckoned with in those parts of the country-side where a conversion to wage labour had been resisted.[55]

The dilemma of the agrarian moderates emerged most clearly during the great agricultural crisis in the last decades of the nineteenth century. The slump destroyed the premises upon which the free-trade liberalism of landlords had been based. Following a generation of steady rises, wheat prices began their descent in 1880 because of cheaper foreign competition. When the same fate befell other sectors of the rural economy, proprietors lost their fascination with the workings of international markets and switched over to the protectionist camp. The world depression also witnessed the first socialist inroads among the dispossessed peasantry in the Lombard and Emilian lowlands, where deteriorating conditions on capitalist estates caused wage labourers to take to collective action in lieu of Christian co-operation. The June strike that brought farming activity to a standstill in basin villages during 1882 alerted Brescian employers to the social costs of commercial relations. Though calm returned to the sleepy countryside after this isolated incident, the labour troubles of their neighbours in Mantua and Cremona prompted landowners to put aside religious differences and present a united front in the form of clerical-moderate electoral coalitions. However useful as a political cement, this reconciliation exposed the crudity of the 'liberty with order' campaign. After demands for government repression replaced a *laissez-faire* stance on the question of public security, fear for property was all that remained of liberalism on the periphery.[56]

Beside the conservative coalition in the countryside stood a progressive alliance of professionals, entrepreneurs, and artisans from the capital and minor manufacturing centres in the uplands. Veterans of the Giovine Italia movement and the Brescia insurrection of 1849, the democrats became the standard-bearers of Mazzinian patriotism. They too saw politics in economic terms, and their formula for material prosperity did not differ greatly from the early agrarian programme. Optimistic about Italy's ability to compete internationally, the radical publicists wanted to liberate industrial resources from haphazard exploitation by expanding communication systems,

---

[55] Ibid., pp. 322-33; L. G. Fabbri, 'Crescita e natura delle Casse Rurali Cattoliche', in *Quaderni Storici*, vol. xii (1977), pp. 789-803.

[56] *La Provincia di Brescia*, 22 and 23 June 1882; L. Preti, *Le lotte agrarie nella valle padana* (Turin, 1955), pp. 92-5; C. Seton-Watson, *Italy from Liberalism to Fascism: 1870-1925* (London, 1967), pp. 95-6.

improving banking facilities, and encouraging private investment. Denouncing protectionism as regionalism, these free-traders had faith that commerce, credit, and capitalism would carry their country into the orbit of the advanced economies. They looked to education instead of religion to win over the masses; enlightenment, not super-stition, would create an intellectual climate conducive to market advance and institutional reform. Unlike the pious rural merchants of the province, of whom Arthur Young had despaired, the urban middle classes which rallied to the national cause opposed the church and its claims to temporal power. When the notables of the hinterland moved closer to the clergy during the 1880s, their bourgeois rivals in town turned hostility to clericalism into something of an obsession.

The oligarchy of moderate counts who went to Rome as deputies more than met their match in the lawyer intelligentsia representing the protests of the parvenus in parliament. The formidable Zanardelli, a famous jurist and eloquent orator who later served as prime minister, led the progressive opposition. So strong was his hold on municipal government by the end of the century that opponents in the chamber referred to the city as his fief.[57] Very much the left liberals' man, Zanardelli enjoyed a solid constituency in his home town. Although he became a partisan of Mazzini in 1848, his republicanism had vanished by 1859, but he stayed an unflinching irredentist as well as an orthodox champion of economic individualism.[58] He made a religion of anticlericalism: his abortive divorce bill shocked associates in parliament. Despite his reputation as Italy's cleanest politician, Zanardelli had clienteles. When news broke of his nomination as minister of public works in the Depretis government of 1876, popular enthusiasm radiated throughout the villages of the Val Trompia, with both arms manufacturers and their employees confident that 'justice' would finally visit local industry. Long concerned that his ill-connected province counted less than 100 kilometres of train track within its borders, Zanardelli managed to commission the construc-tion of two new lines during his second month in office. Steel producers in the area also lobbied for a third line to breach the moun-tains for Trent, but their man in the ministry, pulling against conser-vative resistance, could not oblige them.[59]

[57] G. Giolitti, *Memoirs of My Life* (New York, 1973), p. 60; G. Carocci, *Agostino Depretis e la politica interna italiana dal 1876 al 1887* (Turin, 1955), p. 609.
[58] E. Ondei, *Giuseppe Zanardelli e un trentennio di storia italiana* (Brescia, 1954), pp. 30-3.
[59] R. Chiarini, *Politica e società*, pp. 16-17, 50-60.

The democratic left attempted to capture the loyalties of the lower classes, but a gulf remained between the well-to-do leadership and the populace it sought to galvanize. The radicals countered ecclesiastical charity with subsidized self-help. Resurrecting Mazzinian associationism to cover the cracks in their social base, sympathizers of the progressive opposition gathered in an assembly at the Brescia chamber of commerce in 1860 to found a voluntary mutual benefit society. Created 'for purely philanthropic reasons', this was no proletarian organization.[60] About 300 artisans, operatives, and shopkeepers shared in its insurance schemes, and the presence of a hundred honorary members, who paid the running expenses, gave it a tinge of employer paternalism and patronal intrigue. Ambiguity abounded on the issue of republicanism, since the rank and file rejected the ideological orientation of their benefactors. When the directorate proposed sending money to Mazzini in exile, the workers refused, claiming that they needed it more. In 1870 the group declared itself interested in neither politics nor religion, just mutuality; Mazzini, appalled by the distinction, resigned from the board soon after. Notwithstanding such indifference, Zanardellian canvassers combed the province for recruits to their friendly societies, which by 1880 numbered sixty-three. All were benevolent clubs, though the subscription fee and job requirement kept away the poor and the unemployed. Few of these fraternities enrolled peasants. The urban organizers tried to penetrate agricultural terrain, but sharecroppers converted three brotherhoods into Catholic circles at the suggestion of the local clergy. In one hamlet villagers showed reluctance to join at the first mention of dues, and the Leno league collapsed because of alleged mishandling of funds. Clerical absolutism still reigned supreme in the countryside.[61]

The radicals advocated electoral reform to shift the provincial balance of power, and the national collapse of the right gave them the opportunity to legislate for change. Aided by the abstention of church supporters in the general election, the left scored a stunning victory in 1876 after sixteen years in opposition: nine of the ten deputies returned to Rome ran on the Zanardellian ticket, with the industrial magnate Glisenti upsetting the agrarian leader Count Bettoni. The

[60] O. Cavalleri, *Il movimento operaio e contadino*, pp. 96-7, 103.

[61] Ibid., pp. 108-15, 254-8; B. Benedini, 'De'contratti agrari e della condizione dei lavoratori del suolo nel circondario di Brescia', in *Commentari dell'Ateneo di Brescia*, 1882, pp. 62-3.

papal prohibition, however, did not apply to municipal elections, and democratic forces now saw their chance to enfranchise the *petit-bourgeois* plurality in urban zones as a counterpoise to the Catholic reserve on the periphery. The centrepiece of the 'parliamentary revolution' launched by the Depretis government was a suffrage bill that became law in 1882. Ostensibly designed to make politicians more representative of the people, it came to little more than an instrument to impose the anticlericalism of the city on the voting population of the country. A number of republicans, who had the mutual benefit societies behind them, did hope to extend the franchise to all, but most in the progressive coalition refused to consider any arrangement that would give the peasantry a public voice. Threatened by the persistence of religious loyalties in village life, middle-class reformers wished to conceal their numerical weakness outside the town. Conservatives insisted on the concomitance of property and political rights, and fear of the 'fanatic' rural masses led 'enlightened' legislators to accept this traditional premise, although the minimum property qualification decreased and could be substituted by a certificate of primary education. The enactment increased the electorate to include 10 per cent of Brescia's inhabitants, and 55 per cent of the new voters gained eligibility with their elementary school degrees.[62] Justifying the rule of an informed élite over the primitive rustics in the hinterland, Zanardelli would later call the suffrage battle 'one of the sweetest memories of my life'.[63]

Electoral reform did broaden the base of the provincial ruling class to the advantage of progressive townspeople, yet the half-hearted legislation could not save the left from internal divisions or guarantee it a popular following. Demonstrating the poverty of a secular alternative in a Catholic country, the attack on the church did more harm than good. The intensity of sentiment against religion alienated many a respectable citizen and strengthened the resolve of the conservative coalition. The anticlerical crusade united various democratic groupings in the franchise fight, but when the struggle ended old fissures reappeared. The militant republicans who had pushed for universal suffrage resented the sacrifice of principle for power, while the political ignorance and apathy of the lower middle class made for an unsteady allegiance. Also, the emergence of a workers' party in 1882

---

[62] Istituto Centrale di Statistica e Ministero per la Costituente, *Compendio delle statistiche elettorali italiane dal 1848 al 1934*, vol. i (Rome, 1946), pp. 18-23.

[63] R. Chiarini, *Politica e società*, pp. 263-331.

challenged the radicals' role as protectors of the proletariat. Under the tutelage of the newly formed Partito Operaio in Milan, labourers of Brescia started to reject the leadership of bourgeois parliamentarians and convert their mutual aid associations into 'societies of resistance'. As the economic crisis of the eighties brought rising unemployment and falling wages, these embryonic trade unions parted with their liberal benefactors to raise the banner of socialism.[64]

The continental depression that disengaged labour from the progressive ranks also tried the loyalties of the native business community. Based on a salutary vision of Italy's future as an advanced economy, the free-trade enthusiasm of local industry wore thin with the onset of recession. Brescian industrialists first described their discontents as a defence of the individualist tradition: government hampered private enterprise by underwriting uncompetitive concerns. When the slump deepened, provincial steel producers busied themselves in pressing for high tariffs. The benefits of customs barriers did not appear so axiomatic to the arms manufacturers, who stood to suffer from the steep cost of domestic metals, yet the lawyer politicians they put in office abandoned *laissez-faire* idealism to establish a favourable balance of trade and reduce the dangerous level of unemployment. After the triumph of protectionism in 1887, liberalism boiled down to little more than the bourgeois heresy of anticlericalism.[65]

Proponents of nineteenth-century liberalism wished to bring Italy into the family of industrial powers. Influenced by parallels abroad, the reformers of the middle decades felt that the mobility of money, goods, and ideas would cut a road to modernity through the backwater of peasant routine, undercapitalized enterprise, and primitive belief. This widespread commitment to commercial expansion and free trade joined élites from both town and country in the business of unification. Guided by profit as well as by principle, the local heroes of the Risorgimento looked forward to a domestic market and overseas opportunities untrammelled by restrictions from Vienna. Economic individualism acquired a new mystique. With the Austrian villains out, indigenous investment and initiative could harness the waterways

[64] On the Partito Operaio see R. Del Carria, *Proletari senza rivoluzione*, vol. i (Milan, 1970). pp. 218-20; G. Manacorda, *Il movimento operaio italiano attraverso i suoi congressi: Dalle origini alla formazione del Partito Socialista (1853–1892)* (Rome, 1952).

[65] *La Provincia di Brescia*, 5 August 1876; on protectionist ideology, see S. Lanaro, *Nazione e lavoro: Saggio sulla cultura borghese in Italia 1870–1925* (Venice, 1979), pp. 163-202.

of the province and transform Brescia into another Lowell, Massachusetts; released from import prohibitions on the continent, the silk boom would turn the Lombard town into a second Lyons.[66] As they led the people to material improvement, moderate and progressive spokesmen intended to remain the diviners of the general will. Political contests seemed irrelevant in their vision of a respected and affluent nation. Modifying the basis for their continued rule in the name of economy, optimistic notables saw no need to overhaul the established hierarchy of the old order.

Deferential social relations and customary values could not build the foundations of a mature commercial culture. But over against the force of tradition lay structural factors beyond the control of the best-intentioned patriots. Instability of world markets combined with the deficiency of natural resources to rule out development along the lines of foreign precedents. When the great depression destroyed prosperity and endangered property, threatened interests turned to government for social action and tariff protection. While arch-conservatives sought to repress internal dissent at the very time that progressive leaders wanted to rectify domestic injustice, both placed new emphasis on state intervention to achieve their ends. In a country where steady demographic growth surpassed the quirky rate of production, the desperation of the people and apprehension of employers defeated democratization on the European model. Even as the recession began to lift in the last years of the century, high food prices and low wages brought disturbances throughout the peninsula. Governments in power could only respond by launching a constitutional devolution. With the suppression of workers' associations and the contraction of the electoral register in 1894, the liberal graft showed signs of rejection on Italian soil.[67]

The problem of social unrest remained intractable. Labour troubles continued to haunt the Italian business community despite official reaction. At Brescia eleven strikes escaped erratic government repression between 1894 and 1897, until one textile manufacturer, in the absence of adequate state assistance, took matters into his own hands and called a lock-out which lasted over two months.[68] Not very far away in Milan, an 1898 outbreak of bread rioting that authorities mistook for organized revolution brought down the conservative

---

[66] G. Zanardelli, *Notizie naturali, industriali ed artistiche*, pp. 75, 112-31.

[67] G. Candeloro, *Storia dell'Italia moderna*, vol. vi (Milan, 1974), pp. 424-38.

[68] O. Cavalleri, *Il movimento operario e contadino*, pp. 578-80.

regime of the Marquis di Rudinì, whereupon a caretaker ministry under General Pelloux further compromised civil liberties in an effort to restore public order.[69] The military commander believed that a coercion bill widening executive prerogatives, reviving powers of banishment, and limiting freedom of the press would eliminate the vices of participatory democracy. In the process of expropriating the apparatus and appearance of legality, he also consolidated the forces of opposition. The general, who lost the confidence of parliament, resigned in 1900, but not without having revealed the authoritarian tendencies of the feeble administrative system. Aversion to popular contention stayed as the political legacy of the nineteenth century.[70]

The Rise and Fall of Giolittian Liberalism

By all appearances the economic development of Italy entered a period of unaccustomed perpetuity during the first years of the twentieth century. The two decades between the trough of continental depression and the eve of World War I saw industrial output double and investment treble. Sericulture quickly recovered from the slump as a result of favourable trade conditions, though an expanded and mechanized silk industry lost its prodigious place in the Lombard commercial community to the manufacture of an imported fibre. Fuelled by the hydroelectric power of the Alpine rivers, the fabrication of cotton yarns and cloths soon overtook that of other textiles in the conquest of the home market, forcing linen into a final decline. New public subsidies coupled with old tariffs to encourage the growth of iron and steel, despite the absence of cheap coal, but the emergence of an engineering sector in the North redressed the balance in favour of more competitive concerns. While the high cost of domestic metals seemed to weigh against machine, tool, and motor enterprise on the peninsula, the technically advanced railway shops and mechanical plants before long produced for foreign customers as well as satisfying internal demand. By the side of this dynamic and unprotected branch of metalworking were promising departures in light industry, with chemicals and cement leading the way.[71]

Enduring prosperity still depended upon the country's main source

---

[69] On the Milan rising see L. Tilly, 'I fatti di Maggio: The Working Class of Milan and the Rebellion of 1898', in R. Bezucha (ed.), *Modern European Social History* (Lexington, 1972), pp. 124-58.

[70] B. King and T. Okey, *Italy To-Day* (London, 1901), pp. 88-109; M. Neufeld, *Italy: School for Awakening Countries* (Ithaca, 1961), pp. 219-22.

of human capital and natural wealth, the land. The chronic malaise of poor harvests and summer droughts prolonged the recession in agriculture, and protected wheat could not keep pace with the consumption needs of a growing urban population, even during good years. Grain prices rose at a time when the purchasing power of the rural masses stayed slight, yet the government did not see fit to develop a coherent policy, which might have relieved the resulting social and regional imbalances. Tariff incentives, lower taxes, and easy credit promoted the cultivation of commercial crops, but private investment tended to amplify existing profit rather than exploit neglected resources in impoverished zones. Significant improvement was largely confined to the classic irrigated plains of Lombardy and Emilia, where reclamation works and artificial fertilizers yielded immediate returns. Traditionally depressed areas remained backward. Like the contrasts between town and country, the disparate rates of change which distinguished rich, careful culture from infertile, forbidding scrub kept Italian development uneven and halting, the national public fragmented and poor.[72]

Whatever its limitations in stimulating the economy as a whole, industrial expansion did provide a sympathetic ambience for the emergence of an updated brand of transformist governance. The cabinet formed by Zanardelli in 1901 marked a break with the authoritarian regimes of the depression, which had appealed to force. An advocate of stability through reform and renovation, the statesman from Brescia refused to circumvent or suspend constitutional guarantees in the pursuit of social peace. The masses had to be prodded away from extremist courses by responsible persuasion in the place of blind repression. Confused reaction, he believed, violated the Risorgimento beliefs in liberty and law to expose an already vulnerable democracy to revolution. Zanardelli's hostility to clericalism and distance from socialism, however, doomed him as a relict of another century, and instead the new minister of the interior came to personify the disinterested liberalism of 1900. Giovanni Giolitti, who went on to assume the premiership in 1903 and rule Italy for more than a decade, was a pragmatic politician with little patience for legal purism or

[71] R. Romeo, *Breve storia della grande industria in Italia 1861–1961* (Rocca San Casciano, 1974), pp. 65-114; A. Gerschenkron, *Economic Backwardness in Historical Perspective* (Cambridge, Mass., 1966), pp. 74-6.

[72] V. Castronovo, 'La storia economica', in *Storia d'Italia*, vol. iv, part I (Turin, 1975), pp. 187-9; E. Sereni, *Capitalismo e mercato nazionale in Italia* (Rome, 1966), pp. 3-41; E. Corbino, *Annali dell'economia italiana*, vol. v (Città del Castello, 1938), pp. 78-9.

tiresome passion. He did not intend to eliminate corruption in the chamber, but rather to extend it to those with electoral strengths outside the old establishment. In an attempt to broaden popular acquiescence to state authority, he courted Catholics and socialists alike and offered their leaders a share of the spoils. Giolitti went beyond the contrivances of his clientele to secure the blessings of organized labour. He turned official toleration into a party game. By insisting on public neutrality in trade disputes, recognizing the legitimacy of union representation, and subsidizing the co-operative movement, this manipulator of parliamentary majorities planned to bring a domesticated working-class community into the democratic fold.[73]

The overpopulated and underemployed countryside first tested the government's policies of conciliation. When an end to legal persecution and the beginning of economic revival led to an upsurge of labour militancy, the grievances of the agricultural proletariat found expression once again. Soon after agrarian moderates surrendered their long-standing monopoly over provincial administration to a triumphant alliance of democrats and socialists, rural employers briefly lost control of their estates.[74] During the spring and summer of 1901, close to 5,000 dependent labourers and casual farm hands participated in a series of strikes which broke out in twenty-eight villages.[75] Determined to resist the offence to private property, landlords demanded public assistance in suppressing the peasants. No one would respond to their call. Instead of dispatching troops to clear the fields, the ministry of the interior advised amicable arbitration. In all but two disputes workers successfully obtained higher wages and shorter hours. Despite their speedy victory, the dispossessed of the lowlands remained unorganized. As before, impetus came from the combative Po valley leagues, and the agitation that spread northwards by rudimentary improvisation caught local proprietors unawares. The town socialists, parochial as they were at the turn of the century, did not attempt to co-ordinate the protest of the once Catholic hinterland. Still, the contagious enthusiasms of the neighbouring basin unions gave the impression of a veritable revolution. Interpreting Giolitti's

[73] G. Carocci, *Giolitti e l'età giolittiana* (Turin, 1971), pp. 64-105; A. W. Salomone, *Italy in the Giolittian Era: Italian Democracy in the Making* (Philadelphia, 1960), pp. 42-61.

[74] G. Procacci, *La lotta di classe in Italia agli inizi del secolo XX* (Rome, 1972), pp. 77-9; P. Albertario, *I salari agricoli*, p. 207.

[75] Ministero di Agricoltura, Industria e Commercio, Direzione Generale della Statistica, *Statistica degli scioperi avvenuti nell'industria e nell'agricoltura durante l'anno 1901* (Rome, 1904), pp. 93-4.

sober impartiality as bureaucratic timidity, many notables began to disavow the liberal state, which seemed insensitive to their sufferings.[76]

The industrial population lived far from this. In 1900 textiles still represented the most advanced sector of the local economy. Silk filature returned to its 1890 level of productivity by 1903. In step with the Lombard trend, cotton manufacture tripled its output over the same period, and the size of the payroll reflected the transformation under way. In 1890 Brescia's ten shops in the branch engaged 1,175 workers. Thirteen years later the labour force had trebled to 3,521, while the number of factories increased by just five.[77] The development of electricity, itself a testimony to industrial achievement in a country without coal, mushroomed after the recession: between 1900 and 1911 local emission of hydroelectric energy multiplied more than sixfold.[78] Only classic heavy industry appeared stillborn. Because of the emergence of mining and metallurgical activity in other parts of the peninsula, provincial iron and steel took their time to convalesce. The metalworkers employed during 1903 amounted to a mere 2,755, 40 per cent below the 1890 total, and some 250 firms had been whittled down to fifty-four. But by eliminating the multitude of archaic charcoal-burning enterprises buried in the uplands, the world crisis also set the stage for the expansion of modern, large-scale operations in the suburbs surrounding the town. Finally, during the years 1905-10, Brescian steel broke out of its artisan shell.[79]

The metallurgical and engineering concerns of the province should not be dismissed as congenitally retarded, for their sluggish growth did not simply reflect poor management. Among the conservative family businessmen, there were indeed a few adventurers. Still, the most successful industrial capitalists came from outside the traditional commercial community of the town. Already in 1887 Attilio Franchi, heir to a filature dynasty in the countryside, tried to switch from silk to steel and take advantage of the power facilities under

[76] G. Giolitti, *Memoirs of My Life*, pp. 152-5; see also A. Cardoza, *Agrarian Elites and Italian Fascism: The Province of Bologna, 1901–1926* (Princeton, 1983), pp. 68-122.

[77] Ministero di Agricoltura, Industria e Commercio, Direzione Generale della Statistica, *Statistica Industriale: Riassunto delle notizie sulle condizioni industriali del Regno*, vol. ii (Rome, 1905), pp. 64-5.

[78] Camera di Commercio e Industria di Brescia, *Statistica industriale al 30 Gennaio 1911. Industrie varie* (Brescia, 1911), pp. 5-6.

[79] Camera di Commercio e Industria di Brescia, *Statistica industriale al 30 Giugno 1910. Industrie mineralurgiche, metallurgiche e mecchaniche* (Brescia, 1910), pp. 15-22; A. Gnagna, *La Provincia di Brescia e sua Esposizione: 1904* (Brescia, 1905), pp. 138-45.

construction in the zone. Hoping to install a modern rolling mill, he had to settle for a modest blast furnace because of cash constraints. Inadequate financial backing failed to carry the company through the slump, and all textile operations closed in 1896, though the Banca Commerciale of Milan bailed out the foundry with some long-term credit.[80] By 1899 Franchi had his mill to manufacture rail and trolley equipment, as well as fancy French furnaces which used oil instead of coal. His line of finished steel and pig-iron products gradually expanded until 1905, when he made a real coup and the government opened a major account. The nationalization of the railways and the consequent extension of the network revivified the sector but also set an ominous pattern of dependence on the state for local enterprise.[81]

Another city firm, the Officine Meccaniche Tubi Togni, made a fortune in land reclamation and the harnessing of Alpine rivers for electricity. Born to the 'fountain nobility' of the province, Giulio Togni, like Franchi, started as an outsider in the old industrial establishment; his father Giacomo, an artisan who designed decorative conduits, constructed many of the town's seventy-two public fountains. Young Togni never became a craftsman, but he did take the family business one step further. In 1894 he won a bid to manufacture and install new water mains for the provincial capital, and by 1905 he had moved on to produce seamless tubes and railway axles. When the firm began to dabble in rare alloys during 1906, Togni employed a work-force of nearly 1,000.[82]

Even the arms manufacturers, survivors of a distant past, showed new vigour during those expansive years. Like his father before him, Pietro Beretta entered the trade as a teenage apprentice. The inventor of the famous pistol bearing his family's name decided to branch out beyond firearms, and by 1907 he had gone on to make artillery with his own power plant. He did not break with tradition when it came to his workers, who more than tripled in number during his tenure. In 1910 Beretta operatives still received the highest wages in the valley, and the company housed 170 of its 270 employees.[83]

Another world financial crisis, however, punctured Brescia's indus-

[80] A. Confalonieri, *Banca e industria in Italia 1894–1906*, vol. iii (Milan, 1976), pp. 435-7.

[81] R. Webster, *Industrial Imperialism in Italy 1908–1915* (Berkeley, 1975), pp. 87-8; A. Giarratana, *L'industria bresciana*, pp. 48-9.

[82] *Tubi Togni. Condotti forzati 1903–1923* (Milan, 1926), pp. 2-5; *Le officine metallurgiche Togni in Brescia* (Milan, 1912).

[83] Camera di Commercio e Industria di Brescia, *Statistica Industriale al 30 Giugno 1910*, p. 25; A. Giarratana, *L'industria bresciana*, p. 68.

trial renaissance. The 1907 crash hit the fragile Italian economy especially hard, and silk received the most debilitating blow.[84] Even the modern, mechanized factories suffered catastrophic collapses from which the sector never managed to recover. By 1911 the number of spindles had been reduced to about a third the 1904 figure of 76,000, and after World War I the total did not exceed 20,000.[85] New foreign competition doubled the effect of the slump on cotton, while provincial iron and steel suffered withdrawal symptoms from rail fever. Togni's government orders trickled, but private aqueduct work provided some relief. For those like Franchi and the Giovanni Tempini, both of whom depended exclusively on high state expenditure, operations came to an abrupt halt. The single motor-car company in the district suffered the heaviest capital losses and the Bianchi lorry manufacturers, in business since 1905, went bankrupt.[86] The logical conclusion of all this uneven, feeble growth might have been rationalization and concentration, but by shouldering the burden of over-expansion, the authorities in Rome averted industrial retrenchment. Franchi, Togni, Beretta, and numerous others continued to exercise both ownership and control of their family enterprises, which military contracts salvaged for arms production in 1910. The Metallurgica Bresciana già Tempini represented the only major casualty among the local steelworks; the COMIT group stepped in with foreign partners to buy out the old proprietor.[87]

The fickle behaviour of provincial industry left its mark on the labour movement. The spread of unionism among the Brescian working class was slow and spasmodic, but hardly late by Italian standards. Modelled on similar French councils, the local Camera del Lavoro opened its doors less than a year after the 1891 creation of the parent chamber in Milan. Though managed by the socialists, the Camera did not begin as a subversive group and depended upon the municipality for free space and administrative expenses. The institution first functioned as an employment exchange, catering to the

---

[84] On the 1907 crisis see F. Bonelli, *La crisi del 1907: Una tappa dello sviluppo industriale in Italia* (Turin, 1971), pp. 164-9.

[85] Camera di Commercio ed Arti della Provincia di Brescia, *Sul progetto di un Consorzio per la tutela degli interessi serici* (Brescia, 1908), pp. 3-5; Camera di Commercio e Industria di Brescia, *L'economia bresciana*, vol. ii, fasc. 1, p. 126.

[86] Camera di Commercio e Industria di Brescia, *Costituzioni, modificazioni, scioglimenti di società* (Brescia, 1911).

[87] A. Confalonieri, *Banca e industria in Italia dalla crisi del 1907 all'agosto 1914*, vol. i (Milan, 1982), pp. 517-23.

occupational needs of the urban poor. By 1894 it had assumed an active role in the arbitration of labour disputes, and early in 1898 it started to initiate agitation against intransigent employers. Therefore, when the government declared martial law on the peninsula in the wake of the Milan riots, the organization had moved from finding jobs to dealing with strikes and fighting management.[88]

General Pelloux closed down the Camera to weaken revolutionary solidarity after the 1898 incidents, but eighteen months of clandestine activity completed the transformation of this semi-official employment agency into the militant organ of the local trade unions. Doubling its following to 1,388 workers, a radicalized chamber of labour reopened during 1900, and membership continued to grow in the more liberal climate of the Giolittian period. By 1902 some 2,983 subscribers had joined. In 1903 about 3,500 could be counted, 80 per cent of whom lived in the metropolitan area. In contrast with the final decade of the last century, which saw the bulk of twenty-five work stoppages end unfavourably for the ranks, improved economic conditions stimulated a wave of industrial action quite different from the failures of the depression years. In 1900 alone twelve strikes broke out, with all but three resolved to the advantage of the participants. During 1902 unionists won thirty-four of forty wage disputes.[89] Whatever its record as the bargaining body of the town proletariat, the Camera still could not speak for two important categories of the provincial labour force, even following its return to legality. The landless of the countryside had yet to be conquered, and associationist traditions persisted among the skilled metalworkers.

Official aid became another problem, for few of the town councillors approved of the Camera's union activities. Leaders of the clerical-moderate bloc tried to upstage the workers' council in 1900 by founding an apolitical employment exchange run by the local authorities, but after the socialists and their Zanardellian friends gained municipal control, the situation changed. Eliminating the rival Ufficio del Lavoro's funding in 1902, the new governing coalition reaffirmed the primacy of the old Camera, whose annual allowance increased fivefold. Communal approbation, however lucrative, placed labour leaders in a difficult position, and the doctrinal divergence that developed over their freedom of action adumbrated future tensions

---

[88] *Diario Guida: Brescia e Provincia* (Brescia, 1905), p. 77; see also O. Gnocchi-Viani, *Dieci Anni di Camere del Lavoro* (Bologna, 1899).

[89] O. Cavalleri, *Il movimento operaio e contadino*, pp. 192-6.

between the politicians and unionists of the Partito Socialista Italiano (PSI). The reformists who shared power in city hall welcomed the opportunity to step out of the opposition and intended public support to lend the union movement an air of bourgeois respectability. Yet the syndicalists presiding over the chamber during its hibernation wanted nothing to do with capitalist society and meant to keep their organization an instrument of class struggle. A precarious unity camouflaged conflict for a little over a year. The Camera's militant guardians accepted the municipality's label and money, using both to sustain agitation and finance propaganda, until a nationwide display of revolutionary solidarity brought troubles to the surface in 1904. Called by the syndicalists to protest against police brutality in Sicily and Sardinia, the two-day general strike that left Brescia without light or transport caught moderate socialists on the administrative junta by surprise.[90] While the September incident failed to stir the whole of the urban working class to revolt, it did succeed in alienating democratic opinion. By early October progressive liberals broke with their proletarian partners on the board, and subventions to the Camera stopped.[91]

Not only in Brescia but all over the country, discord between revolutionists and reformists reduced the strength of the socialist movement. Internecine bickering took its toll of the ranks, and a decline in strikes coincided with the start of employers' reaction. During this impasse PSI officials attempted to reimpose a measure of control over the radical chambers of labour by founding a central organization to synchronize the activities of the national trade federations and local union groupings.[92] The creation of the General Confederation of Labour (CGL) in 1906 provided institutional leverage against direct action by extremists, but the problem of political hegemony lingered. Unable to convert the lower ranges of the working class, for whom syndicalism retained an appeal, party moderates sought only to neutralize the temper of the masses.

Since the traditional divisions of the labour world proved so difficult to bridge, instead of offering to co-ordinate the Brescia Camera from Turin, the confederation gave it competition at home. Concentrating

[90] G. Savoldi, 'I primi passi del socialismo a Brescia', in *Brescia Nuova*, 30 August 1952.
[91] O. Cavalleri, *Il movimento operaio e contadino*, pp. 234-5.
[92] G. Arfé, *Storia del socialismo italiano (1892-1926)* (Turin, 1965), pp. 113-22; A. Pepe, *Storia della CGdL dalla fondazione alla guerra di Libia* (Bari, 1972), pp. 10-13, 62-76.

their efforts on the proletarian aristocracy of metalworkers, provincial spokesmen for the CGL could not draw the semi-skilled, the state-employed, or the jobless from radical courses. Only when the syndicalists seceded to form a splinter movement in 1912 did the Camera's career as an independent institution end, and even then die-hard militants managed to maintain their autonomy from the national organization.[93] The Camera's first moderate secretary, who got appointed by default, bungled the job and soon left the post, which remained vacant until 1914. Unwilling to subsidize a flaccid agency, many old members disowned their local association altogether.[94] The failures of the reformists went beyond the administration of the chamber of labour, for their unionists could not round up participants for most strikes. The CGL may have drawn its strongest following from the working-class élite, but the support of this privileged minority was by no means general: before the Great War the Italian Federation of Metalworkers (FIOM) enrolled just 16 per cent of those engaged in heavy industry.[95] After 1912 labour militancy did increase, but not under the sponsorship of CGL affiliates. Small, local disputes involving workers at one factory or village accounted for the majority of conflicts. The announcement of wage reductions and lay-offs in textiles ignited agitation by female operatives in Catholic leagues, while wildcat stoppages occurred in the numerous steel shops of the mountain valleys to protest against deteriorating conditions of work.[96] The national metallurgical federation successfully pressed for economic concessions in three strikes during 1914 and 1915, but the settlements affected no more than the employees of two companies.[97]

The geographic dispersion of the proletariat and the seismic fluctuations of the economy do much to explain the CGL's inability to mobilize the labour community of the province. The location of most factories and workshops outside the town limits made unionization complicated enough, and the gradualist tactics advocated by re-

[93] G. Savoldi, 'I primi passi del socialismo a Brescia'.

[94] ACS, Min. Interno, DGPS, Serie G1, Associazioni 1896-1897 e 1910-1934, b. 8, fasc. Camera del Lavoro, 16 May and 17 September 1913, 17 January and 23 June 1914.

[95] A. Pepe, *Storia della CGdL dalla guerra di Libia all'intervento 1911–1915* (Bari, 1971); in 1912 Brescia also reported the lowest percentage (33.8) of strike participants in all Lombardy, p. 350.

[96] M. Rossi, *Le origini del partito cattolico*, pp. 222-3; unsuccessful strike action in textiles more than halved membership in the provincial white leagues between 1910 and 1914.

[97] *La Provincia di Brescia*, 16, 21, and 23 September 1914; *Avanti!*, 16 and 20 March 1915.

formists could palliate the grievances of the working class only in conditions of full employment and high wages. But native manufacture
was still limping from the blows of 1907, and the recession deepened in
the aftermath of the Libyan War. In September 1914 the Züst automobile firm dismissed two-thirds of the 300-odd men on the payroll,
and the largest steel combine in the area threatened to fire all of its 790
employees.[98] The modernized button industry of Palazzolo suffered
from a changing export market whose ill effects had already resulted in
the liquidation of three companies. Once foreign textile business
began to fade, the pay scales of cotton and wool workers contracted;
jobs as well as salaries underwent further reductions in the silk sector.
During this period of pessimism, those engaged in chemical and
cement production alone looked forward to a small share of prosperity, thanks to growing domestic demand. Subject to such ups and
downs of industrial development, the unions were powerless to better
the material circumstances of their recruits.[99]

Notwithstanding the dejection of organized labour, the propertied
classes did not hesitate to react against the violent style of proletarian
politics. The syndicalist initiatives of 1904, as well as the agricultural
strikes which ensued a few years later, discredited Giolitti's policy of
socialist *rapprochement* when they demonstrated the insecurity of the
reformists' position. The practical premier recognized the popular
strength of religious sentiment, and he turned new attention to the
church in an attempt to establish a parliamentary balance against the
extreme left. Weaned from anticlerical demagoguery, liberalism
became more dispassionate than ever. The Vatican's relaxation of the
non expedit permitted the third ministry of the Piedmontese statesman
to rest upon a centre majority, but the active participation of papal
supporters at the polls ineluctably changed the nature of the Italian
governing system. The ultramontane presence proved especially
imposing at Brescia. There, much to the horror of the old-school
democrats in the Masonic lodge, untold votes flooded the urns during
the 1909 general elections to return seven clerical-moderates out of
eight deputies. Universal suffrage completed the massive entry of
Catholics into public life. The 1911 extension of the franchise to
uneducated commoners may have bolstered the socialists in some

[98] ACS, Presidenza del Consiglio, Prima Guerra Mondiale, fasc. 17.2, sfasc. 1,
8 August and 20 September 1914; sfasc. 4, 2 October 1914; sfasc. 6, Società Lombarda
Ligure, 4, 9, and 29 September 1914.
[99] *La Provincia di Brescia*, 5 and 8 July 1914.

urban zones of the North, but an evangelical spirit possessed the Brescian electorate, and by 1914 not one Zanardellian could be found on the administrative council of the province.[100]

The increasing turbulence of the class struggle also prompted agrarian moderates to connive with the church. For those who had counted upon state assistance to contain the advance of the socialist movement in the countryside, the syndicalist labour troubles of 1907 served as a rude awakening. When the absence of public auxiliaries forced basin farmers to accept the first collective agreement in Brescian agriculture, a number of rural entrepreneurs advocated active resistance, but more intelligent landlords preferred to promote 'professional', Christian unionism in place of the 'political', revolutionary brand.[101] Just as negotiations for a new peasant pact drew near, average per hectare yields of wheat jumped from 11.3 quintals in 1911 to reach 18.5 two years later, while grain prices stayed inflated by the import duty. The determination of proprietors to appropriate profit redoubled accordingly.[102] Inviting the confessional leagues to the bargaining table, the employers' association agreed to eliminate the more vexatious terms of tenure for sharecroppers and salaried workers, who, together with small leaseholders, made up the mass following of social Catholicism, in exchange for impunity from binding settlements at the provincial level.[103] Since the National Federation of Land Workers (Federterra), which represented the interests of unskilled farm labourers, had yet to establish itself in the Bresciano, decentralized arbitration forestalled the entrance of the socialist organization into trade disputes.

Italian labour survived the offensive of employers and the crisis of the Libyan War, but both developments distanced the socialists from the bourgeois parties of order. Neither Giolittian reform nor Catholic co-operation could restrain the working class from revolutionism, for as social conditions failed to improve, the position of the moderates within the PSI weakened. The formation of a conservative cabinet

---

[100] A. Vezzoli, *Il Partito Popolare a Brescia visto attraverso 'Il Cittadino di Brescia' (1919–1926)* (Brescia, 1966), p. 31.

[101] P. Albertario, *I salari agricoli*, pp. 201-2, 208; *La Provincia di Brescia*, 17 March 1907.

[102] Sindacato Nazionale Fascista Tecnici Agricoli, *Il frumento* (Rome, 1929); see also Ministero di Agricoltura, Industria e Commercio, Ufficio di Lavoro, *Le organizzazioni. I: Le agrarie* (Rome, 1912), p. 48; *L'Agricoltura bresciana*, 14 March 1913.

[103] Cattedra Ambulante di Agricoltura, *Patto colonico per la pianura bresciana* (Brescia, 1912); *L'Agricoltura bresciana*, 8 November 1913; *Il Contadino*, 1 February, 16 May, and 1 June 1913.

under the premiership of Antonio Salandra in March 1914 confirmed
the civic isolation of the left, and the policy of internal appeasement
pursued by progressive liberals ultimately collapsed in the so-called
'red week' during June of that year. The antimilitarist demonstrations
which caused minor disturbances at Brescia resulted in barricades
throughout Emilia and the Marches as well as in the major cities,
disclosing open hostility to the democratic state.[104] By the eve of the
world conflagration, all attempts to keep proletarian militants from
subversive action had clearly come to grief.

The Intervention Crisis

In the wake of the riotous general strike came news of the Sarejevo
assassination. As the Balkan crisis unfolded into a general European
war during the summer of 1914, the Salandra government found itself
caught in the polemical crossfire between supporters of Germany and
those of the Allies. Military unpreparedness, a cooling of relations
with Austria, and domestic instability led the prime minister to
declare Italy's neutrality in August. At first public opinion seemed to
bear out the sagacity of his decision. The socialists vociferously
opposed involvement in what appeared to be a purely imperialist
venture. Democrats and irredentists alike wanted little to do with the
dynastic ambitions of the Triple Alliance. Despite clerical deference
to the Habsburgs, Catholics too preferred to stay out of the conflict.[105]
Only spokesmen for the bellicose nationalist movement, which had
long disowned the inveterate complacency of liberal parliamentarianism, and a handful of conservative politicians advocated participation
in the campaigns of the Central Powers.[106]

The unanimity of the left disintegrated, however, after the Austrian
retreat in September, and arguments for intervention on the side of
the Entente acquired a new cogency. Democrats began to abandon
neutrality in the struggle against German imperialism; irredentists
joined nationalists to call for the rescue of unredeemed lands from the
Dual Monarchy. Although the vast majority of socialists remained
committed to pacifism, the PSI lost some of its more dynamic

[104] On 'red week' see L. Lotti, *La settimana rossa* (Florence, 1965).

[105] F. Meda, *I cattolici italiani nella prima guerra mondiale* (Verona, 1965), pp. 3-16;
B. Vigezzi, *L'Italia di fronte alla prima guerra mondiale*, vol. i (Naples, 1966), pp. 200-8, 588-
99.

[106] A. Salandra, *Italy and the Great War: From Neutrality to Intervention* (London, 1932),
pp. 75-7; A. De Grand, *The Italian Nationalist Movement and the Rise of Fascism in Italy*
(Lincoln, 1978), pp. 60-71.

members when a group of revolutionary interventionists, including the editor of the party newspaper, Benito Mussolini, repudiated the official policy of passivity. The liberal establishment continued to resist embroilment with the belligerents, but before long the demand for entry had plunged the governing class into a national debate that portended the political destiny of Italy. Apart from territorial gain, war now seemed to promise an end to the pettiness of parliamentary life and the indiscipline of social relations. A broad coalition, stretching from monarchists to syndicalists, united in antipathy to the neutralist Giolitti. By winter non-alignment had become synonymous with proletarian cowardice, transformist intrigue, and patriotic abjuration.

The spring of 1915 witnessed the growing polarization of provincial politics as the defenders of public order flung overboard every remnant of the Giolittian system. April marked the adoption of a new labour militancy, stimulated by full employment in the war industries, and the town democrats decided to cut loose from their proletarian ties. When workers at the Franchi Griffin steel company went on strike to obtain not wage increases but indemnity from dismissal and the regulation of overtime, the advanced liberals who used to promote moderate unionism were overcome with indignation. The progressive *Provincia di Brescia* cast aside its old reformism to 'deplore, in the name of the fatherland, citizens taking part in such agitation'.[107] The FIOM representatives in turn regarded this patriotic posture as a sham, since no one expected the industrialists to foresake profit in the interests of the nation. Seeking preservation through a period of short, sharp military rule, the constitutional left had simply exhausted its programme of social toleration and governmental reform.

The pacifist cause proved inexpedient for even the socialists in a province where jobs depended upon war production. The political defence of the working class came into conflict with the immediate material interests of labour, and the reticence of the rank and file reflected the awkwardness of the PSI position. The passive neutrality of 'neither support nor sabotage' helped to clothe the practical dilemma of the party leaders and the unemployed members. And the interventionist demonstrations of radiant May certainly reinforced the quietism of the socialists: anticipating energetic resistance from the bourgeoisie, they would not take their antimilitarism to the streets. The fate of Italy's liberal élite, declared the local moderate Arturo

---

[107] *La Provincia di Brescia*, 19 and 29 April 1915.

Reggio, rested with the fortunes of war, and the masses could not be allowed to stand in the way: 'For when in history have great decisions been made by the majority? . . . The Italian people will become what the ruling class wants them to be.'[108]

The socialists were not the only casualties of the political altercation, which also saw the attrition of the clerical consensus. The initial alliance with Giolitti disguised the divergence of opinion among provincial Catholics, who divided on allegiance to Austria.[109] Papal loyalists showed reluctance to take arms against the Central European bulwark of the faith, while such hawks as the nationalist Carlo Bresciani pressed for intervention to maintain Italy's territorial integrity.[110] By April 1915 the leaders of the white labour movement had gone over to the right, with just a few church pacifists behind on the neutralist bench. On the verge of entry into war, the Christian democrats still seemed unable to follow a common line. The *Cittadino* ran two pieces on the controversy: its front page carried an editorial urging participation, the second page an article in praise of peace.[111]

While destroying the cohesion of the church laity and throwing progressive liberalism into disarray, intervention did provide a unique rallying point for the traditional parties of order. Catholics and conservatives came together with democrats for the first time in Brescian history. The crisis fused urban and rural élites 'in expectation of the glorious hour', as a minority creed turned into the generalized protest of the provincial bourgeoisie. Industrialists drawn by the pull of high state expenditure on arms stood by agrarians hoping to curb the advance of socialism in the countryside. Free-traders as well as protectionists imagined that war might bring salutary change to a sluggish economy, and Masons found themselves working next to clerics in the business of national regeneration. This collective commitment to the gospel of upper-class salvation had to be forged even through use of the piazza, and the usually civilized *Provincia* went so far as to applaud a hanging of the philistine Giovanni Giolitti in effigy.[112]

The excitement created by the interventionists evinced a new awareness of common class alignments. National events, not local

---

[108] *La Sentinella Bresciana*, 14 May 1915.

[109] *Il Cittadino di Brescia*, 14 November 1914 and 7 January 1915.

[110] Ibid., 19 November 1914; G. De Rosa, *Storia del movimento cattolico in Italia*, vol. i (Bari, 1966), p. 586.

[111] *Il Cittadino di Brescia*, 15 May 1915; see also A. Fappani, *La guerra sull'uscio di casa: Brescia e bresciani nella prima guerra mondiale* (Brescia, 1969).

[112] *La Provincia di Brescia*, 2 April 1915.

developments, inspired the preoccupation with bourgeois strength and survival. For Brescia somehow managed to resist the ascendancy of maximalist socialism and the spread of organized labour. In a province of 586,000, manufacturing occupied 93,969 people, 51,742 of them workers, yet the reformists could claim just 4,548 members and the revolutionaries counted only twenty-two.[113] Despite noticeable change in the structure of industry, the agricultural population withstood the mass conversion to wage labour and remained fragmented. Farming engaged about 143,000 of the active population: 21,000 proprietors and 122,000 generic peasants. Though its numbers multiplied, the countryside stayed passive, unaffected by the transformation outside. It was this state of affairs that the provincial notables sought to preserve.[114]

[113] L. Lotti, *La settimana rossa*, table III.
[114] Camera di Commercio e Industria di Brescia, *Cenni sulla struttura economica della provincia di Brescia* (Brescia, 1924), pp. 8-9.

2

Workers and Warriors

WHEN on 20 May 1915 parliament granted the Salandra government full powers for war, the public accepted the call to arms with resignation. Four days later Italy was fighting on the side of the Triple Entente. The mobilization against Austria lulled the interventionist crowds, who likened their victory to the triumph of privileged patriots fifty-five years before. Recalling the campaigns of the liberation movement, during which a heroic élite imposed its notion of the general will on a passive populace, the renunciation of neutrality allowed an ardent minority to serve as the embodiment of the civic conscience. Belligerence, as the Brescian nationalist Filippo Carli understood it, represented yet another episode in the struggle for independence that began with unification: Germany threatened the peninsula's economic and political autonomy, and only by meeting the Teutonic challenge abroad could sovereignty at home ensue.[1] Whereas their liberal predecessors had placed premature optimism in free trade and constitutional monarchy to Europeanize the country, the apostles of war suffered from the delusion that controlled markets and rule by decree could rescue the infant state from oblivion as a second-rate empire. But whatever the divergence in agenda, the demeanour of the regenerative forces appeared the same. Again, a narrow yet influential group of partisans prevailed over the lower classes without having to play the plebiscitary card. So long as the real nation remained highly localized and loosely integrated, the patrimony of the Risorgimento would linger.

Instead of touting the benefits of agricultural development as the liberal oligarchs of the nineteenth century had done, conservative interventionists saw in industrial expansion the basis for prosperity. Commercial independence, according to the nationalists, required imperialist drive to release the energies of domestic enterprise from acknowledged inferiority. Until obstacles of location and cost

---

[1] F. Carli, *La riforma della tariffa doganale e le industrie meccaniche e chimiche* (Brescia, 1915), pp. 25-8.

vanished, the homeland stayed condemned as a 'pastoral field' for German dumping. Defence spending alone promised to force up consumption of goods and thereby free the country from vassalage to foreign trade. With the wide distribution of armaments contracts to the multitude of iron and steel companies throughout Italy, the martial effort did succeed in eliminating outside competition for the duration of hostilities. Military expenditure went beyond glorified protectionism and compelled government regulation. To the jaundiced eye of General Alfredo Dallolio, master-mind of the mobilization programme, the native metallurgical sector never really existed: it was for all practical purposes a fictitious entity.[2] Hoping to cure this fundamental weakness of the lop-sided economy, he sought to insert heavy industry into an advanced capitalist order which would be superintended by the state to improve and accelerate output. War, then, offered not only the opportunity to safeguard existing manufacture, but also the possibility of propelling new departures. Under public guidance and control, private interests could finally forsake anarchic individualism to rationalize and modernize within a corporative framework.[3]

External aggression brought with it internal repression. After intervention came a host of emergency measures that restricted constitutional liberties. Although the right to association remained, the authorities forbade public assembly, and prefects reserved the prerogative to confiscate printed matter which even seemed to endanger national unity and civilian morale. Military surveillance and press censorship proved particularly cumbrous in districts designated as war zones, including Brescia. Compulsory arbitration did away with strikes, while job abandonment became punishable by a special court. Workers avoided active service through employment under government contract, but those exempt from induction had to respect the army disciplinary code on the shop floor. Administrative hindrances and labour regulations limited criticism during preparation

[2] Camera dei Deputati, *Atti Parlamentari del Regno d'Italia*, Legislatura XXVI (1921-1923), documento XXI, fasc. 2 (Rome, 1923), p. 108.

[3] Ibid., p. 109; the Comitato Centrale di Mobilitazione Industriale, set up in 1915 under Dallolio's direction, controlled the negotiation of war contracts, the distribution of supplies to industry, and the mediation of labour relations. See A. Caracciolo, 'La crescita e la trasformazione della grande industria durante la prima guerra mondiale', in G. Fuà (ed.), *Lo sviluppo economico in Italia*, vol. iii (Milan, 1975), pp. 205-10; M. Clark, *Antonio Gramsci and the Revolution that Failed* (New Haven, 1977), pp. 15-16.

[4] L. Einaudi, *La condotta economica e gli effetti sociali della guerra italiana* (Bari and New Haven, 1933), pp. 99-121.

for combat, and foreign conflict served as a pretext to disarm domestic opponents for the duration of hostilities.[4]

Boom and Bust in Wartime Brescia

As peasants answered conscription summonses to the front, draft deferrers and employers stayed behind to undertake a crash programme of industrial expansion. Between equipment and carriage costs, Italy spent an estimated 13,761 million gold lire on defence, and after decades of neglect Brescian entrepreneurs began to receive favoured treatment from Rome.[5] The first year and a half of the military buildup saw capital investment increase by 60 per cent in the machine and steel concerns of the province, and new corporations accounted for more than 40 per cent of that accretion.[6] Seventeen metallurgical and engineering outfits sold exclusively to the armed forces ministries just months after intervention. Most of the Val Trompia gun-makers signed subcontracts with the Gardone arsenal, and three firms in the Val Sabbia did piece-work for FIAT.[7] Area manufacturers, lamed no longer by transport difficulties, peacetime markets, and inexpensive imports, experienced boom profits. Only labour shortages and technical constraints could limit output during the early stages of the mobilization. Employers tried to offset the scarcity of skilled hands by recruiting untrained help and by standardizing production, so the process of proletarian dilution accompanied the push of plant enlargement. The number of wage-earners engaged in the metal and the mechanical trades swelled almost overnight from 8,059 in 1915 to 20,534 by the second half of 1916.[8] This rapid growth of unskilled manpower kept up through much of 1917.

Rearmament modified the balance between public and private initiative in the economy. The urgency of full mobilization demanded the imposition of bureaucratic checks to convert inefficient local manufacture into a centralized system of production. In 1915 the state

[5] A. Caracciolo, 'La grande industria nella prima guerra mondiale', in A. Carracciolo (ed.), *La formazione dell'Italia industriale* (Bari, 1969), pp. 197-8; estimate also cited in M. Clark, *Antonio Gramsci and the Revolution that Failed*, p. 13.

[6] Camera di Commercio ed Industria di Brescia, *Problemi e possibilità del dopo-guerra nella provincia di Brescia. III: Inchiesta sul capitale e sulla tecnica* (Brescia, 1917), pp. 5-6, 21-3.

[7] ASB, Fondo Camera di Commercio, R. Arsenale, Contratti di Guerra, b. 11-21, April-September 1915; ACS, Min. Armi e Munizioni, CCMI, b. 2, fasc. Brescia, sfasc. 6 (catalogue, n.d.).

[8] Camera di Commercio ed Industria di Brescia, *Problemi e possibilità del dopo-guerra nella provincia di Brescia. II: Inchiesta sui salari nel 1915 e 1916* (Brescia, 1917), pp. 14-15.

moved beyond the mere provision of lucrative contracts and protective tariffs to claim new regulatory authority over labour, prices, and raw materials. But the business community did not fret at government sovereignty in the wartime market-place. Industrialists on the brink of bankruptcy before intervention suddenly found privilege and preferment bestowed from above. A special decree banned all imports, with the exception of primary goods and certain foodstuffs, and German finished steel parts ceased to haunt the Lombard firms as a result.[9] High, unrestrained military expenditure reduced the pressures of domestic competition, and salvage operations helped eliminate dependence on foreign investment. Attilio Franchi, for example, acquired controlling interest in the Mannesmann steelworks at Dalmine without having to increase his capital stock, when the Banca Commerciale arranged to place the seamless tube plant in Italian hands.[10] The Brescia ironmaster also absorbed the Gregorini company of Lovere and the Metallurgica Bresciana combine by exceeding peacetime credit barriers. Official guide-lines, encouraging expansion with minimal cash outlays on the part of the entrepreneur, sanctioned the suspension of normal loan requirements for defence contractors. Banking institutions, cushioned by guarantees from the ministry of arms and munitions, went on to sponsor development through short-term financing and advances against shares.[11]

In the twenties a spate of popular literature portrayed all entrepreneurs as war profiteers, who hoarded vast reserves under monopoly conditions. Apart from a notable few, however, local businessmen realized modest returns from the feverish activity and the spectacular price rises that rewarded the integrated conglomerates instead. Medium-sized firms could compete for artillery commissions only by undercutting the larger outfits. Franchi, perhaps the most successful owner-operator in the zone, offered to deliver what giants such as Vickers-Terni and Armstrong furnished, but at two-thirds their rate. The Naples arsenal did accept the lower bid, although the Brescian supplier lacked equipment to meet navy specifications and

[9] R. Bachi, *L'Italia economica nel 1916* (Città del Castello, 1917), pp. 212-15; S. Golzio, *L'industria dei metalli in Italia* (Turin, 1942), p. 55.

[10] ASIG, Società Anonima Franchi Gregorini, Consiglio di Amministrazione, verbale, 21 August 1917.

[11] A. Fossati, *Lavoro e produzione in Italia dalla metà del secolo XVIII alla seconda guerra mondiale* (Turin, 1951), p. 522; G. Scagnetti, *La siderurgia in Italia*, pp. 281-2; R. Webster, *Industrial Imperialism in Italy*, pp. 88-9.

pig-iron for projectiles had to be processed elsewhere.[12] For utilization of its facilities in treating the metal, the Ansaldo shipyard of Genoa exacted immediate payment. Franchi's fussy clients, on the other hand, took months and sometimes years to disburse: by the declaration of the cease-fire, the armed forces had run up an account of nearly 100 million lire.[13] Expecting inflation to cancel his debts, Franchi continued to buy out smaller machine and steel shops to fulfil defence needs despite delays in remuneration. Soon munitions orders fell off, and even with the latest technology he would have trouble finding peacetime customers for military hardware. Management made little attempt to curb plant enlargement until the spring of 1918, when it tried to reduce costs while increasing, not redressing, productivity. As victory approached and the Banca Commerciale proceeded to recall 80 million lire in short-term promissory notes, Franchi's industrial structure remained hopelessly distorted and he appealed to government to help discharge his financial obligations. Like numerous other manufacturers on the peninsula, he could not escape the shadow of speculative overexpansion. A long failure to rationalize and reconvert exposed the rickety foundations of the brief boom in the capital goods sector. The mobilization, which at its apogee had brought prosperity to secondary metallurgical concerns, ended by promoting the power of big investment banks over independent companies.[14]

Whereas armaments policy confirmed the marginality of provincial iron and steel by creating an artificial market that disappeared with the cessation of hostilities, military procurement in light industry stimulated sound expansion. Corporate investment gains were slight in textiles, where the work-force decreased by one-fifth over the course of war. Still, the privations of an austere and closed economy quickened modernization in this consumer sector.[15] The final collapse of hand-weaving and silk-spinning attended the concentration of large, mechanized factories capable of expanding operations, for only

[12] Camera dei Deputati, *Atti Parlamentari*, Legislatura XXVI (1921-1923), documento XXI, fasc. 2, p. 47; Archivio della Camera dei Deputati, Inchiesta 1921-1923 (manuscript source for the parliamentary inquest on war profits), b. 70, fasc. Franchi, 3 March 1921.
[13] ACS, Presidenza del Consiglio, 1918, fasc. 3.986, Prefettura di Bergamo, 29 October 1918.
[14] A. Caracciolo, 'La crescita e la trasformazione della grande industria durante la prima guerra mondiale', pp. 241-7.
[15] Camera di Commercio e Industria di Brescia, *L'economia bresciana*, vol. ii, fasc. 2, p. 76.

the very vigorous mills could recover from the slump in foreign trade or survive the drop in domestic demand. One such installation belonged to Vittorio Olcese, who moved from Milan during 1896 to manage a cotton company headed by the Feltrinelli brothers.[16] A decade after his arrival in Brescia, the mechanical engineer left the job to set himself up in business, backed by a Catholic financier. Starting out with 120,000 spindles, he intended to take full advantage of the hydroelectric resources held by the Oglio river. Economy of scale put Olcese in an excellent position later to compete for government contracts, so at the outset of armed conflict he successfully bid to provide uniforms for soldiers. The credit opportunities that accompanied state orders let him swallow up six failing manufactories nearby, and in 1919 he bought out his former employers to command a total of 234,000 spindles.[17] The year 1907 saw Emilio Antonioli found the Lanificio di Manerbio with funds from two wool merchants of Roubaix. Between 1912 and 1915 the firm's capital stock rose from 2 to 3 million lire, and units of production doubled. Antonioli cashed in on the mobilization too by clothing the Italian army, but growth did not stop once the combatants returned home. Following the armistice he paid off his French partners to acquire sole ownership, and the number of spindles under his control increased by close to 60 per cent.[18]

Attempting to emancipate Italy's cheapest raw material from foreign domination, wartime policy also drove on the process of concentration in the field of electricity. Under the Bonomi decree of 20 November 1916, private contenders could vie for sixty-year concessions to transform the utility from public waterways.[19] Although the energy programme aimed eventually to repossess all power plants, it balked at nationalization, and banking giants did not hesitate to pump money into the development of electrification networks. Bolstered by government grants and corporate connections, one holding company edged out smaller distributors in satisfying local kilowatt demand. The Società Elettrica Bresciana, by 1917 part of the Edison con-

---

[16] *Il Cotonificio Vittorio Olcese nelle sue origini, nelle sue vicende e nella sua attività* (Milan, 1939), pp. 3-10.

[17] Camera di Commercio e Industria di Brecia, *L'Industria Tessile al I Gennaio 1923* (Brescia, 1923), pp. 50-5.

[18] A. Giarratana, *L'industria bresciana*, pp. 88-9, 92-3.

[19] L. Einaudi, *La condotta economica*, pp. 157-9; see also G. Mori, 'Le guerre parallele. L'industria elettrica in Italia nel periodo della grande guerra (1914-1919)', in *Studi Storici*, vol. xiv (1973), pp. 319-35.

glomerate, monopolized the heavy industrial traffic and state expansion schemes created by rearmament. As independent competition fell away during the first eighteen months of combat, the subsidiary augmented its capital stock, the increments of which ended by representing 14 per cent of recent investment in the province.[20]

Agriculture in Brescia shared the wartime conditions of the rest of the Italian countryside. The draft more than halved the number of men on the land. Shortages of imported fertilizers, insecticides, and machinery made the adoption of modern methods difficult.[21] In spite of the contracted labour market and impediments to improvement, yields stayed only slightly below pre-war harvests since women worked to maintain production.[22] Cereals continued to dominate provincial cultivation, supported by a 42 per cent increase in grain prices on the Milan market during 1915.[23] The local cost of beef went up by two-thirds that same year, and wine became twice as dear.[24] Rather than unite those cultivators who had avoided military service in a common prosperity, the new profitability of farm commodities accentuated old divisions in the rural community. Conscription may have eliminated chronic unemployment by draining the reservoir of manpower in the fields, yet hired hands paid in monetary wages suffered a significant loss of purchasing power due to greater outlays on food. Peasants compensated in kind, on the other hand, could double earnings if they sold surplus staples at the going rates. Commercial leaseholders of the basin showed prodigious gains during the mobilization. Government controls allowed them to benefit from rents frozen at peacetime levels as well as from inflation, but the fixing of contracts that enriched such tenant entrepreneurs also emptied the pockets of absentee landowners. Because estate income remained stationary while property taxes and living expenses climbed, the economic status of non-resident proprietors deteriorated and the distribution of wealth shifted, to the advantage of their ambitious lessees.[25]

---

[20] Camera di Commercio ed Industria di Brescia. *Problemi e possibilità del dopo-guerra nella provincia di Brescia. III: Inchiesta sul capitale e sulla tecnica*, p. 7.

[21] L. Einaudi, *La condotta economica*, p. 85.

[22] A. Serpieri, *La guerra e le classi rurali italiane* (Bari and New Haven, 1930). p. 95.

[23] Sindacato Nazionale Fascista Tecnici Agricoli, *Il frumento*, pp. 116-20.

[24] Camera di Commercio e Industria di Brescia, *L'economia bresciana*, vol. ii, fasc. 2, pp. 36-7.

[25] A. Serpieri, *La guerra e le classi rurali italiane*, pp. 113-55.

Class Conflict on the Home Front

Intervention ended, for a time, the determination of employers to fight
the workers' movement. With all the material and human resources of
the country geared to national defence, business leaders tolerated the
participation of organized labour in a bargaining system overseen by
the state. The army, when it established the industrial mobilization
programme in the summer of 1915, created machinery for the settlement of trade disputes. Delegates of both sides sat next to civilian
experts and a presiding military officer on regional boards of arbitration. Collaboration on these mixed committees altered the strategy of
social conflict in factories under ministerial contract. Industrialists
consented to conclude wage agreements in return for a guaranteed
market and restrictions on job mobility. The socialist CGL sacrificed
its strike prerogatives to secure government recognition and full
employment. Eager to preserve order and negotiate reform, the unions
rallied behind public authority as Italy prepared for war.[26]

Organized labour thus abandoned the threat of the general strike
for the language of legalism, but at the cost of internal dissension.
Though bargaining with the military accredited the CGL as the
legitimate representative of the proletariat, active support of state
policy clashed with the passive neutrality of the PSI. Governmentally-
minded unionists prevailed in the resolution of discord since they
retained the only effective means of improving wages and conditions
during the mobilization, and the basis of revolutionary solidarity
weakened as a result. The maximalist socialist party consented to limit
involvement to strictly political issues while the moderate trade federation dealt exclusively with the economic concerns of the working class.
Reasonably successful at the national level, the temporary truce permitted both groups to enjoy a considerable degree of autonomy and to
advocate incompatible positions on the intervention question. In
Brescia, however, the arrangement failed miserably. The party there
slid languidly into torpor, and activity at the Camera del Lavoro came
to a standstill when local militants ignored instructions from Rome to
distribute patriotic literature on the shop floor.[27] PSI membership
continued to shrink through 1918, whereas the FIOM increased enrolments fivefold over the first two years of combat.[28] The primacy of the

[26] ACS, MRF, b. 81, fasc. Confederazione Lavoro, 24 September 1915 and 29 May
1916; M. Clark, *Antonio Gramsci and the Revolution that Failed*, pp. 28-9.
[27] ACS, MRF, b. 81, fasc. Confederazione Lavoro, 12 August 1915.
[28] *Almanacco Socialista Italiano* (Milan, 1921), pp. 480-1.

CGL and its affiliates in the province demonstrated how little the antimilitarist cause weighed in balance against the arguments for collaboration with the war effort.[29]

The attitude of the rank and file towards mobilization reflected the ambivalence that tore the organizational fabric of the labour community. The neutrality of the Brescia workers during May 1915 was indubitably as genuine as it had been unanimous. They resented the harsh discipline and military surveillance in the war industries, all equipped with little gaols on the premises, but preferred unpleasant factory conditions to the front. Until the summer of 1917, when scarce supplies and crop failures exacerbated the pressures of inflation and overcrowding, their mood remained one of resignation. Earlier full employment and rising wages do much to explain this apparent indifference (Table 1).[30]

Table 1. *Real wages in industry, 1915–1926*

Year	Brescia all sectors	Brescia heavy industry	Italy all sectors
1914	100.00	100.00	100.00
1915	103.69	99.71	93.73
1916	134.63	125.08	85.25
1917	135.87	114.73	73.28
1918	108.96	88.66	64.79
1919	94.62	83.66	93.41
1920	114.37	100.27	114.75
1921	125.65	109.91	127.39
1922	129.92	107.79	123.98
1923	132.82	121.95	116.40
1924	126.60	122.52	112.96
1925	126.16	121.67	112.15
1926	124.37	114.30	111.82

Labour leaders should not be accused of having sold out to the state. Edgardo Falchero, a FIOM activist from Milan, planned the few partial strikes that broke out at Brescia in the first year of war. Anxious to use his position as CGL delegate to extract concessions from industry with the assistance of government, he also had no qualms about agitating for better terms should arbitration fail. On

[29] ACS, Min. Interno, DGPS, Serie G1, Associazioni 1896-1897 e 1910-1934, b. 8, fasc. Camera del Lavoro (Brescia), 4 and 26 July 1917; see also A. Malatesta, *I socialisti italiani durante la guerra* (Milan, 1926).

[30] Source: Camera di Commercio e Industria di Brescia, *L'economia bresciana*, vol. ii, fasc. 2, pp. 50-126; A. Fossati, *Lavoro e produzione in Italia*, p. 634.

25 November 1915 the unionist staged a walk-out of nearly 800 operatives at an engineering plant, but the participants voted to resume production after one day of illegal job action.[31] He waged a campaign for fixed pay scales in the capital goods sector, but the indiscipline of his followers amplified the resistance of employers, who exploited the insecure hold of the moderate. By 1917 the rank and file had dumped Falchero as their spokesman, for the economic downturn and occupational instability caused them to lose confidence in those installed by the reformist establishment.[32] Workers instead resorted to frequent absenteeism, a practice especially popular among women as a means of expressing grievance. Whatever unity provincial radicals managed to muster usually entailed rejecting the guidance of the central organization. Already in January 1917 the Val Trompia metallurgical league had independent recourse to the Lombard mediation board after an indemnity scheme devised by the FIOM was shelved, and not much later proletarian protesters from an armaments combine presented their own set of demands directly to the mixed committee. While the combative temper of the local militants reinforced opposition in single factories and individual municipalities, the credibility of socialist officialdom suffered at the bargaining table. The national federation could not control the conduct of its own members.[33]

Territorial rivalry lay behind the bolder spirits of hard-core militants on the shop floor. Unionists from the zone resented the growing influence of foreign authority. The Brescia leagues threatened secession from the FIOM twice, once because the federation failed to secure a draft deferment for a member.[34] When the national directorate named Falchero secretary of the Camera del Lavoro, organizers in town accused the outsider of bourgeois careerism.[35] During a general strike of metallurgists in Lombardy, local activists refused to bring out the masses in sympathy.[36] The force of tradition prevailed over the pull of class consciousness, and the bulk of skilled metalworkers stayed loyal to their old comrades and accepted the decision

[31] ACS, Min. Interno, Casellario Politico Centrale, fasc. 1932, E. Falchero, 26 November 1915.

[32] ACS, Min. Armi e Munizioni, CCMI, b. 232, Comando di Brescia, 19 February 1917.

[33] Ibid., b. 215, Unione Professionale Triumplina, 7 January 1917; *Almanacco Socialista Italiano* (Milan, 1919), p. 336.

[34] ACS, MRF, b. 14, fasc. Comitato Regionale Lombardo, 13 September 1918.

[35] Ibid., 11 October 1918; the local league also charged that the national federation 'only knew how to sponge money off the Brescian working class'.

[36] ACS, Min. Armi e Munizioni, CCMI, b. 171, fasc. 43, verbale, 8 September 1918.

to limit agitation to provincial issues. As the labour leaders fell to fighting among themselves, the regional committee in Milan found itself arbitrating internal disputes instead of negotiating wage settlements.[37]

Employers endured the enthusiasms of the rebellious Brescians. The strength of the national federation declined at a moment when severe shortages of steel supply and electric current incapacitated industry, and arms manufacturers took advantage of the organization's disarray by enforcing regular, unpaid furloughs.[38] On the grounds that it lacked sufficient primary materials to maintain full production, the Metallurgica Bresciana company reduced the working week from six days to five and thus avoided indemnifying 9,000 employees.[39] Not only did such tactics increase the mutual hostility between management and personnel, but they also heightened tensions within the labour movement. The obligatory abstentions first affected the proletariat's most expendable elements, rural migrants who had come off the land and into the factories only three years before. The high salaries and overtime hours of qualified metalworkers, the FIOM's staunchest supporters, aroused the suspicions of unskilled operatives, who argued that the union had made a deal with business and the state at their expense. Disparities in wage scales did little to alter this image of partiality. During the spring of 1918 the daily pay of a semi-skilled labourer in artillery averaged about 9 lire.[40] Most workers at the MIDA steel combine made 12 to 15 lire, and some got as much as 40.[41] Although the going rate at the Metallurgica Bresciana plant continued at 10 lire a day for women, a number of male specialists received 90 to 98 lire and a few foremen took home 120 lire.[42] Inequalities in earnings and conditions of employment infuriated recent recruits, many of whom began to disown agreements concluded by their representatives.[43]

Uniform but less favourable conditions of work in other sectors could produce a sense of occupational solidarity. With speculation

[37] Ibid., 6 July and 8 September 1918.

[38] Ibid., b. 215, Comando di Brescia, 24 September 1917.

[39] Ibid., b. 222, Comitato Lombardo, 16 April 1918.

[40] Camera di Commercio e Industria di Brescia, *L'economia bresciana*, vol. ii, fasc. 2, p. 96.

[41] ACS, Min. Armi e Munizioni, CCMI, verbale, 21 May 1918.

[42] Ibid., b. 216, 16 April 1918; Camera di Commercio e Industria di Brescia, *Variazioni nel costo della vita e nei salari a Brescia prima, durante e dopo la guerra* (Brescia, 1920), table II.

[43] ACS, Min. Armi e Munizioni, CCMI, b. 215, Comando di Brescia, 1 February 1918.

and profiteering accompanying the massive influx of metallurgists to the province, the cost of living in Brescia rose 15 per cent above that in Milan during 1917.[44] Doubtless the salaries of an élite in heavy industry outstripped prices, yet the real wages of railway workers plunged below the 1914 level, a drop which members of the trade shouldered almost evenly.[45] This common lament both stimulated and sustained militancy during the war. State employment, moreover, made the railwaymen invulnerable to the divisive ways of private owners.

The masses in the consumer sector proved more difficult to organize. Oppressed by intermittent crises in foreign markets and by wartime shortages in supplies, textiles offered scant security to the unskilled labourer. By 1918 real wages sank to 58 per cent of the 1914 standard, and the numbers on the payroll slipped from 11,085 at the outbreak of hostilities to 8,401.[46] While the move of trained female hands to lucrative positions in factories under government contract initially offset the decline of traditional manufacture, women also fell first victims to unemployment once arms production decelerated. A vicious cycle had been created. Because the attractive pay tendered by the metal, machine, and chemical companies drew experienced hands away from the countryside, clothiers relied upon casual help, in large part local farm girls. The high turnover in the branch would have presented the most vigorous union with a formidable task. Perhaps aware of the odds against converting them, the CGL made no attempt to recruit the new marginal members of the proletarian population. The socialist textile federation FIOT occupied a small room at the Camera del Lavoro and enrolled a minority in the provincial wool concerns, which outfitted Italian soldiers. The Catholic leagues founded before intervention disappeared during the mobilization, leaving the rank and file to their own devices. On four occasions spinners and weavers in the foothills called wildcat strikes, but the spontaneous protests lasted only a couple of hours. Detached from the industrial world of the town, peasant workers usually confined discontents to old, individualist channels of rural wrath, since agriculture

[44] Ibid., b. 133, fasc. 1, 'caroviveri', September 1917.

[45] ACS, Min. Interno, DGPS, Serie G1, Associazioni 1896-1897 e 1910-1934, b. 8, fasc. sindacato ferrovieri, 22 July 1914; Camera di Commercio e Industria di Brescia, *L'economia bresciana*, vol. ii, fasc. 2, p. 123; see also L. Guerrini, *Organizzazioni e lotte dei ferrovieri italiani* (Florence, 1957).

[46] Camera di Commercio ed Industria di Brescia, *Problemi e possibilità del dopo-guerra nella provincia di Brescia. II: Inchiesta sui salari nel 1915 e 1916*, pp. 18-20.

remained their primary interest. Women still toiled in the evening on plots at home and, when conditions deteriorated in the cotton shops, several attempted to forsake their jobs and return to the land.[47] Absenteeism became a serious problem during the summer months, and some smaller mills closed down during the seasonal return to the fields.[48]

Popular disturbances occurred with great frequency in the provincial hinterland. The hunger and want brought about by what seemed an endless war revived peasant mistrust and resentment, yet civilian officials managed to control and dilute the rage of isolated rural folk.[49] Urban unrest required special attention. The year 1917 witnessed an explosion of petty violence and crime in the town, where pitched brawls between workers and soldiers broke out almost nightly.[50] Though conservative patriots believed that disruptive draft-dodgers should be shipped from the factories to the front, most businessmen recognized the importance of continuity and co-operation on the shop floor for the success of the economic effort. At a time when class relations showed signs of strain, those who banked on order and hierarchy intended to subdue seditious sentiment by demonstrating the consequences of radical courses. Edgardo Falchero, authorities complained, had abused his position on the mixed committee to damage discipline and productivity, and one ironmaster summoned the police to persecute the FIOM representative.[51] To oblige Attilio Franchi, the military command prohibited the trade unionist from re-entering the city limits following a day trip to the Val Trompia.[52] After Falchero informed against the harsh measures adopted to restore deference at the Sant'Eustacchio plant, the industrialist retaliated by convincing Tito Bacchetti, the prefect, to remove the trouble-maker from the zone.[53] Falchero's notoriety in Milan circles, however, gave him too much clout. The prefect also tried to transfer Chiaffredo

[47] ACS, Min. Armi e Munizioni, CCMI, b. 70, fasc. mano d'opera femminile, Comando di Brescia, 13 June 1918; b. 232, verbale, 21 July 1917.

[48] Ibid., b. 215, verbale, 24 January 1917; b. 232, Comando di Brescia, 12 and 14 July 1917.

[49] ACS, Presidenza del Consiglio, Prima Guerra Mondiale, fasc. 17.2 Brescia, sfasc. 9; Min. Interno, DGPS, AGR 1914-1918, b. 16, cat. A5G fasc. Brescia, 23 January and 1 February 1917; b. 51, cat. A5G 1918, fasc. Brescia, sfasc. maggio 1917, 1 and 9 May 1917.

[50] ACS, Presidenza del Consiglio, Prima Guerra Mondiale, fasc. 19.1, G. Graziotti, 31 January 1917.

[51] ACS, Min. Armi e Munizioni, CCMI, b. 171, fasc. 43, verbale, 1 April 1918.

[52] Ibid., Comando di Brescia, 5 May 1918.

[53] Ibid., 20 June and 6 July 1918.

Baudino, secretary of the local metallurgical league, from Brescia to the Adriatic. Again, Franchi insisted on banishing the metalworker, but Bacchetti revoked the recommendation within weeks. The idea of combat appeared too awful to contemplate, so Baudino became more practical in outlook and agreed to struggle in a less offensive manner.[54]

The prefect's policy of neutralizing prominent militants might have succeeded in the first years of war, when the interests of the proletariat seemed to converge with the concerns of industry. By 1918, however, the end was visibly near and the quick profits over. The reduced demand for labour, which started to touch all categories in the capital goods sector, reflected the cut in government spending, and skilled metalworkers grew restive. Businessmen also developed symptoms of distress. Feeling the after-effects of a boom economy, employers petulantly assumed a more obdurate posture. Just as the unions saw their support surge, management moved to break them.[55]

The refusal of Franchi's new manager to discuss wage claims with the internal commission at the Metallurgica Bresciana plant sparked revolutionary agitation in the spring of 1918. Hand-picked by the industrialist, who had just acquired the controlling interest in the installation, Mario Jarach aimed to reduce costs and increase productivity. This technician intended to get the most out of his employees by enforcing discipline and tightening pressure. The factory gaol swelled during his first month in the job, and by Jarach's ninth week offenders had to queue for days to serve their time. The programme, albeit severe, did improve efficiency and performance. The workers, of course, expected pay bonuses for their extra labours. Rather than grant any further concessions, however, the company preferred to retract previous ones.[56]

The old paternalism had disappeared, yet industry would not play by the changed rules of the game. Anxious for the protection of public authority in trade disputes and ready to collaborate with the state in a planned economy, such dated liberal stalwarts as Franchi objected to collective bargaining, the other side of the corporatist coin. Dwindling profits and wage demands led the employer to the conclusion that organized labour would drive him out of business, while management's belligerent tone left the strike as a last resort. On 10 May 1918

[54] Ibid., 15 May 1918.

[55] M. Abrate, *La lotta sindacale nella industrializzazione in Italia 1906–1926* (Turin, 1967), pp. 176-81.

[56] ACS, Min. Armi e Munizioni, CCMI, b. 171, fasc. 43, Falchero e Arbizzati, 1 and 2 April 1918.

half of the Metallurgica Bresciana workers initiated agitation, and a few hours later Jarach decided to talk with their elected representatives. The engineer and the internal commission reached a tentative agreement, unfavourable to the unskilled masses. Male operatives picked up their tools, but the women refused to return to their positions until the company guaranteed indemnity against obligatory abstention. When the police tried to push the crowd behind the factory gates, they met violent resistance. Hoping to circumvent formal FIOM intervention, Jarach called a lock-out, and the immediate arrest of leading activists put an end to his troubles. Combativeness withered in the wake of dissension and repression.[57]

Franchi continued his battle against the labour movement. Instead of pestering militants with national connections, he now concentrated on eliminating grass-roots organizers. Bacchetti dutifully translated the employer's instructions into action, and before long the local metallurgical league found itself purged of potential leaders. Soldiers discovered at public meetings of the FIOM risked transfer from the province. Civilian members of government-sponsored factory commissions lost their jobs upon election to office. Franchi first charged the workers with some disciplinary violation, which police confirmed in a detailed report under separate cover. Against the collusion of industry with the lower levels of state authority, the unions had no defence.[58]

The FIOM's usual recourse to the war office in Rome failed to protect three comrades from getting the sack. Faliero Squarci went to the capital to see the under-secretary Nava, who assured the Brescian unionist that Franchi would be censured by the ministry of arms and munitions, but the militant returned home only to learn of his impending departure from the zone.[59] Chastened by employer obstinacy, local organizers became circumspect. Throughout September 1918 Falchero urged a strike, though the metallurgical league foiled his assemblies by holding rival meetings. As the national delegate lurched further to the left, the provincials showed more caution. Internecine bickering increased in the face of intimidation from above.[60]

[57] Ibid., 10 and 11 May 1918; see also b. 71, fasc. 78, Operai: Ditta Franchi, 23 July 1918.

[58] ACS, Presidenza del Consiglio, Prima Guerra Mondiale, fasc. 19.25, F. Turati, 12 December 1918.

[59] ACS, Min. Armi e Munizioni, CCMI, b. 215, verbale, 5 July 1918.

[60] Ibid., Federazione Nazionale Metallurgica, 13 August 1918.

To cut corners, other firms adopted Franchi's antiquated policy of containing the advance of centralized bargaining. Both the MIDA and the Tettoni steelworks had labour at their mercy, when management fired militants, ignored collective agreements, and reduced salaries through the exaggerated use of unpaid furloughs.[61] That same year the Acciaieria Danieli bypassed the mixed committee in Milan altogether.[62] During the autumn industry pugnaciously pressed its advantage. The FIOM crew, powerless to curb secret negotiations between independent workers and individual employers, steadily lost ground. Such autonomous action embarrassed delegates of the national federation, since few disputes found their way to the regional board of arbitration. Unable to prevent the slide in real wages, Falchero turned his attention to the dilemma of demobilization.[63] He scheduled rallies to publicize insurance schemes and redundancy benefits, but many in the audience landed in gaol. Filippo Turati, the socialist parliamentarian, petitioned the government to halt the violation of civil liberties in Brescia, yet the prime minister's promises did little to restrain the offensive against the union movement.[64]

Internal divisions widened as the strength of opposition declined. Conflict persisted on the stale issue of collaboration. The heated debate over participation in the industrial mobilization programme found its post-war counterpart in a battle about co-operating with the parliamentary commission set up to study the transition to peace. The dispute that nearly split the national socialist leadership from its trade federation stemmed from the reformist Rigola's decision to take part in the Orlando government initiative, which the PSI directorate denounced as a whitewash. Discord between ideologues and unionists, maximalists and moderates, again threatened common action, only this time the radicals prevailed. The revolutionaries forbade all comrades to assist in the official inquiry. Rather than acknowledge the primacy of political purism over economic expedience, Rinaldo Rigola resigned as secretary-general of the CGL, and his successor Ludovico D'Aragona concluded a pact of alliance with the party. Castigated for bureaucratic timidity but unwilling to repent, labour organizers in Italy agreed to a condominium arrangement.[65]

[61] Ibid., b. 71, fasc. 78. Comitato Lombardo, 23 July 1918.

[62] Ibid., b. 215, verbale, 12 June 1918.

[63] Ibid., b. 171, fasc. 43, Falchero e Arbizzati, 8 September 1918.

[64] ACS, Presidenza del Consiglio, Prima Guerra Mondiale, fasc. 19.25, F. Turati, 13 and 27 December 1918.

[65] ACS, MRF, b. 14, fasc. Comitato Regionale Lombardo, 11 October 1918; b. 81, fasc.

Socialist militants of the Bresciano declined to share sovereignty and instead used the national conflict as a scourge for CGL spokesmen at home. Deriding collaboration as a bourgeois vice, maximalists in town portrayed Falchero as a traitor to his own class. If the unionist found it difficult to muster much enthusiasm for a new government commission after his harrowing experience as a Lombard arbiter, then reluctance to promote the supremacy of the party led him to favour participation in the state agency. For support of the reformist position he earned the obloquy of the local metallurgists. Their new secretary Cristoforo Venturini challenged the authority of the FIOM official, though the provincial could not command a popular following even within his own trade.[66] Arturo Maestri, head of the railway employees, had the makings of a gifted leader, yet his extremist rhetoric caused concern among the more sober metalworkers.[67] These three men, all of whom presumed to represent the masses but never really did, fought out the decisive action. In October 1918 Falchero acquiesced to the pressures of the other two and returned to Milan 'for fear of contamination'.[68] The war ended as control of the labour movement reverted to native hands.

Business Interests during the Industrial Mobilization

Industry discovered too comfortable an ambience during wartime military rule. Entrepreneurs consumed dividends with little concern for the future. The disappearance of the foreign competitors under conditions of a guaranteed market made profit easy to come by and reinvestment seemed unnecessary. The unsuccessful wage claims and ineffective labour strikes that reinforced the political confidence of businessmen also sanctioned organizational complacency. The protection offered by the prefect and the police allowed local magnates to remain loosely grouped. Able to cope with working-class unrest on their own terms, employers felt no need to look to association. The mobilization, which harmonized public and private enterprise for

Confederazione Lavoro, riunione del consiglio direttivo, 16 July 1918; R. Bachi, *L'Italia economica nel 1918* (Città del Castello, 1919), p. 309; for Rigola's correspondence with Filippo Carli on class collaboration see Archivio Rigola, Istituto Giangiacomo Feltrinelli, b. 1918, 17 April 1918.

[66] ACS, MRF, b. 14, Comitato Regionale Lombardo, 11 October 1918.

[67] ACS, Min. Interno, Casellario Politico Centrale, fasc. 2908, A. Maestri, 29 October 1917.

[68] ACS, MRF, b. 14, Comitato Regionale Lombardo, 13 September 1918; *Avanti!*, 15 and 20 September 1918.

national defence, fomented conflict among the arms manufacturers themselves.

In their clumsy, haphazard attempts to diversify and expand in the Brescia and Bergamo area, the ironmasters of the province began to step on each other's toes. The greatest subterranean dispute in the business community concerned state concessions to local operators for the development of water-power plants under the Bonomi decree. Given the scarcity and the expense of imported fuels, manufacturing output came increasingly to depend upon hydroelectric reserves. Lake Idro promised to be the richest source of 'white coal' around, so Franchi, Togni, and the Società Elettrica Bresciana all entered the contest for the right to harness it.[69] Franchi counted on his Commerciale connections to win him the bid, but he lost the bank's favour to Togni, another COMIT customer with FIAT links to boot. The controversy between the three reached a climax in 1917, when the electrical company took the offensive. The utility supplier initiated cuts in kilowatt-hours. Approved by the Lombard mobilization board, whose member Carlo Esterle happened to manage the parent company Edison, the reductions principally affected the installations of the other contenders. The bureaucratic partiality that had helped build his local dominion now turned against Franchi, whereas Togni possessed enough acumen to see the writing on the wall. The steelman stood to lose tubing contracts for aqueduct work, so he yielded to the Società Elettrica Bresciana. The joint venture with the Università del Naviglio Grande resulted in the formation of the Società Lago d'Idro.[70] Continued insufficient supply limited the productive capacity of their rival's enterprises.[71] By October 1918 Franchi's tab at the Banca Commerciale had passed the 80 million lire mark and Pietro Fenoglio, a representative of the Milan creditor, presided as chairman of the board.[72]

Franchi did not hesitate to capitalize on his injured position and

---

[69] A. Giarratana, *L'industria bresciana*, p. 53; see also E. Barni, *Per una politica delle acque* (Brescia, 1917), pp. 14-15.

[70] ACS, Min. Armi e Munizioni, CCMI, b. 197, Provvedimenti: Società Elettrica Bresciana, 28 December 1918; Credito Italiano, *Società Italiane per Azioni: Notizie Statistiche 1914* (Milan, 1915), p. 567; *Le società idroelettriche la recente legislazione* (Brescia, 1917), pp. 14-15, appendix.

[71] ASIG, Società Anonima Franchi Gregorini, Consiglio di Amministrazione, verbale, 5 January 1918.

[72] ACS, Presidenza del Consiglio, 1918, fasc. 3.986, Prefettura di Bergamo, 13 November 1918. Franchi did obtain smaller hydroelectric concessions in the Bergamo area; see G. Scagnetti, *La siderurgia in Italia*, p. 339.

bully organized labour.[73] In addition to using energy shortage as a pretext to lay off employees without indemnity, he threatened to dismiss two-thirds of the Metallurgica Bresciana staff unless the government procured special subsidies and long-term credit. Munitions orders declined, and the owner responded to waning returns by tightening the screws on his work-force. Already in 1917 Franchi had become a notorious exploiter of women and children for cheap, untrained help. His factories registered the highest turnover of casual hands. At one plant females accounted for over 41 per cent of the operatives, a figure 16 per cent above the national wartime average, which included some light industry.[74] He also instituted new methods of payment to keep the wage gap between skilled and unskilled categories the widest in the province.[75]

Franchi, whose shop stewards earned the best pay in their sector, did not regard the inflated salaries given to a minority of qualified metallurgists as concessions to the labour movement because he fought the growth of unionism by trying to divide the loyalties of the rank and file. Rather, the industrialist believed the other employers guilty of appeasement in recognizing the socialist trade organization as the legitimate representative of the working class. Acceptance of collective agreements, to his mind, spelled the intrusion of bureaucratic machinery into management functions. The Idro affair bred a second conflict of mentalities in the local business community. Togni chose to aid the penetration of outside capital into the area, while Franchi preferred to fight the trust. Though Franchi had long opposed the marked concentration of the great conglomerates in the province, transparent self-interest reinforced his old-style liberalism. Jealous of the hydroelectric power plant, he felt cheated, for corporate monopoly strategy had been advanced at his expense. A number of family entrepreneurs, notably the manufacturers of the Val Trompia and the Val Sabbia, belonged to the Franchi faction.

As the traditional spokesmen of protectionist heavy industry, the Brescia nationalists instead promoted the electrical group's cause. Filippo Carli, secretary of the chamber of commerce, argued that the

[73] ACS, Min. Armi e Munizioni, CCMI, b. 71, fasc. 78, Operai: Ditta Franchi, 17 March 1918.
[74] Ibid., b. 70, fasc. mano d'opera femminile, 13 June 1918; b. 232, Comando di Brescia, 12 January 1917. On female employment in the war industries, see A. Camarda and S. Peli, *L'altro esercito: La classe operaia durante la prima guerra mondiale* (Milan, 1980), pp. 21-46; C. Gino, *Problemi sociologici della guerra* (Bologna, 1921), pp. 203-8.
[75] ACS, Min. Armi e Munizioni, CCMI, b. 232, Comando di Brescia, 13 April 1918.

government had already behaved with gross partiality on behalf of local steelmen, who should never have received hefty war contracts in the first place. To surrender control of Italy's 'hydraulic patrimony' to small conservative companies would seal the fate of the whole economy.[76] Concentration and bureaucratization of production must be made concomitants of state intervention, since provincial operators could not maintain efficiency and profitability, let alone improve techniques.[77] Close ties to Giacinto Motta of the Edison complex inspired, to some extent, this defence of monopolistic competition. The Società Elettrica Bresciana, for its part, subscribed to the nationalist myth through support of the newspaper *Idea Nazionale*.

Discord between the nationalist camp and the old liberals generated great friction. Professional rivalry heightened hostility. For all his money and influence, the self-made Franchi could never rise to the stature of Togni, the authoritative leader of the provincial industrial establishment. His colleague's foresight deepened Franchi's resentment. Togni stood among the few Brescian manufacturers to anticipate demobilization when he balanced operations early in 1917. Co-ordinating factory dismissals with military discharges, he eased the transition to peacetime normality and managed to avoid the labour problems that so plagued Franchi. The uniformed workers moved to the artillery plant, where lay-offs would later occur.[78] Not only did all civilian employees have the option to stay with the firm and continue the production of seamless tubes, but returning conscripts received their former positions again. Since the lucrative contract that he had extracted from his Edison friends for the construction of water mains required about 500 more people on the assembly line, Togni could afford to be magnanimous with those on the payroll. He opened a company co-operative in the hope of saving wage-earners from the clutches of 'miserly shopkeepers speculating on the hunger of others'.[79] Rather than ignore the presence of trade unions, management hastened their growth 'in the interests of class collaboration'. Togni's refusal to admit the newly formed Catholic metallurgical league to the Lombard mixed commission revealed an inclination towards corporatism. Unlike Franchi and the majority of local entrepreneurs, who welcomed the entrance of a confessional contender on

[76] *Idea Nazionale*, 10 December 1916; see also D. Civiltà, *Il problema idroelettrico in Italia e l'attività delle Imprese Elettriche* (Rome, 1922).

[77] F. Carli, *L'altra guerra* (Milan, 1916), p. 297.

[78] *La Provincia di Brescia*, 23 January 1919.

[79] ACS, Min. Armi e Munizioni, CCMI, b. 223, verbale, 5 September 1918.

the side of the proletariat, he would recognize only the FIOM, the federation of the 'organized' metallurgists.[80] Instead of stubbornly resisting change, the modern manufacturer followed the fashion. Notwithstanding record earnings in 1918, which also saw the firm's capital double, Togni let the ILVA trust buy a substantial portion of company stock one year later.[81] He stayed on as managing director and chairman of the board, but partial resignation to post-competitive concentration protected him from the general malaise afflicting North Italian steel enterprise at the end of the war.

The textile manufacturers showed even less interest in association than employers in iron and steel, but the war forced them to attempt organization. The ministry of arms and munitions assured the metal-lurgical and machine shops skilled manpower, making the mainten-ance of trained and permanent personnel impossible in consumer goods.[82] The high rates that lured experienced help to the metal trades raised the standard pay in the province, so the iron law of wages underwent revision. Mill owners wished to handle trade disputes independently of socialist unions and government agencies, but conciliatory paternalism no longer seemed to resolve conflict. The fluidity of the labour pool established in the sector during the Euro-pean conflict terminated any influence management once had over the work-force, especially since military surveillance and austerity measures radicalized many operatives. Unable to exert an institutional leverage against heavy industry or state bureaucracy, clothiers could achieve nothing better than ineffective alliances limited to petty and parochial concerns. Giorgio Mylius, president of the Associazione Cotoniera Italiana, appreciated the need to co-ordinate the claims of local companies in this climate of pessimism. In 1917 he tried to form a regional pressure group, yet his colleagues made poor recruits. While the free-traders demanded an end to intervention as well as the suspension of controls on exports, their impatience and individualism delayed the development of prolonged campaigns and collective action. When entrepreneurs in the area responded to the 1918 crisis of the clothing market with their usual indiscipline, the Brescian cotton lobby collapsed.[83]

[80] *La Provincia di Brescia*, 27 December 1918.
[81] Credito Italiano, *Società Italiane per Azioni: Notizie Statistiche 1920* (Rome, 1921), p. 777; R. Bachi, *L'Italia economica nel 1919* (Città del Castello, 1920), p. 181.
[82] ACS, Min. Armi e Munizioni, CCMI, decreti di ausilarità, b. 2, fasc. Brescia, sfasc. 6, cc. 13, complaint, 10 September 1915.
[83] *La Provincia di Brescia*, 15 February 1915.

Farmers looked more aggressively to organization. Provincial agriculture, according to the nationalist Ferrata, remained a backwater of
landed property and conservative capital; the state ought to take a
tougher line with the lethargic Brescians and 'coerce' patricians in the
countryside to mechanize their operations.[84] The technocrat's image
of rustic life hid the fact that underneath the apparent stagnation and
sloth real struggles smouldered. Power eluded the old guard of
nostalgic landowners, and the initiative passed to capitalist leaseholders, numerically in the minority. Proprietors nostalgically whined
about their greedy peasants, 'who once were contented with half the
crops but now erroneously think they are entitled to the security of
contracts'.[85] Tenant farmers elected to marshal their forces through
propaganda and action. Although the basin lessees lagged behind
their impetuous neighbours in Mantua and Cremona, they did enjoy
considerable influence, since nine served as village mayors. The issue
of taxation on war profits prompted these entrepreneurs to start their
own association and, under the leadership of Tomaso Nember, they
also concerned themselves with labour relations.[86] The group
favoured an agricultural mobilization programme which would
provide government protection to employers while regimenting
workers for the benefits of rural modernization.[87] Despite the pressures of agrarian spokesmen throughout the Po valley, the authorities
in Rome refused to intervene in estate management. On the Brescian
plain, however, leaseholders summoned up all their connections in
municipal politics to succeed where Emilian associates had failed.
Public policing for private ends began at the local level. During the
spring of 1917, the prefect finally gave permission for a seasonal migration of sorts when hundreds of soldiers, paid at the daily rate for casual
help, left the barracks to toil in the fields. At the height of a shortage in
manpower for wool manufacturing, the ability to take male hands
away from textiles displayed a new collective sophistication
unmatched by other businessmen.[88]

Almost imperceptibly, the countryside had changed. The quiet life

---

[84] M. Ferrata, *La Mobilitazione Industriale e il dopo guerra* (Brescia, 1918), pp. 6-7.

[85] *La Provincia di Brescia*, 24 August 1918.

[86] Ibid., 11 April and 2 September 1916; for parallel developments in the Veneto, see
F. Piva, *Lotte contadine e origini del fascismo* (Venice, 1977), pp. 66-85.

[87] *La Provincia di Brescia*, 14 January 1917; F. Piva, 'Mobilitazione agraria e tendenze
dell'associazionismo padronale durante la grande guerra', in *Quaderni Storici*, vol. xii
(1977), pp. 805-35.

[88] *La Provincia di Brescia*, 21 March 1917.

was over, the old indifference gone. The organizational coherence of the leaseholders testified to a growing public sensitivity. Aware of their marginal position in the provincial order of things, these prosperous farmers sought to assume a political importance on the municipal scene in spite of their small numbers. The rising rural bourgeois did not confine themselves to agriculture, and from a spread of interests they derived strength. Giovanni Bianchi, mayor of Maderno, held the purse-strings of four small cotton manufactories in the Veneto.[89] Emmanuele Bertazzoli, founder of the Consorzio Agrario di Bagnolo Mella, toyed with speculative land reclamation projects in Cremona and helped set up two local chemical companies.[90] Few ever ventured into national politics, but the village clienteles of these self-made men secured them a hold over community affairs.

As the war drew to a close, notables in both the basin and the town spoke confidently of the future. The last three years, Filippo Carli believed, had invigorated the upper reaches of society by restoring patriotic sentiment and providing a sense of common purpose. Intervention reversed free-trade liberalism and recouped foreign investment, allowing native industry to flourish. He advocated workers' participation in profit instead of parliament to compensate for the owners' avidity during dimmer decades. The bourgeoisie had used the wrong bait to entice the masses, trying to 'seduce' the proletariat with political liberties when wage-earners really wanted economic ones.[91] The nationalist urged management to loosen rigid hierarchies and expose employees to the pleasures of the business world; labour would get non-voting shares in enterprise while capital maintained control. The peacetime emphasis should be on producer partnership, not class conflict.

Other members of the chamber of commerce refused to adopt such a conciliatory approach. The influence of industry perhaps widened after intervention, but the government had served as a buttress. Spoiled by state mediation during the mobilization, many in management now seemed afraid to go it alone. They banked on continued protection and compulsory arbitration to make Carli's corporative

---

[89] See G. Bianchi, *Per l'agricoltura a per i contadini nel "dopo guerra"* (Brescia, 1919), pp. 13-14, 20-1.
[90] ASB, GP, b. 28, fasc. 21, sfasc. Bertazzoli (n.d.); see also ACS, Presidenza del Consiglio, Prima Guerra Mondiale, fasc. 17.2, sfasc. 2, Camera di Commercio, 7 August 1917.
[91] F. Carli, *La partecipazione degli operai alle imprese* (Brescia, 1918), pp. 4-5, 18.

paternalism superfluous.[92] With discharged soldiers returning home and local workers freed from disciplinary restrictions on the job, the initial optimism of more businessmen began to fade. No longer a rump body, the Camera del Lavoro suddenly boasted over 10,000 adherents and, after a two-month slump, the provincial PSI section increased pre-war enrolments fivefold.[93] Popular discontent, particularly acute in the countryside, stimulated non-socialist militancy as well. The CGL soon had clerical competition, and the numerical possibilities of white unionism made the town's liberal guardians jumpy.[94] Catholic and lay organizations challenged managerial absolutism in private enterprise just as the steel-yards lay empty and the machine shops tooled down. At the ebb of fighting on the front, the simultaneous pressures of falling wages and rising unemployment unleashed a social war in the factories.

World War I placed provincial class relations in a new frame of reference, and Brescia slowly synchronized with the rest of the peninsula. Peasant infantrymen regarded conscription as a heavy tribute to pay an alien and oppressive state, and survivors from the trenches demanded recompense for their sacrifices. Urban operatives who had avoided the draft faced long hours under military watch in the factories; bureaucratic chicanery during the settlement of trade disputes turned them against the government. Harsh, insecure conditions of employment radicalized a large part of the industrial labour force, but the divergent interests of its members deferred the development of a strong associationist tradition. Local activists parted company with representatives of the national federation, and the moderate leadership of skilled metallurgists could not cope with the influx of militant masses. While collaboration with the economic effort inflated union enrolments, complicity in the rearmament programme also laid bare the weakest fibre of the workers' movement for the separation of reformist and revolutionary strike action would limit radical alternatives long after the armistice. The structural provincialism of proletarian politics remained intact during the mobilization, which did no more than incorporate doctrinal disputes and post-mortem debates into the organizational stuff of Italian socialism.

The effects of war went further. The momentum of arms production provoked the rapid but precarious expansion of provincial iron and

[92] M. Ferrata, *La Mobilitazione Industriale*, p. 11.
[93] *Almanacco Socialista Italiano* (Milan, 1921), p. 481.
[94] *La Provincia di Brescia*, 19 December 1918 and 15 February 1919.

steel, since improvisation rather than careful planning informed official policy. State support allowed the problems of industrial rationalization and employer association to be eluded, although more prescient manufacturers recognized the need for both. Ultimately, what seemed to present opportunities for small, competitive business doomed local entrepreneurial autonomy: the mobilization disturbed Brescia's economic seclusion by ushering in concentration. As government assumed an activist role in the amalgamation of resources and the resolution of social discord, public and private domains began to overlap under centralized control. And with the return to normality, military bureaucracy retreated from civilian life, leaving an administrative vacuum that dated liberal caucuses could not fill.

3

Political Alignments in Post-War Brescia

THE collapse of the Austro-Hungarian army in Venetia brought hostilities to an end during the early days of November 1918. The defeat of the Dual Monarchy moved the Italian frontier north to the Brenner, completing unification. Yet despite the demise of an old foe and the conquest of new territory, the fruits of three and a half years of human suffering and material destruction seemed slight. Trent and Trieste had been reclaimed, but Fiume stayed in foreign hands. The sacrifice of the Adriatic showed that the tricolour remained a minor power. Economic exhaustion, political impoverishment, and social strife figured as the domestic costs of the Allied campaign, a price that developing nation-states could ill afford.[1]

News of the Bolshevik success in Russia and rumours of socialist revolution in Central Europe gave the general instability of government in Rome a universal significance. Influenced by stirrings of rebellion throughout the continent, proletarians and peasants on the peninsula came to expect radical change in Italian political life. As the country switched from military to civilian rule, demands for democratic legitimacy, social justice, workers' control, and agrarian reform dominated public opinion. Collective bargaining during the mobilization suggested alternatives to traditional hierarchies and solidarities in the factory, and those engaged in war industry looked to the trade union movement to organize their interests. Active duty in the name of national allegiance did away with the inertia and isolation which had once accounted for rural indifference, so constituents in the countryside grew difficult to manipulate and to confuse. Infantrymen returned from the front lines to promises of land reform and resettlement; they waited for the Opera Nazionale per i Combattenti to make them smallholders of formerly state-owned properties. The programme, founded in 1917 with a capital of 300 million lire, proved a bitter disappointment to most, simply because the agency had too few plots to

[1] R. Vivarelli, *Il dopoguerra in Italia e l'avvento del fascismo (1918–1922). I: Dalla fine della guerra all'impresa di Fiume* (Naples, 1967), pp. 169-218, 385-435.

redistribute.[2] In Brescia bureaucratic mismanagement and administrative favouritism foiled even the sale of draught horses to veterans at discount rates. The exclusive disposal of these animals to prominent landlords over the winter of 1919 revealed that the liberal establishment did not see fit to reduce the great gap between wealth and poverty in the farming community.[3]

Post-war economic realities pushed labour leaders further to the left. Factory organizers, who had hitherto limited protest to propaganda against demobilization procedure, soon abandoned the passive posture adopted during rearmament. The Brescia Camera del Lavoro advocated sacking all women in the steel-yards in order to leave room for male recruits, but within weeks of the armistice unionists recognized that nothing would protect the membership from dismissal.[4] Transport problems and coal shortages hindered production in the capital goods sector, and the number of positions in provincial heavy industry dropped by more than half during the first months of 1919.[5] Franchi fired some 5,000 operatives from the Sant'Eustacchio installation, while the Metallurgica Bresciana management let 6,800 workers go.[6] The decline of the lira abroad aggravated conversion difficulties at home. The cost of living soared as lay-offs mounted.[7] The arguments of the maximalists for an aggressive platform gained ground, and militants pledged their opposition to the bourgeois state.[8] Although demands for an eight-hour day and unemployment benefits did little to attract jobless veterans to the socialist cause, such immediate objectives permitted the local party directorate and the metallurgical league to bridge tactical differences, which appeared during the interventionist period, in common action after victory.

As elsewhere on the peninsula, demobilization, unemployment, and inflation provoked the radicalization of other groups too. Post and

---

[2] L. Einaudi, *La condotta economica*, p. 292, 307-9.

[3] *La Provincia di Brescia*, 25 January 1919; *Il Combattente*, 31 May 1919, 1 August 1920. See also A. Papa, 'Guerra e terra 1915-1918', in *Studi Storici*, vol. x (1969), pp. 29-45; L. Einaudi, *La condotta economica*, pp. 282-6.

[4] *La Provincia di Brescia*, 10 January 1919; R. Vivarelli, *Il dopoguerra in Italia*, pp. 299-321.

[5] Camera di Commercio e Industria di Brescia, *L'economia bresciana*, vol. ii, fasc. 2, p. 76.

[6] ASIG, Società Anonima Franchi Gregorini, Consiglio di Amministrazione, verbale, 25 January 1919; *La Provincia di Brescia*, 9 and 16 February 1919.

[7] Camera di Commercio ed Industria di Brescia, *Variazioni nel costo della vita e nei salari a Brescia*, p. 6; L. Einaudi, *La condotta economica*, pp. 354-5.

[8] ACS, Min. Interno, DGPS, AGR 1919, b. 47, cat. C2, fasc. Brescia, 12 January and 3 February 1919.

telegraph employees initiated agitation to obtain pay increases, and workers at the municipal cafeteria went on strike for better conditions.[9] Salesmen of the province held a meeting to establish a bargaining organ that would negotiate uniform wage scales in the private sector.[10] The white leagues did not escape the recriminatory mood of 1919. Catholic militants, perhaps unsuccessful in deflecting the FIOM's following in heavy industry, won a strong position among textile operatives in the foothills to the west of the capital.[11] The Unione Cattolica del Lavoro also commanded support from the intermediate categories of rural labour. Sharecroppers, small tenants, and petty proprietors, all of whom wanted to keep their farms, found it difficult to get excited about socialist talk of collectivization. The UCL agenda of class collaboration through the extension of co-operative marketing and credit facilities appealed to the individualistic cultivators. Those peasant veterans without land sought fraternity in the Associazione Nazionale dei Combattenti. Based on a loose coalition of disparate political tendencies, the ANC focused its attention on placing inactive servicemen in the public works projects of the subalpine Valcamonica zone, which had deteriorated over the course of war.[12]

Socialist, Catholic, and combatants' spokesmen did agree on one issue. They expected the rich who benefited from the boom economy to pay the social costs of demobilization. In 1919 the ministry of Vittorio Emanuele Orlando, struggling with a massive budget deficit, commercial transport breakdown, and unprecedented labour unrest, became trapped between popular pressures and conservative resentment. The announcement of plans to charge a surtax on war profits, designed to hush the public outcry for disapprobation, ended by alienating the business community. The proposed impost made employers feel insecure and indignant but never brought government closer to the people. The old political machine had broken, for no class would respond to its call.

Employers and the Transition to Peace

Divisions among the agrarian élite widened during the return to normality. The attempt to penalize profit met resistance from the rural

---

[9] *La Provincia di Brescia*, 14 and 16 December 1918.

[10] Ibid., 17 December 1918.

[11] Ibid., 15 February 1919; *Il Cittadino di Brescia*, 14 and 15 February 1919.

[12] *Il Combattente*, 15 May 1919; G. Sabbatucci, *I combattenti nel primo dopoguerra* (Bari, 1974), pp. 62-4; G. Tassinari, *L'influenza dello stato di guerra sulla economia di un comune montano di confine* (Brescia, 1919), pp. 22-3.

bourgeoisie of the plains and approval from absentee landlords in town. Having taken full advantage of fixed contracts and rampant inflation, commercial farmers considered the taxation programme economic anathema. Estate owners, on the other hand, pointed to the scandalous relation beween high produce prices and low realty returns. As elsewhere in the Po basin, hostility to the proposed fiscal measure stiffened the mood of local agricultural entrepreneurs. Discontents, however, stopped short of conspiracy. The line of attack was defensive: the middling tenant, 'that obscure and misunderstood hero of the war', had been made a scapegoat for popular sentiment.[13] Tomaso Nember's Associazione Conduttori di Fondi, which had earlier attempted to placate traditional notables by favouring a 5 per cent increase in rents, assumed a tougher, less conciliatory stance.[14] Although the state finally tabled its revenue recommendation, the leaseholders' escape reflected the impotence and indifference of the new cabinet, headed by Francesco Salverio Nitti, rather than any discipline or determination mustered by provincial lobbyists. The heated surtax debate formalized the rift between old proprietors and upstart lessees. While both groups dismissed ministerial oscillation as governmental weakness, they had yet to settle their differences in resolute reaction.

Complaints of profiteering extended to heavy industry. Organized labour declared employers guilty of extortion for earning maximum dividends with wages at minimum levels, and criticism of capitalist warmongers became a leitmotiv for radical propaganda. But if some large firms made quick, speculative gains under monopoly conditions, most smaller concerns faced financial ruin due to expensive over-expansion. In Brescia the MIDA steelworks flagrantly abused public patronage by jacking up prices to more than double those charged by the Terni complex for an identical rifle.[15] The Metallurgica Bresciana company concluded contracts to furnish machine-guns at non-competitive rates, yet it approached bankruptcy by making steep outlays for producing what could be manufactured by foreign outfits more cheaply. Franchi ignored calculations of comparative cost and absorbed the failing business, inheriting its double-edged position. He acquired controlling interest to diversify operations and process rare alloys, which would draw peacetime customers. The government,

[13] *La Provincia di Brescia*, 17 February 1919.

[14] Ibid., 3 January and 25 March 1919; *La Sentinella Bresciana*, 25 January 1919.

[15] Camera dei Deputati, *Atti parlamentari*, Legislatura XXVI (1921-1923), documento XXI, fasc. 2, pp. 47, 52-3, 57.

however, took time to pay. Franchi received advances for military orders through long-term credit vouchers on the Banca Commerciale, whereas such great armaments combines as Ansaldo and Breda got cash.[16] Even in the absence of the windfall surtax, the local entrepreneur lacked the assembled reserves to ward off his creditors, let alone carry out essential improvements. During September 1919, a time which seemed to mark the beginning of a deflationary downturn, the Franchi Gregorini supervisory board moved to convert debt to equity by diluting company stock.[17]

Franchi resisted efforts to exact a capital levy by threatening to discharge 5,000 workers unless the armed forces ministries paid up first. Instead of moving toward association in times of trouble, the Brescian refused to join the General Confederation of Italian Industry and the Lombard steel consortium because both seemed inclined to concede an eight-hour day and institute profit-sharing schemes.[18] When the authorities in Rome spoke of sponsoring a redundancy benefit fund, they came under fire for using the mood of the masses as a political compass. The employer's intransigence, hailed and followed by many associates during the mobilization, now served further to isolate the old-fashioned entrepreneur from more informed leaders of provincial industry. Men like Carli and Togni recognized that the war had irrevocably altered the terms of labour relations. They favoured the formation of national syndicates, roughly horizontal cartels, in which Franchi's individualism simply had no place.[19]

Businessmen in light industry went through a difficult period immediately following the war. Since the primary interest of textile manufacturers remained the reduction of labour costs, the eight-hour day and minimum wage regulations won by metallurgists had serious repercussions for the consumer goods sector, dependent on exports. Ambrogio Ambrosi, a first-generation hosiery magnate who employed a work-force of over 2,000, actually encouraged the extension of weaving at home to keep wages down while increasing output. The

---

[16] ACS, Presidenza del Consiglio, 1918, fasc. 3, n. 986, Banca Commerciale (n.d.); *La Provincia di Brescia*, 16 February 1919; F. Bonelli, *Lo sviluppo di una grande impresa in Italia: La Terni dal 1884-1962* (Turin, 1974), pp. 113-27.

[17] ASIG, Società Anonima Franchi Gregorini, Consiglio di Amministrazione, verbali, 3 and 28 September 1919.

[18] For the activities of the CGII, established in April 1919 and known also as the Confindustria, see R. Sarti, *Fascism and the Industrial Leadership in Italy, 1919-1940* (Berkeley, 1971), pp. 10-16.

[19] ACS, Min. Armi e Munizioni, CCMI, b. 215, 14 February 1919.

modern, mechanized mills, anxious to recapture foreign markets, supported the employers' movement. Ambrosi and the owners of Montanari e Studer, another local company, helped found the Unione Calzifici di Milano. Less concerned with the issue of taxation, the organization planned to lobby for better tariff concessions.[20]

Attitudes on the question of association differed among the makers of consumer and producer goods. The food, cloth, and paper manufacturers preserved the mentality of the middle-class merchant. They disliked government interference in the bargaining process and opposed infringements on management in peacetime. For Pietro Wührer, whose beer factory closed down during the war, Rome had come to represent 'those big bureaucrats placed everywhere to block the best and healthiest of private initiative'.[21] The Folonari brothers, turning from the clothing business to create the largest viticulture dynasty in Lombardy, intended to benefit from public investment in the reclamation projects of Apulia but denounced official intervention in labour relations. The commitment of cotton notables such as Mylius and Olcese to employer unionism proved conditional too. With neither interest nor faith in social welfare as a responsibility of the state and capital, the textile industrialists wanted only to revive foreign trade. Above all, their lethargic pressure-group tactics aimed to lift the controls on exports introduced during the mobilization.[22]

At first industrialists in iron and steel applauded the entry of the state to referee class relations in the name of economy. Government intervention appeared the 'inevitable' concomitant of a new capitalism which sought to 'rationalize' and 'discipline' the market by setting up employer syndicates.[23] Convinced that social legislation would fall in frank favour of management, many producers saw interest-group politics as the peacetime equivalent of the war mobilization. They could abide by official mediation of trade disputes in return for high tariff walls and continued military spending, but sales and prices had to be 'free, untrammelled by all obstacles'. In contrast to the textile manufacturers, who stayed condemned to compete abroad by the archaic law of supply and demand, defence contractors depended upon full protection and public purchase to offset the cost of domestic labour.

---

[20] *La Provincia di Brescia*, 15 February 1919; ASB, GP, b. 26, cat. 21, n. 1023 (n.d.).

[21] *La Provincia di Brescia*, 11 February 1919; Camera di Commercio e Industria di Brescia, *L'economia bresciana*, vol. II, fasc. 1, pp 109-10.

[22] A. Giarratana, *L'industria bresciana*, pp. 127-30; see also R. Bachi, *L'Italia economica nel 1919*, pp. 286-8; R. Sarti, *Fascism and the Industrial Leadership*, p. 16.

[23] E. Spagnolo, *I sindacati di importazione e di esportazione* (Brescia, 1918), pp. 2-3.

Following the spring of 1919 the attitude of heavy industry soured. Inflation reduced the burden of debts acquired during the mobilization, but coal imports contracted and demand dropped. State regulation of labour relations ended in March and a succession of strikes soon after revived conservative unease. The Orlando cabinet seemed to tolerate the new militancy of the workers' movement. A body of liberal opinion advocated mild social reform, but companies could appease the multitude on the payrolls with wage increments, profit participation, and full employment only if they benefited from significant armaments expenditure and complete market isolation. The reality of reconversion precluded both provisos. At the same time that post-war political circumstances forced public authorities to acknowledge the mandate of the masses, peacetime economic exigencies produced in management a resolution to resist. A change of government in June did not reassure the bourgeoisie. Nitti's draft of a capital levy lost what little commercial support had surrounded the inception of his ministry. Business leaders rallied to reverse this financial prestidigitation as their loyalties to the regime in Rome began to falter.

Socialism, Syndicalism, and the Strikes of 1919

The national metalworkers' agreement of 20 February 1919 established the eight-hour day, secured pay increases, and recognized internal factory commissions as agencies for the settlement of grievances on the shop floor.[24] Employers expected the concessions to inoculate management against immediate labour troubles. The technical victory won by the FIOM moderates in fact bolstered the urban power base of the maximalist militants, who preached the violent destruction of capitalist society as the ultimate aim of union activity. Not much later reformist members of the Camera del Lavoro found themselves out of office for having postponed the revolutionary moment. Agitation by which strikers obtained economic demands developed into demonstrations of proletarian solidarity unrelated to wage disputes.[25]

When national government declined to place the army behind property during displays of class cohesion, industrialists called upon the local mouthpiece of civilian rule to keep the peace. The laments of private parties led the prefect to recommend repressive courses for public safety. Still, in the atmosphere of the armistice, the usual

---

[24] M. Abrate, *La lotta sindacale*, p. 211; M. Clark, *Antonio Gramsci and the Revolution that Failed*, pp. 40-2.
[25] ACS, Min. Interno, DGPS, AGR 1919, b. 47, cat. C2, fasc. Brescia, 19 March 1919.

solution of indiscriminate imprisonment could test the temper of the ranks rather than dissuade aspiring extremists. Bacchetti instead petitioned the transport commissioner to promote the PSI leader Arturo Maestri and the propagandist Attilio Prignachi from linesmen on the Brescia tracks to positions at some station in a remote corner of the country. The railway authorities failed to comply. Central administration no longer deferred to the influence of individualistic interest, and subversive politics did not merit professional advancement. Unable to eliminate the proselytizers of the left, businessmen lay silent while the provincial socialists became terrorist in tone.[26]

Negotiated in the final days of the mobilization system, the national agreement that made employers feel so magnanimous toward metallurgists concealed the dissatisfaction of the FIOM membership. Stipulations for obligatory overtime accompanied the conquest of the forty-eight-hour week. The contract pitched wage improvements at reasonable levels but proved problematic on two other scores. Unionists had yet to claim back the right to strike, and the cumbrous machinery created to resolve disputes before job action recalled the mixed committees used during the war. Procedural constraints undermined the independence of the controversial internal commissions, which functioned more as instruments for material gain than as organs of workers' control.[27] The document, written by the labour and management representation already accredited by government in 1915, countenanced the extension of the industrial truce after the withdrawal of state sponsorship. Ambiguities abounded in the agreement, leaving plenty of room for interpretation. To the moderate unionists of the CGL, who wished to collaborate peacefully, the concordat signified success to the full since it guaranteed tangible gains. From the maximalist point of view at the Camera del Lavoro, the organizational triumph forestalled a revolutionary struggle to be settled in the streets.

Once again conflict between national union bureaucrats and provincial party spokesmen confused the politics of the proletariat. And as FIOM delegates and Camera maximalists continued to collide over definitions and tactics, new contenders for a factory constituency exposed the equivocal terms of the collective accord. Although the conquest of the eight-hour day strengthened the position of organized labour, management retained the prerogative of compensating for lost

---

[26] Ibid., 26 March 1919; L. Einaudi, *La condotta economica*, pp. 310-11.

[27] M. Clark, *Antonio Gramsci and the Revolution that Failed*, pp. 38-43; G. Maione, *Il biennio rosso: Autonomia e spontaneità nel 1919-1920* (Bologna, 1975), pp. 10-14.

hours through the enforcement of compulsory overtime. Attilio Franchi, who had yet to join the Lombard steel consortium, refused to accept the March concordat on any terms, and he viewed the internal commissions with particular hostility. Benito Mussolini first tested the loyalties of the masses at the industrialist's Dalmine plant in an attempt to capitalize on the employer's intransigence and the workers' fragmentation. Presenting conflicting sets of demands to the Milan mixed commission during the mobilization, operatives at the combine had been divided since the war. The Unione Italiana del Lavoro, the trade confederation of Alceste De Ambris and Edmondo Rossoni, boasted grass-roots support among their ranks. *Popolo d'Italia* reported the deplorable conditions on the shop floor as early as 1918, despite Franchi's patronage of the newspaper, since his isolation within the business community made him a safe target. Interventionist syndicalists simulated an occupation of the Dalmine steelworks, calling a 'creative strike' on 15 March 1919, in protest against the owner's failure to observe the eight-hour law. Mussolini appreciated the possibilities of an appeal to the aristocracy of metallurgists and gave his blessing to the agitation four days later. He applauded the 'heroic initiatives' of the shop stewards, but immediately after his appearance at a public meeting in Bergamo, an anxious Franchi went to talk to the FIOM representatives.[28] The UIL's sit-in soon fizzled out, and all the instigators returned home.[29]

Franchi signed the concordat, hoping to exploit the ambiguities of the document to his advantage, and by 27 March 1919 the FIOM resumed agitation. The dispute originated over his interpretation of the settlement. The industrialist tried to establish a new pay scale for the forty-eight-hour week by calculating old salaries on the basis of fifty-seven hours, instead of sixty, and he also attempted to incorporate fixed overtime into the contract. When four other employers followed his example, the metalworkers' federation could only respond by a strike.[30]

The unity of the left, forged in the face of employers' obstinacy, disappeared during the doctrinal fights on strike tactics, in which the

---

[28] *Popolo d'Italia*, 19-21 March 1919; B. Mussolini, *Opera Omnia*, vol. xii (Florence, 1953), pp. 314-16.

[29] *Corriere della Sera*, 19 March 1919; G. B. Pozzi, *La prima occupazione operaia della fabbrica nelle battaglie di Dalmine* (Bergamo, 1921); A. Scapelli, *Dalmine 1919* (Rome, 1973), pp. 87-103.

[30] ACS, Min. Interno, DGPS, AGR 1919, b. 54, cat. D13, fasc. Brescia, 29 March 1919; *Brescia Nuova*, 5 April 1919.

deep divisions between the revolutionist and more moderate labour traditions surfaced. While the leadership of the Camera del Lavoro passed to the maximalists, its constituent unions remained in reformist hands, so organizational fissures persisted. The local FIOM section intended the stoppage to secure economic concessions. Recognizing the federation's right to negotiate collective bargains independently of the provincial party, the Camera's directorate at first accepted the decision to limit the campaign to wage arbitration, but the secession of 3,000 of the chamber's members followed.[31]

Under the tutelage of anarcho-syndicalists, the semi-skilled dissidents formed the splinter Camera del Lavoro Sindacale. This group maintained that the agreement sought by the metallurgical federation would create more bureaucratic checks on strike action and thereby weaken the basis of proletarian solidarity. The anarchists hit upon a real deficiency in the evasive truce between militant politicians and sober unionists, and the old Camera had to act fast if it hoped to preserve credibility with wartime recruits. Backed by FIOM representatives, the chamber's executive board entered the dispute by demanding that a provincial unemployment fund be guaranteed in the contract. The socialists' attempt to obtain benefits already promised by industry before the 1915 mobilization proved suicidal, for Franchi now refused to concede any indemnity measures to compensate the jobless. He was prepared, however, to meet the original claims of the strikers, and the 7,000 metalworkers returned to the factory on 3 April 1919.[32] The terms, materially expedient for the rank and file, represented a psychological defeat for local activists. The Camera's intervention played a marginal role in the deliberations, and employers enjoyed the upper hand throughout. None the less, the PSI weekly *Brescia Nuova* described the settlement as 'better than most stipulated in other regions of Italy'.[33]

The political consequences of the March agitation heightened the discouragement of labour. According to *Brescia Nuova*, the Franchi Gregorini and the Metallurgica Bresciana companies systematically laid off members of the socialist party, and maximalists found their

[31] ACS, Min. Interno, DGPS, AGR 1919, b. 54, cat. D13, fasc. Brescia, 2 and 3 April 1919; on the secessionists see ACS, Min. Interno, DGPS, Serie G1, Associazioni 1896-1897 e 1910-1934, b. 8, fasc. Camera del Lavoro Sindacale, 8 and 13 June 1919; *Avanti!*, 29 March and 2 April 1919.

[32] *La Provincia di Brescia*, 3 April 1919.

[33] *Brescia Nuova*, 5 April 1919.

daily wages reduced by 2 lire.[34] Franchi asked the prefect to arrest
Domenico Viotto, the new secretary of the Camera del Lavoro, but
higher authority denied the request. Local influence continued to
condition justice all the same. Bacchetti simply waited for a patriotic
demonstration on 25 April, where he expected disruptions to occur
because of the vigilante burning of the Milan headquarters of *Avanti!*
less than a fortnight before.[35] When the old Camera joined forces with
the splinter Camera del Lavoro Sindacale to counter the rally of young
officer-students, the leaders of both chambers landed in jail on
charges of 'verbal abuse'.[36]

Against the pre-emptive tactics of management and civilian
authority, the socialists remained powerless. Employer intransigence
and police repression left labour with no means of redress and confirmed the futility of moderate courses. The provincial PSI protested
at the arrests by calling the usual eight-hour strike, but the appeal
failed to break the brute partiality of local officialdom. Although the
prefect released nineteen of the twenty-five militants detained, the
Camera's most vigorous spokesmen stayed imprisoned. In Viotto's
absence the socialists focused their attention on the problems of
unemployment and inflation, about neither of which they could do
very much. The acting Camera leadership seemed blind enough to
believe in the therapeutic effects of female withdrawal from the industrial work-force. The demand of the '*via le donne*' meant an implicit
acceptance of the marginal position occupied by the 'cumbersome
feminine dilettanti' in the labour market, which had been transformed
during the war.[37] On a more practical level, the Camera's attitude
towards the 'second-class workers' revealed a desperate attempt to
enrol the support of jobless veterans while contending with Catholic
unionists, who had organized a number of successful strikes by
women in the textile sector.[38]

For the socialists the provocations from the left became as trouble-
some as those from the right. The splinter chamber of labour, which
earlier had declared a truce with the maximalists as a result of the

[34] Ibid., 7 June 1919.
[35] ACS, Presidenza del Consiglio, Prima Guerra Mondiale, fasc. 19.25, sfasc. 2, 2 May
1919.
[36] ACS, Min. Interno, DGPS, AGR 1919, b. 47, cat. C2, fasc. Brescia, 1 May 1919.
[37] *Brescia Nuova*, 10 May and 30 August 1919; *Guerra di Classe*, 19 April and 28 June
1919.
[38] ACS, Min. Interno, DGPS, AGR 1919, b. 39a, cat. C1, fasc. Brescia, 10 and 12 May
1919; *Il Cittadino di Brescia*, 23 April and 9 May 1919.

recent arrests, now passed to the offensive. With Viotto conveniently in gaol, the anarcho-syndicalists saw their chance to capture the federated Camera del Lavoro and called a 'political strike' in all factories owned by Franchi. The organizers expected the rank and file to come out in sympathy and discredit the official leadership, but the plot backfired miserably. Enlisting the aid of the employer and the prefect, FIOM representatives escorted the metalworkers past the picket lines. The anarcho-syndicalists made great play of this new alliance, chiding the bureaucrats of the CGL for co-operating with the forces of reaction. The Camera del Lavoro Sindacale, however, found itself in a position no happier, since its efforts to permeate the labour movement in heavy industry by planting revolutionary activists there alienated potential support. Rather than admit defeat, the hard core of militants preferred to extend the agitation to other sectors, in the hope of receiving a more favourable reception, but the membership remained faithful to the traditional socialist unions.[39]

The defeat suffered by the secessionists temporarily postponed further feuding within the local labour movement and strengthened by default the position of the old leadership. The political eclipse of anarcho-syndicalism coincided with the spread of popular unrest and violence throughout the peninsula. Uncontrolled inflation more than tripled 1914's retail prices in the province and, as elsewhere in Italy, the hopeless inadequacy of Orlando's economic measures exacerbated tensions.[40] On 3 July 1919 women began to invade food shops in the centre of town. Although this spontaneous expression of discontent erupted independently of the socialist organization, the Camera del Lavoro intervened to co-ordinate the incident and announced a general strike against the rising cost of living. But the agitation that culminated with the pillage of the municipal market escaped the maximalists' control. The mayor agreed to establish a compulsory price ceiling and the Camera called off the stoppage to maintain credibility in bargaining with the city council. Again, revolutionary unionists tried to take matters into their own hands and urged the rioters to repudiate the command and continue the protest. Unable to restrain the militancy of the new left, the PSI officials failed

[39] ACS, Min. Interno, DGPS, AGR 1919, b. 54, cat. D13, fasc. Brescia, 6 and 8 May 1919; *La Provincia di Brescia*, 7 and 8 May 1919.

[40] Camera di Commercio e Industria di Brescia, *L'economia bresciana*, vol. ii, fasc. 2, pp. 50-126; A. Fossati, *Lavoro e produzione in Italia*, p. 634; Ministero dell'Economia Nazionale, Direzione Generale del Lavoro e della Previdenza Sociale, *I conflitti del lavoro in Italia nel decennio 1914–1923* (Rome, 1924), pp. 153, 167.

to bring a compromise solution to the problem of public disorder. The socialist directorate may have lost its hold over the piazza, but the prefect did not, since troops arrived to keep the peace. Killing a child and seriously wounding several demonstrators, the soldiers suppressed the outbreak with great effect.[41]

In other provinces of the North, the cost-of-living incidents during July prompted an increase in membership for the socialist-affiliated leagues.[42] At Brescia, though, the Camera del Lavoro emerged weakened by the episode. Its sole instrument to protest against the police violence which accompanied the riots remained a parade of revolutionary solidarity, yet the prestige of the maximalists had already declined and they could not afford another display of their inability to subdue wayward spirits. Arturo Maestri stalled for time and delayed agitation until 20 July, the day of the infamous 'international strike' which organizers thought would bring production on the peninsula to a standstill.[43] The result still proved disastrous since the replay of disorder and repression exhausted the ranks. When the French trade confederation refused to participate, Italian railwaymen withdrew their support from the labour front. Threatening to leave the CGL if censured, post and telegraph employees defied the Camera's directive as well. Then, thousands of textile workers in the province announced their intention to stay at the mills. Only in heavy industry did the stoppage assume nearly general proportions.[44]

The strikes encouraged by factiousness within the union camp not only divided the workers' movement against itself, but they also horrified the bourgeoisie. The July incidents fed the fears of the propertied élite and provoked a sense of real crisis. Provincial notables who months before had spoken about policies of appeasement towards organized labour began to assume a defensive posture, and maximalist mention of burning the 'old, decrepit, and putrid frying-pan of capitalism' did little to reassure them.[45] Conservative liberals

[41] ACS, Min. Interno, DGPS, AGR 1919, b. 39a, cat. C1, fasc. Brescia, 6-8 July 1919; *La Provincia di Brescia*, 9 July 1919; *La Sentinella Bresciana*, 9 July 1919; *Brescia Nuova*, 12 July 1919.

[42] See, for example, P. Corner, *Fascism in Ferrara 1915-1925* (London, 1975), pp. 62-3; M. Vaini, *Le origini del fascismo a Mantova* (Rome, 1961), p. 67; R. Vivarelli, *Il dopoguerra in Italia*, pp. 414-15.

[43] ACS, Min. Interno, DGPS, AGR 1919, b. 59a, cat. K5, fasc. Brescia, sfasc. sciopero generale, 14 and 16 July 1919; *La Sentinella Bresciana*, 18 July 1919; *Avanti!*, 17-20 July 1919.

[44] ACS, Min. Interno, DGPS, AGR 1919, b. 59a, cat. K5, fasc. Brescia, sfasc. sciopero generale, 21 July 1919; *La Provincia di Brescia*, 22 July 1919.

[45] *Brescia Nuova*, 12 July 1919.

retaliated by attributing inflation solely to high wages, and some industrialists accused the government of putting up with 'bolshevik antics' at management's expense.[46] Blame fell on the prefect, making him vulnerable to criticism from the right as well as from the left. Giacomo Bonicelli, a moderate deputy, complained that *agents provocateurs* hired by the socialists for 1,200 lire monthly had been allowed to 'incite class hatred' undisturbed by public authority.[47] Shopkeepers, whose stores had been damaged during the cost-of-living riots, demanded that Bacchetti secure state funds to compensate for their losses 'due to the complete absence of police protection'.[48] Concerned citizens founded the Lega di Tutela Civile two weeks after the mob action. The civil defence league vowed to 'bring back that sense of order and national discipline ... and to oppose with propaganda and deed all forms of political immorality'.[49]

The increasing violence of social conflict spurred employers to arrange private protection for their threatened interests. Attilio Franchi, who habitually resisted any government interference in labour relations, stood among the first to revive wartime disciplinary prerogatives and clamp down on high wages. With profit margins under severe pressure, he held the advent of the eight-hour day responsible for his financial difficulties and jumped at the chance to retract the concession. The businessman had recently lost the controlling interest in the Dalmine operations, and family shares in the Metallurgica Bresciana passed to the Banca Commerciale as collateral. Franchi's continual evasion of credit barriers now became a liability. Since labour remained the only flexible item upon which he could impose a measure of control, on 26 August he announced plans to reinstate the regulations used during the industrial mobilization, even through use of a prison on the shop floor, and to bring back the ten-hour day. Franchi appealed to the foremen, encouraging them to stay by offering inflated salaries, but he recruited cheap peasant help on the assembly line to compensate for the pay increase.[50]

[46] *La Sentinella Bresciana*, 22 July 1919.

[47] Only two activists at the Camera were on the regular payroll, and their salaries averaged about 500 lire a month. ACS, Min. Interno, DGPS, AGR 1919, b. 47, cat. C2, fasc. Brescia, 28 July 1919.

[48] Ibid., b. 39a, fasc. Brescia, 2 and 29 October 1919.

[49] M. Faini, *La marcia su Brescia 1919–1922: Nascita e avvento del fascismo bresciano* (Brescia, 1975), pp. 66–7; *La Sentinella Bresciana*, 5 August 1919.

[50] ACS, Min. Interno, DGPS, AGR 1919, b. 54, cat. D13, fasc. Brescia, 31 August and 1 September 1919; *Avanti!*, 24 and 27 August 1919; *Brescia Nuova*, 27 August and 4 September 1919.

Although typical of the industrialist's limited outlook, the decision to revert to wartime organization nevertheless caught trade unionists off their guard. The Camera del Lavoro responded by declaring a general strike. Yet even under the determined leadership of the PSI directorate in Brescia and FIOM representatives from Milan, the socialists proved no match for management, strengthened by the troops the prefect placed at the company's disposal. The other employers, who had seemed reconciled to collective bargaining months earlier, could no longer be persuaded to stand still either. Blaming the reduced work-load for the drop in productivity, they followed Franchi's example, against the arguments of Togni. The federated firms now refused to negotiate with the delegates of labour unless the metalworkers accepted the nine-hour day as a precondition.[51]

When armed force accompanied the belligerence of management, labour became more circumspect. The Camera del Lavoro called off the general strike and instead limited agitation to the Franchi enter-prises. On the first day of the stoppage, police intervened to combat unionists and enlist peasant blacklegs. Military assistance allowed the intransigent employer to mobilize 1,231 scab workers in his Sant'Eustacchio factory and 461 at the Metallurgica Bresciana plant. War-surplus lorries provided daily transport from the countryside for the new recruits.[52]

The presence of the military on the shop floor made the stewards nervous. Soon they began to abandon their positions and join the strikers. After the majority of foremen had gone over to the side of organized labour, the Camera opted for a factory occupation as its next move. Yet Franchi, unable to continue production with only unskilled blacklegs, intensified his campaign and called a lock-out on 15 September 1919.[53] The socialists took four days to announce another general strike in retaliation, but by then the federated industrialists threatened to shut down their operations as well. The arrest of leading militants completed the defeat of the FIOM, which came to a temporary agreement with the steel consortium and ordered

[51] ACS, Min. Interno, DGPS, AGR 1919, b. 54, cat. D13, fasc. Brescia, 3 September 1919; Camera di Commercio e Industria di Brescia, *Variazioni nella produzione industriale della Provincia di Brescia a causa degli scioperi e della diminuizione degli orari di lavoro* (Brescia, 1920), pp. 7-10.

[52] ACS, Min. Interno, DGPS, AGR 1919, b. 54, cat. D13, fasc. Brescia, 4 and 8 September 1919; *La Provincia di Brescia*, 3-5 September 1919.

[53] ACS, Min. Interno, DGPS, AGR 1919, b. 54, cat. D13, fasc. Brescia, 15 and 16 September 1919.

its members back to work. Police partiality at the local level confused the policies of unionists and consolidated the victory of employers.[54]

The settlement that ended the partial work stoppage on 1 October included no technical sacrifices for labour. It guaranteed management recognition of the forty-eight-hour week, internal factory commissions, and employment exchanges in which both sides would be equally represented. But all these concessions had been won nationally by the FIOM in March, so the new contract essentially protected old gains and did not entail any real advances. Employers still reserved the right to enforce compulsory overtime, and many only paid lip-service to the mixed committee set up to superintend hiring and dismissal. Franchi served as a governing member of the Ufficio di Collocamento, though he never once used the official agency to recruit help.[55] After the September strike, the industrialist resigned as a delegate to the board and continued to fill job vacancies independently. The Palotti machine shop neglected to observe the eight-hour day stipulation until 1 January 1920, while Francesco Tecchiolo ignored the reform altogether.[56] The Danieli steel company and the Miani e Silvestrini engineering firm successfully foiled the functioning of the workers' councils for months.[57] Such tacit violations of the FIOM accord went unnoticed by the prefect, and the trade federation lacked the power to contain the infractions. Whatever formal assurances the union had been given, the offensive of individual owners continued.

Social Movements in the Countryside

Class relations seemed less polarized outside the provincial capital. The persistence of artisan and domestic industry made union recruitment difficult for the socialists, and during much of 1919 the Camera del Lavoro devoted little energy to organizing in the sweated trades throughout the countryside. Women comprised the vast majority of those employed in textiles, where the antifeminist platform of the PSI did not meet with great enthusiasm. Moreover, the interests of peasant workers in consumer manufacture diverged greatly from the concerns of skilled operatives in the capital goods sector. Most came

---

[54] Ibid., 25 and 28 September 1919; ASB, Corte d'Assise, b. 54, fasc. 11, procedimento penale contro Domenico Viotto e Luigi Galli; *Brescia Nuova*, 20 September and 4 October 1919.

[55] Ibid., 20 September 1919; *La Provincia di Brescia*, 1 October 1919.

[56] Camera di Commercio e Industria di Brescia, *Variazioni nella produzione industriale*, p. 8.

[57] *Brescia Nuova*, 14 February 1920.

from families of small proprietors and tenants, for whom the Catholic co-operative programme had real appeal. The church played a vital role in ending the political isolation of landed labourers before the war and, as they were never fully integrated into the CGL during the mobilization, they looked to the white leagues for direction after the armistice.

The militancy of the white leagues varied with each village, and peasant circles in the basin sympathetic to Guido Miglioli's scheme for workers' participation in profits coexisted next to conservative unions in the foothills maintaining close ties to employers. Never fully independent of church authority, the Unione Cattolica del Lavoro saw the solution of the social question in terms of Christian charity rather than class conflict. Giovanni Maria Longinotti, a clerical-moderate deputy in parliament and a rabid antisocialist, served as secretary of the UCL and co-ordinated its syndical operations. Noted for an exceptional skill in obtaining limited yet tangible reforms, he had built an unshakeable structure of co-operatives and mutual benefit societies before the war. He used work stoppages, often partial, as a last resort and vehemently opposed the instrument of the general strike. His organization condemned both FIOM and UIL militants for their support of the March agitation at Dalmine: collaboration and compromise should supplant the dangerous course of direct action.[58]

The conservative character of the local Catholic hierarchy did not escape the socialists, who accused their competition of being inspired and subsidized by employers. Dismissed as the '*carabinieri* of capitalism', the UCL organizers were grossly underestimated by their red rivals.[59] The anticlerical liberals of the left also charged the Christian syndicalists with trying to dupe the workers into an isolated movement, not noticing that the church militants had assumed a combative and populist posture in parts of the province.[60] In May 1919 the white leagues experienced their most febrile expansion, and this surge of enthusiasm found expression in the pay disputes that broke out in light industry. Cotton producers, slow to recover from the crisis which hit their international markets during the latter half of 1918, refused to come to terms with labour and abide by collective agreements. Although the larger firms in the foothills conceded such reforms as the eight-hour day and minimum wage scales by April, small enterprise

---

[58] *Il Cittadino di Brescia*, 24 March 1919; A. Vezzoli, *Il Partito Popolare a Brescia*, pp. 27, 80, 108-10.

[59] *Brescia Nuova*, 10 May 1919.

[60] *La Provincia di Brescia*, 2 February 1919.

paid little attention to the demands of union representatives. The obstinacy of mill owners caused walk-outs at two shops and, when the response of the ranks became unanimous, management capitulated on all points.[61] Longinotti, who preached caution and co-operation, received news of the offensive with some hostility, and only after its success appeared certain did he publicly support the action.[62] Similar agitation erupted throughout the wool sector over routine economic grievances. Nearly 700 of one factory's 800 operatives took part in a proper, disciplined strike, and the Catholics used this numerical strength to conclude a favourable settlement one week later.[63]

The radical course of white syndicalism was more a reflection of rank-and-file embitterment than an indication that the leadership had abandoned its Christian social moderation. A situation of genuine economic discontent plagued rural industry. Real wages in textiles dropped steadily during the war, and in 1919 they remained below the 1914 level. If the leagues failed to turn grievances into action, individual workers simply took matters into their own hands. An important strike arose against the will of the central organization when Catholic unionists could not prevent the dismissal of three women. The firm responded to the spontaneous outburst by firing participants in the short-lived stoppage.[64] Soon after, unorganized spinners at the Pirola silk mill followed the cautious course of abstention in protesting against the heavy fines imposed by the management, but the outcome of this agitation at first seemed equally disastrous too. The employer called a lock-out, which lasted until church proselytizers saw the opportunity to win recruits by intervening in the dispute one week later. The UCL exacted some nominal changes in the company's strict disciplinary code, and its new members dutifully returned to the shop.[65]

Aiming at a religious rather than an occupational solidarity, the Catholic syndicates meant to keep the congregation away from Marxist materialism. Because the church activists owed their success to the policy of negotiating with individual employers for practical remedies and confining agitation to one factory at a time, the

---

[61] ACS, Min. Interno, DGPS, AGR 1919, b. 39a, cat. C1, fasc. Brescia, 12, 22 and 27 May; *Il Cittadino di Brescia*, 19, 20 and 28 May 1919.

[62] Ibid., 13, 14, 22 and 24 May 1919.

[63] ACS, Min. Interno, DGPS, AGR 1919, b. 39a, cat. C1, fasc. Brescia, 16 and 23 May 1919.

[64] ACS, Min. Interno, DGPS, AGR 1919, b. 39a, cat. C1, fasc. Brescia, 4 August 1919.

[65] Ibid., 9 September 1919; *Il Cittadino di Brescia*, 8-10 September 1919.

'professional' labour movement tended to be more fragmented and less contentious than the socialist organization. The UCL settled grievances peacefully, and members received immediate economic benefits in the majority of cases. But the localized nature of the disputes and of their resolution did little to advance the development of a centralized, stronger form of unionism. Dependent on individual militants in isolated circumstances, the political face of social Catholicism changed from parish to parish.[66]

Although the UCL remained ideologically fractured, its parliamentary affiliate, the Partito Popolare Italiano, emerged with a decidedly conservative colour at Brescia. Founded early in 1919 under the guidance of the Sicilian priest Don Luigi Sturzo, who saw his work as a crusade to capture the masses through modest reform, the PPI began as a Christian democratic organization.[67] At its first national congress in June, however, all the delegates from the province came out in defence of collaboration with the liberal right. And when the Cremona peasant organizer, Guido Miglioli, made his famous appeal for a proletarian party platform, a local notable serving as vice-chairman of the Bologna proceedings walked away in disgust, while the editor of the *Cittadino* prepared a vicious attack on the militant's left-wing position.[68] If the views of the centre prevailed over both extremes during the meeting, the Brescian deputation still stood united in sanctimonious sympathy with the old political establishment.

In some areas the socialists exploited the clerical-moderate complexion of the provincial PPI to good advantage. Popular Catholicism failed to penetrate the eastern basin, where capitalist relations exacerbated class antagonism. Lacking a cohesive élite of aristocratic landowners and a permanent population of peasant cultivators, this zone had never been a church stronghold. Farmers continued to resist all concessions to landless wage labour in order to maintain wider margins of profit at the expense of social stability. Since casual workers had no fixed interest in the soil they tilled, the UCL co-operative programme appealed less to them. It was from the agricultu-

[66] ASB, GP, b. 15, cat. 24, ricorso n. 195, 21 April 1924 (details of 1919 strikes in silk shops); F. Piva, *Lotte contadine e origini del fascismo*, pp. 100-6; M. Fabbro, *Fascismo e lotta politica in Friuli (1920–1926)* (Padua, 1974), pp. 27-30; A. Zanibelli, *Le leghe 'bianche' nel Cremonese (dal 1900 al 'Lodo Bianchi')* (Rome, 1961), pp. 49-64.

[67] R. Webster, *Christian Democracy in Italy 1860–1960* (London, 1961), pp. 62-3; E. Pratt Howard, *Il Partito Popolare Italiano* (Florence, 1957), pp. 155-66.

[68] *Il Cittadino di Brescia*, 15 and 16 June 1919; G. De Rosa, *Storia del movimento cattolico*, vol. ii, p. 78.

ral proletariat of the plain bordering Mantua that the Federterra claimed the most recruits.

The spread of the socialist movement to the Brescian countryside owed its new momentum to the organizing efforts of local railwaymen. Members of the town Camera del Lavoro stationed in the hinterland would tour villages during their spare time and set up Federterra leagues. The progress of these activists in engaging hired hands proved patchy in the western plain, as peasants on yearly contracts predominated there. As Calvisano in the eastern basin, however, the captain of the train depot scored success with casual day labourers. Enlisting the help of a fellow linesman, he tried to ape the initiatives of the Po valley unions, which sought to establish uniform pay scales and an eight-hour day in farming.[69] A partial strike broke out in the district during May 1919, and within days the agitation extended to the central flats above Cremona. The radical upsurge of collective action found the rural élites unprepared, and growers immediately conceded defeat.[70] Unlike their colleagues in Emilia, Federterra leaders in the provincial lowlands could not gain control of employment exchanges, but instead they exacted the imposition of a labour quota. Under the terms of the new contract, all irrigated farms had to maintain a fixed number of salaried workers during the winter months. The arrangement represented the first pledge to employ that was enforced on the peninsula, and it significantly circumscribed the prerogatives of management.[71]

Enrolments in the red leagues soared after the May accord. The police urged the transfer of the railway activists, so great seemed the 'pernicious effects of their extremist theories on the rural masses' following the agitation.[72] Another militant at Manerbio led a group of salaried workers into a strike and the proprietors capitulated after five days.[73] This first ingress into church territory got UCL leaders anxious, since many dependent labourers of the area left the white unions in the hope of obtaining better terms with the socialist competition. At Castenedolo the local Camera del Lavoro claimed over a hundred new members during the course of a week, and when two PSI spokesmen from town held a public meeting in Orzinuovi,

[69] L. Preti, *Le lotte agrarie*, pp. 228-34; A. Serpieri, *La guerra e le classi rurali italiane*, pp. 413-16.

[70] P. Albertario, *I salari agricoli*, pp. 209-11; *La Sentinella Bresciana*, 4 May 1919.

[71] L. Einaudi, *La condotta economica*, p. 304.

[72] ACS, Min. Interno, DGPS, AGR 1919, b. 47, cat. C2, fasc. Brescia, 21 May 1919.

[73] *Brescia Nuova*, 7 June 1919.

they drew a crowd of 2,000.[74] After PPI organizers failed to shout down the socialist speakers, the prefect suspended the rally and authorized the arrest of its most receptive participants.[75]

The general expansion of the socialist agricultural unions stopped short of the Catholic citadel in the foothills, where the intermediate categories of rural labour prevailed.[76] Peasant ties to the parish stayed close and the hold of the priest remained uncontested. In this district the church traditionally played a democratizing role, which the Camera del Lavoro tried desperately to assume, but sharecroppers, small tenant farmers, and petty proprietors showed little interest in the PSI objective of collectivization that would convert the flock into landless workers. The very name of the Lega di Miglioramento e di Mutuo Soccorso at Bornato, founded by local railwaymen, emphasized the associationist rather than the revolutionist spirit of the proletarian cause, yet attempts to conjure away Catholicism still amounted to naught. When representatives from the Federterra arrived to inaugurate the league in June, only 150 villagers showed up and most of them came to heckle.

Catholic peasant conscripts returning from the front often became the *popolari*'s most impetuous militants. And those former servicemen who suspected the PPI of covert clericalism joined the local Associazione Nazionale dei Combattenti, founded in Milan just days after the armistice. With both popular and patriotic appeal, the ANC expanded rapidly throughout the province during 1919. In early May the village veterans' groups numbered seventeen, but two weeks later twenty-seven had been formed.[77] By July the federated legionnaires in the Brescia area numbered well over 10,000 and the Breno association, under the leadership of the left radical Guglielmo Ghislandi, boasted the unanimous support of all 2,900 veterans in the Valcamonica.[78]

Discharged officers usually set up the rural combatants' circles. The provincial socialists used the preponderance of commissioned veterans on the organizational ladder as a pretext to denounce the ANC as 'audaciously interventionist'. For the Camera del Lavoro, the new group proffered yet another variant of bourgeois liberalism, only this time under a populist guise. Maximalists pointed to the ex-

[74] Ibid., 14 June 1919.
[75] ACS, Min. Interno, DGPS, AGR 1919, b. 47, cat. C2, fasc. Brescia, 11 June 1919; *Il Cittadino di Brescia*, 12 June 1919.
[76] A. Serpieri, *Studi sui contratti agrari* (Bologna, 1920), pp. 210-12.
[77] *Il Combattente*, 15 May 1919.
[78] Ibid., 30 August 1919.

servicemen's newsletter, which received subsidies from individual employers and parliamentary oligarchs. The Bonomi fuse firm, whose owner made a fortune during the economic mobilization, actually started the Val Sabbia section at Vestone.[79] Financial aid to soldiers' associations protected the smaller, more obscure industrialists from charges of profiteering under boom conditions, while patronage on the part of politicians represented a convenient, however superficial, expression of patriotic solidarity. The ANC managed to exploit both sources of support but avoided surrendering its institutional independence. The resolute denunciation of war speculators and corrupt liberals became a persistent theme in *Il Combattente* and, unlike the multitude of conservative combatants' clubs throughout central Italy, the Brescian movement maintained its distance from nationalism.[80] Although critical of the PSI's rigid dogmatism, the local legionnaires did not foreclose collaboration with the party of the proletariat until the September occupation of the factories in 1920.

Dismissing nationalism for its close links with heavy industry and bolshevism as crude class interest, the Brescia ANC assumed the defence of 'the fifth estate'. The combatants' association stood somewhere between moderate socialism and left liberalism. The organization claimed to be an autonomous pressure group of the neutral masses and sought the allegiance of those citizens previously excluded from genuine political participation. Professor Augusto Monti, the group theoretician, singled out the peasant proprietor, the small shopkeeper, the independent artisan, and the white-collar worker as potential recruits.[81] He looked to a practical programme of public works projects, subsidized mutual benefit societies, and ameliorative legislation to mitigate the uneasy isolation of the middle ranks from civic life. This identification with the plight of the *petit bourgeois* merged the opposition of demobilized soldiers with the discontents of poor cultivators farming the subalpine zone. The veteran reformers gathered strength throughout the provincial uplands, where they threatened to deflect the following of the PPI. The centrist alliance of concerned patriots attracted not only those who had fought and survived but also friends and family of those who had served and died. In a region with strong communal traditions of open-field agriculture, the ANC alone

[79] Ibid., 16 July 1983; A. Giarratana, *L'industria bresciana*, p. 133.
[80] G. Sabbatucci, *I combattenti*, pp. 64-78; R. Vivarelli, *Il dopoguerra in Italia*, pp. 329-38.
[81] *Il Combattente*, 12 December 1920; in 1922 Monti began collaboration with Piero Gobetti on *Rivoluzione Liberale*, the antifascist weekly.

proposed to relieve structural unemployment, by way of state grants to restore the ruined pasture and timber resources of the mountainous war zone.

Although the ANC owed its initial success to the geographical dispersion and social heterogeneity of its following, the conflicting political tendencies in the movement soon became a permanent source of tension. While the popular base of the association widened in the countryside, the executive council remained largely the monopoly of men capable of securing public funds and private donations. The steering committee included Carlo Bonardi and Annibale Tinti, both town notables of the liberal left with connections in provincial government.[82] Divisions deepened between the Brescia-based leadership and the rural folk it represented over the debate on electoral participation. The urban faction that favoured collaboration with the Zanardellian radicals encountered overwhelming resistance from the majority of peasant members backing the formation of an independent combatants' party. Before long, established parliamentarians such as Bonardi undertook to separate their destinies from those of the veterans' lobby.

Under the control of Ghislandi and Monti during the autumn of 1919, the provincial ANC drifted to the left. Alienating the old executive council, the association declared itself antimilitarist and anticlerical. *Il Combattente* bitterly reviled the higher ranks of the armed services for war profiteering and right-wing subversion, with generals denounced for their aristocratic and reactionary trappings.[83] The radical enthusiasm of the Brescia veterans, who had won the support of liberal spokesmen and paternalistic employers after the cease-fire, now troubled conservatives. That this progressive party of rural levellers could pull the lower middle-class vote away from the old liberal bloc did not augur well for drawing-room parliamentarians during the forthcoming elections.

The Elections of November 1919

September 1919 saw an interventionist minority again endeavour to interpret the general will, when Gabriele D'Annunzio attempted military sedition at Fiume in the name of national salvation. But, in contrast to May 1915, the chamber showed reluctance to entrust the

---

[82] The ANC secured much of its public works funding through Ugo Da Como. The deputy, Nitti's commissioner of pensions, was a close friend of the Bonardi family.

[83] *Il Combattente*, 19 October and 2 November 1919.

fate of the country to an indignant few over the Adriatic question. To the dismay of the right, late in the month the government received a vote of confidence, and the next day Nitti proceeded to dissolve parliament in preparation for new elections. A system of proportional representation, whereby Italy was divided into fifty-four constituencies with five to twenty deputies each, had become law in August.[84] This legislation threatened fundamental change at the polls, since the mass parties looked forward to a plebiscite against the ministerial reshuffles of mainstream liberalism.

At Brescia the moribund parties of order felt particular pressure from the Christian co-operative movement. The Zanardellian left urged responsible citizens to resist the evangelical spirit in casting their vote. Liberal concern over Catholic sentiment in the province developed not from traditional hostility to conventional religiosity, but from fear of church promises to the peasants.[85] All five PPI candidates had been interventionists in 1915, and four of them would have passed as reactionaries even in confessional circles.[86] Given the conservative character of the *popolari* leadership, which aimed to bring workers closer to management through class collaboration, the obsession with the politics of popular democracy reflected the insecurities of the old parliamentary prima donnas.[87]

The moderate party chose not to risk liquidation at the polls, so Brescia became the only metropolis in all of Italy where the stale administrative alliance of Catholic notables with right liberals had been renewed after the war. Most large landowners backed the coalition, and *Il Cittadino* served as a mouthpiece for proprietors in their controversies with capitalist leaseholders. Though the electoral rhetoric of the PPI proposed change through rural democratization, the countryside could be conquered for clericalism only if the peasantry stayed isolated and illiterate.[88]

Attempting to break the hold of the church over the province, the socialists focused their energies on exposing the pretensions of popular Catholicism. A campaign of calumny against the white competition ensued. Aware of the PPI as the party to beat, the local PSI toned down the radical implications of the national programme in

[84] C. Seton-Watson, *Italy from Liberalism to Fascism*, p. 547.
[85] *La Provincia di Brescia*, 1 November 1919.
[86] *Brescia Nuova*, 15 November 1915; *Il Cittadino di Brescia*, 5 and 16 November 1919; A. Vezzoli, *Il Partito Popolare a Brescia*, p. 77.
[87] *La Voce del Popolo*, 1 November 1919.
[88] *La Fiaccola*, 3 November 1919.

an effort to capture the loyalty of veterans and farmers. The maximalists spoke of soviets and Lenin while denouncing the bourgeois state, but they declined to force change by right of violence.[89] If this meant delaying the revolution until all peasants and workers voted the proletarian ticket, the threat of left-wing subversion appeared a very superficial one in 1919.

The Concentrazione Democratica worried about the cancellation of the papal *non expedit*, and the sheer number of new voters overwhelmed civilian authority. Electoral registration closed ahead of schedule, since improper practices at the polls remained the only means of conservative redress in an age of universal suffrage. In addition the prefect ordered 2,500 troops to keep the crowds in line should the socialists stage an insurrection, but the ministry of the interior judged the request excessive. Two hundred soldiers instead left for Brescia, and Nitti urged administrative impartiality in all provinces.[90]

The military reinforcements in fact proved unnecessary. The old parties of order found defeat not in the piazza but at the polls. The November elections of 1919 gave the PPI in the district of Brescia 44,818 votes, which totalled 46 per cent, against the 23,406 of the PSI. The alliance of reform socialists and anticlerical liberals received 18,929 ballots while the ANC got 12,224. Proportional representation saved the Zanardellian democrats from political extinction, so Carlo Bonardi went to parliament. The moderates fared no better. Giacomo Bonicelli, the most venerated politician of the constitutional right, lost the seat he had held since 1902. In all the province returned eight deputies to Montecitorio: four *popolari*, two maximalists, one democrat, and a veteran.[91]

The November results represented a popular mandate for social change. The PPI lost momentum only in those communes where the new party's ties with conservative clienteles came to light. The *popolari* performed poorly in the city, since clerical and moderate forces had controlled the municipal council since 1905. Still closely

[89] *Brescia Nuova*, 11 October and 8 November 1919.

[90] ACS, Min. Interno, DGPS, AGR 1919, b. 55a, cat. E1, fasc. Brescia, 26 October, 6 and 9 November 1919.

[91] *La Sentinella Bresciana*, 18 November 1919; *La Provincia di Brescia*, 18 and 19 November 1919; U. Giusti, *Le correnti politiche italiane attraverso due riforme elettorali dal 1909 al 1921* (Florence, 1922), p. 109. Bazoli, Longinotti, Montini, and Salvadori comprised the *popolari* elected. The socialists returned were Bianchi and Maestri. Bonardi became the only Zanardellian victor, and Ghislandi went to Rome on the ANC ticket.

associated with the traditional right alliance in town, the Christian democrats did not offer a real alternative to the traditional establishment there. The Catholics triumphed in the foothills and the central basin, encountering serious competition from their socialist rivals in the eastern plains, and the PSI came out ahead in all industrialized zones near the provincial capital. In the process of partition between red and white strongholds, the old liberal bloc vanished from electoral geography.

Although the triumph of the mass parties proved much less imposing than the socialist challenge in other provinces, at Brescia too the elections clearly showed that workers, peasants, and veterans expected much more than the compromise and gradualism advocated by conservative bloc politics. The constitutional parties initially tried to ignore the radical implications of their set-back. The Zanardellian left blamed the poor turnout of voters.[92] The moderates claimed credit for the PPI victory, although the running of their two candidates actually put a drag on the Catholic slate. Da Como and Bonicelli, the outgong deputies abused by the ignoble classes, were portrayed as the 'undeserving victims' of proportional representation.[93] It became increasingly difficult, however, for even the more obtuse and obstinate notables to overlook the pathos of post-war Italian liberalism.[94]

While the constitutional parties hesitated to concede defeat, they could not forge new alignments. The old rift between the Concentrazione Democratica and the moderate camp deepened after November 1919. Instead of unifying the liberal establishment, electoral disaster confirmed former divisions. Hoping to steal a share of Catholic success in provincial administration, conservatives fell under the tutelage of their clerical allies. The Zanardellians, who clung tenaciously to their grand secular traditions, found the temporary surrender of the right to the PPI bandwagon appalling.[95] Still convinced of the Giolittian ideal of disinterested bourgeois renovation, they preached reconstruction through cautious reform. The transformed style of interest-group and mass-base politics obliterated the liberal mission, but a fragmented Italian centre would offer no new or coherent course of action.

[92] *La Provincia di Brescia*, 20 November 1919.
[93] *La Sentinella Bresciana*, 21 November 1919.
[94] A. Lyttelton, *The Seizure of Power: Fascism in Italy 1919–1929* (London, 1973), pp. 33–5; C. Maier, *Recasting Bourgeois Europe: Stabilization in France, Germany, and Italy in the Decade after World War I* (Princeton, 1975), pp. 128–33.
[95] *La Provincia di Brescia*, 21 November 1919.

4

Labours of the Left

THE elections of 1919 made stable civilian rule a political impossibility. The PSI and the PPI topped the lists throughout most of the
country to win more than half the seats in Rome, so the success of any
coalition came to depend upon these two inexperienced parties.
Because the maximalists refused collaboration with any bourgeois
regime, no cabinet could expect participation from the largest elected
group in the chamber. Socialist withdrawal from ministerial responsibility bequeathed the charge of leading the new legislature to the
popolari, yet the divided Christian democrats acted with weakness and
indecision. Catholic hesitations then, in addition to the abdication of
the left, allowed established statesmen to stay as the executors of the
commonweal, even though they recognized the legitimacy of their
defeat at the polls. Nitti put together a patchwork ministry, which
survived the November returns for seven months. The mandate of the
masses confirmed the exhaustion of the traditional liberal programme,
but representative institutions failed to channel popular discontent
into administrative reform. Against this background of parliamentary
stalemate must be set the impotence and indifference that came to
characterize central government in Italy during 1920.[1]

Peacetime economic troubles did not abate. While textiles and
engineering showed signs of recovery, the European coal shortage
combined with the world-wide deflation to keep production and
expenditure in heavy industry down. The lira depreciated abroad as
the price of foodstuffs at home continued to rise. Giolitti's resumption
of power in June 1920 signalled a return to pre-war normality for
many. The programme for reconstruction which he pushed through
the chamber included a capital levy, compulsory registration of stocks
and shares, and expropriation of profits made during the mobilization.
These fiscal measures, welcomed by the left opposition in parliament,

---

[1] A. Lyttelton, *The Seizure of Power*, pp. 34-5; C. Seton-Watson, *Italy from Liberalism to
Fascism*, pp. 550-1

hampered investment and caused businessmen to lose confidence in government.

The wave of working-class violence that swept the peninsula during the first months of 1920 accelerated the breakdown of the state machine. In January public servants in transport and communications began agitation under the anarcho-syndicalist banner. By spring Catholic and socialist militants had organized strikes which touched all sectors of agriculture and industry in the most prolonged period of proletarian protest since the turn of the century. The disputes stemmed in part from urban inflation and rural underemployment, yet political paralysis in Rome and labour feuds in the provinces contributed to the confusion and gave the impression of revolutionary insurrection. Membership in the CGL leagues climbed as a result of favourable settlements, and the Federterra in particular experienced remarkable growth. The massive influx of new recruits stretched resources and made discipline difficult, while competition between unions complicated and encouraged street activity. Government efforts at mediation collapsed and clashes erupted between police and demonstrators as terrorism grew. Social tensions sharpened when troops arrived to restore calm in trouble-spots. The swing from disorder to repression alienated supporters of the left and put a weapon in the hands of the right. Maximalists refused to respond to *rapprochement*, and conservatives denounced officialdom for feebleness. The return of Giolitti temporarily softened bourgeois opposition, but discontent reached the point of conspiracy by the end of the year.

The Territorial Division of Organized Labour in Industry

November 1919 inflated the political confidence of the apparent victors. For the PPI 'courageous antibolshevism' had triumphed at the polls.[2] But, according to the PSI weekly, Brescia finally belonged to the proletariat.[3] This euphoria did not stay confined to the printed word, since a recrudescence of labour militancy from its autumn slump accompanied the electoral success of the mass parties. Catholics energetically tried to penetrate the union movement in heavy industry, while the maximalist-controlled Camera del Lavoro ventured into the world of textiles. The advance of the white organizers remained slight among urban metalworkers, however, and the UCL began to lose its following in consumer manufacture as well.

---

[2] *Il Cittadino di Brescia*, 22 November 1920.
[3] *Brescia Nuova*, 22 November 1920.

The Camera's headway in the cotton and silk sectors reflected the new footing of the red leagues. Viewing the church congregation as genuine members of the working class, maximalists took Catholic competition seriously after the general elections. For the first time since the war, *Brescia Nuova* abandoned its contempt for female labour in a pitch to '*compagne*'.[4] The local branch of the textile federation played down revolution and instead concentrated on economic gains as part of a general plea for practical reform.[5] Its organizers undertook strike action in zones already dominated by the Camera like Gardone Val Trompia, a municipality governed by PSI councillors. At the village of Iseo, where a clerical-moderate coalition prevailed, FIOT activists intervened in one dispute only when the timid UCL proved unable to prevent the seasonal closing of a mill without indemnity to the operatives.[6] After the white syndicalists conceded defeat, the socialists resumed agitation and drafted new demands. Threatening to bring out the Alto Milanese spinners in sympathy, the CGL affiliates got the frightened owner to change his tune within three days, during which time the employees changed their union.[7]

This sophistication in bargaining did not result from any home-grown talent. Support and stimulation came from outside. The national federation in Milan dispatched two tireless troupers to co-ordinate the labour offensive and stir the *isola bianca*.[8] The same FIOT delegates brought about another conversion in December at the Villa Cogozzo cotton factory, favourably situated in the Val Trompia. A routine cost-of-living increase, cautiously presented by the Catholics, met the unyielding opposition of Giorgio Mylius, himself a prominent patron of the parish.[9] When negotiations between the white syndicates and the president of the Associazione Cotoniera Italiana broke down, the CGL entered the contest with a November agreement, already signed by the upper Lombard cotton producers, in hand. The contract guaranteed salary supplements greater than those requested by the Catholics. The socialists chided the employer for duplicity and indiscipline, and they announced plans to extend the partial stoppage into a regular strike unless management abided by the accord. Against the organizational superiority of its rival, the confessional union had

[4] Ibid., 29 November 1919.
[5] Ibid., 13 December 1919.
[6] *Il Cittadino di Brescia*, 25 November 1919.
[7] *La Provincia di Brescia*, 28 November 1919; *Brescia Nuova*, 29 November 1919.
[8] *Avanti!*, 12 December 1919.
[9] *Il Cittadino di Brescia*, 10 and 12 December 1919.

no defence. Just days after the UCL's failure, Mylius admitted defeat and most of the firm's 900 workers passed to the Camera del Lavoro.[10] Actually doubling the earnings of semi-skilled help, the Milanese missionaries extracted wage concessions from the Ghedi cloth manufacturers after more than a month of agitation.[11] In early January FIOT representatives demanded that the owner of a large Villanuova fabric company compensate his operatives for inflation. So scared seemed the Cavaliere Strozzini that he immediately capitulated to the proletarian propagandists.[12]

The attitude of cotton manufacturers to the renewed militancy of the working class remained individualistic and backward-looking. Doggedly avoiding any changes in labour relations, most preserved the mentality of upstart entrepreneurs. Reluctance to recognize trade unions made their support of industrial associations transient, and the national defeat suffered by the Associazione Cotoniera Italiana in March of 1920 revived restiveness. The protracted dispute, prompted by questions over management supervision and by demands for better wages, ended favourably for the FIOT. As a result local employers lost faith in their organization and failed to observe the settlement negotiated by the ACI.[13] Instead of depending upon their colleagues collectively for support, conservative employers simply ignored centralized bargaining and took matters into their own hands.

The FIOT taught manufacturers the need to reorganize into an industrial pressure group. Failure to observe the cotton association's agreements meant more agitation and boycotts; after individual employers finally conceded defeat, the prestige and support of the red union increased on the shop floor. The Cotonificio Bresciano Ottolini stalled the elections for internal factory commissions for almost two months, but by the time it got around to setting up the workers' councils in May, the allegiance of labour had shifted to the left. The company's 730 operatives, all members of the Catholic syndicate only a year earlier, gave 674 ballots to the socialist slate.[14] When the Ghedi fabric firm decided to reduce wages by 5 per cent in June, the FIOT responded by calling a strike that lasted for weeks and exhausted management. Compelled to join the ACI and honour the March

---

[10] *Brescia Nuova*, 13 and 20 December 1919.
[11] Ibid., 24 January 1920; *La Provincia di Brescia*, 3 and 22 January 1920.
[12] *Brescia Nuova*, 7 February 1920.
[13] *Brescia Nuova*, 13 and 20 March 1920; *La Provincia di Brescia*, 14 March 1920.
[14] *Brescia Nuova*, 22 May and 12 June 1920; *La Provincia di Brescia*, 10 June 1920.

settlement, the owner Falciola also watched his employees sign up at the Camera del Lavoro.[15]

The collective roles assumed by industry and labour in textiles at first seemed to hurt the Catholic social movement. FIOT representatives frequently insisted upon the removal of competition at the mills, but only in the knitwear branch did they succeed in excluding the rival leagues from strike activity.[16] Pressures to eliminate the parish presence kept opposition alive in other sectors, since dissident manufacturers had every reason to encourage divisions among workers. Conniving with management at the expense of the Camera del Lavoro, Longinotti's syndicate tried to hoist the socialists with their own petard. The FIOT lost silk-spinners to the church and encountered serious set-backs in the cotton-weaving areas of the western foothills.[17] The independent stance of a few employers presented obstacles for the UCL too.[18] One company, hesitant to advance the monopoly of any trade union, actually refused to ban the red federation. The price the owner eventually exacted for dismissing Camera militants was the imposition of an unfavourable contract on the weavers. As a result, the membership paid the cost of the organizational struggle that split the provincial proletariat.[19]

The socialists attempted in vain to break the UCL's hold in the wool industry. There, the poor performance of the FIOT resulted from the foresight of businessmen in the sector and was not because of any effective resistance mustered by the white leagues.[20] Long the most active entrepreneurs in consumer goods, these manufacturers had boasted modern, mechanized factories based on large units of production. They enthusiastically supported the employers' movement and showed a specious concern for social problems. Rarely denying the moderate demands put forth by Catholic syndicalists, industrialists in the branch advocated co-operation with 'professional' unions to exorcise the red spectre.[21] The Camera del Lavoro complained about the conciliatory attitude adopted by mill owners toward their 'black allies'. Given the encouragement of management,

---

[15] Ibid., 14 June 1920.
[16] *Il Cittadino di Brescia*, 18 April 1920.
[17] *Brescia Nuova*, 19 June 1920.
[18] *Il Cittadino di Brescia*, 16 and 18 June 1920; *La Provincia di Brescia*, 25 July 1920.
[19] *Brescia Nuova*, 31 July 1920.
[20] *La Provincia di Brescia*, 3 and 16 January 1920.
[21] *Il Cittadino di Brescia*, 4 and 11 January 1920.

little could be done to undermine the church's monopoly of workers in the trade.[22]

The batting average of organized labour registered somewhat higher in heavy industry. The FIOM brought out its following almost regularly. The succession of local stoppages launched in January, coupled with the maximalist tongue of the provincial socialist party, left the impression of an increasingly aggressive and revolutionary movement. Closer examination of the individual strikes, however, revealed a wary and weakened posture. Virtually all job action protected members against widespread violations of the March concordat, while a number of spontaneous walk-outs proceeded without the federation's consent. Skilled operatives at the Züst automobile shop undertook agitation, which the union later backed, when management at the parent Officine Meccaniche in Milan declined to apply wage increases negotiated nationally months before.[23] The recalcitrant employer eventually succumbed to the pressures of the Camera and the prefect. This technical victory hid the lassitude of the workers' movement, bred in the absence of concrete gains.

The determination of business to fight centralized bargaining made the enforcement of negotiated settlements difficult. On 1 October 1919 Attilio Franchi finally consented to sponsor the controversial unemployment fund that all federated Lombard firms had established with the March accord. The socialists became terribly excited about their valiant triumph over industrial intransigence, but it seemed obvious by January 1920 that the employers had no intention of subsidizing the jobless.[24] The urban FIOM section began agitation at two Franchi concerns located within the town limits, and management would not move. The owner happened to control six firms in the greater Bergamo-Brescia area, yet the idea of co-ordinating labour action in the isolated factories eluded the metalworkers until one month after the failed strike, by which time the Banca Commerciale had repossessed the old Mannesmann operations at Dalmine.[25] At the Danieli steel combine and the Miani e Silvestrini machine shop, unionists felt compelled to endorse an unsuccessful walk-out through fear that reluctance to make collective bargains stick would damage

[22] *Brescia Nuova*, 17 January 1920.

[23] Ibid., 10 January 1920; see also R. Bachi, *L'Italia economica nel 1919*, pp. 182, 405-6.

[24] *Brescia Nuova*, 17 January 1920; *La Provincia di Brescia*, 15 and 18 January 1920.

[25] Ibid., 20 February 1920; the COMIT group entrusted management of the Dalmine plant to FIAT; see ASIG, Società Anonima Franchi Gregorini, Consiglio di Amministrazione, verbale, 13 February 1920.

the leadership's position with the rank and file.[26] All efforts to prevent the tacit sabotage of the internal factory commissions by the Tubi Togni company proved fruitless. The overall effect of the strike wave in heavy industry amounted to one of profound discouragement.[27]

Although the divisive tactics of employers in heavy industry subverted agitation in the sector, the ineffective strike assaults continued. Carli began to complain of the production costs incurred by the metalworkers' disorderly behaviour. At the onset of the European coal crisis and an international recession, local businessmen saw no end to the relentless demands of labour. The mood of management hardened. Resistance, never very slack, now became resolute.[28] Two entrepreneurs in rural areas persuaded a local government official to disband three routine rallies scheduled by the FIOM, but a formal delegation of Brescian manufacturers failed to convince the prefect to outlaw public meetings of the federation in town.[29] The reluctance of civilian authority to protect propertied interests as a matter of course accentuated conservative dissatisfaction with the liberal regime in Rome.

The disarray of organized labour accelerated in the city as industrialists tried to recapture the initiative on their own. The Camera del Lavoro called three separate metallurgical strikes, all of them provoked by the failure of individual employers to pay cost-of-living compensation negotiated regionally weeks earlier. In contrast to the Piedmontese general strike of April, unionists at Brescia settled their grievances at different times and in a variety of ways.[30] Agitation ensued at the Franchi Gregorini plant of Forno d'Allione when management retracted wage increases conceded in March. The subalpine branch of the FIOM appealed to the owner, who ignored the union's letters and proceeded to dismiss 150 militants from the factory. The UCL stepped in with a new set of demands, while the socialists made vague preparations to riposte. Franchi, himself a clerical-moderate, remained averse to any compromise.[31] Longinotti's

---

[26] *Brescia Nuova*, 7 February 1920.

[27] Ibid., 14 February 1920; *La Sentinella Bresciana*, 23 February 1920.

[28] M. Abrate, *La lotta sindacale*, pp. 249-69; R. Bachi, *L'Italia economica nel 1920* (Città del Castello, 1920), pp. 332-3.

[29] *La Provincia di Brescia*, 20 February 1920.

[30] ACS, Min. Interno, DGPS, AGR 1920, b. 74, cat. D13, fasc. Brescia, 12 and 19 April 1920; M. Clark, *Antonio Gramsci and the Revolution that Failed*, pp. 96-115.

[31] ACS, Min. Interno, DGPS, AGR 1920, b. 74, cat. D13, fasc. Brescia, 26 and 28 April 1920.

organization enjoyed a reasonable following among metallurgists in the solidly Catholic Valcamonica. There the local section had cultivated good relations with revolutionary syndicalists, whose leader advised immediate action. Announcing its intentions to hold the first '*sciopero bianco*' in the sector, the white union passed to the offensive. The industrialist, low on supplies anyway, retaliated in kind and threatened a lock-out.[32]

When they could draw upon the co-operative traditions of the pious proletariat isolated in the mountains, Christian syndicalists in heavy industry gathered strength. At nearby Darfo in the uplands, Catholic activists instructed their 200 adherents at the Ferriere Voltri to occupy the factory until management at the ironworks accepted union demands.[33] Local railwaymen belonging to the CGL soon came out independently in support of the strike. The FIOM felt compelled to follow suit, even though it refused to recognize the UCL as a legitimate representative of labour in the sector, so the socialists launched a simultaneous stoppage with a separate programme of objectives.[34]

Faced with a temporarily unified labour front as well as the absence of soldiers to occupy and run the plant, Franchi abandoned plans for a show-down. Inspector-general Renato Malinverno, who replaced Bacchetti at the prefecture, refused to send in troops and tried to dictate a settlement, but the employer would not budge on any point. Negotiations dragged on for weeks, and finally the FIOM called a regional strike of all Franchi operatives in Bergamo and Brescia, with the blessing of the UCL.[35] Reluctant to handle such a massive onslaught during a personnel switch, local officialdom made the industrialist revoke the dismissals and apply national pay standards to manpower in the backwoods. On 15 June the owner finally agreed to respect concessions promised three months before. Catholic support in the mountains forced the socialists to fight an allied campaign throughout the province, and the unwillingness of civilian authority to risk social peace caused Franchi to come to terms.[36] Where the police

[32] Ibid., 17 and 24 May 1920; *Il Cittadino di Brescia*, 16, 18 and 25 May 1920.

[33] ACS, Min. Interno, DGPS, AGR 1920, b. 74, cat. D13, fasc. Brescia, 24 and 25 May 1920; *Il Cittadino di Brescia*, 25-28 May 1920; *La Provincia di Brescia*, 26 May 1920.

[34] *Brescia Nuova*, 1 June 1920.

[35] ACS, Min. Interno, DGPS, AGR 1920, b. 74, cat. D13, fasc. Brescia, 12 June 1920; *La Provincia di Brescia*, 13, 14, and 15 June 1920.

[36] ACS, Min. Interno, DGPS, AGR 1920, b. 74, cat. D13, fasc. Brescia, 15 June 1920; *Il Cittadino di Brescia*, 16 June 1920; *Brescia Nuova*, 22 June 1920; see also ACS, MRF, b. 80, fasc. Lovere (n.d., but June 1920), on the Catholic metalworkers' federation at Franchi's Bergamo combine.

showed greater partiality towards management and the workers' movement stayed divided into two hostile camps, job action ended less conclusively for the rank and file.[37]

The socialist federation of transport workers boasted a better record. Employers accepted the union's ambitious programme, which included minimum wage scales, indemnity benefits, and an eight-hour day, with hardly a murmur.[38] As in textiles, sponsorship and supervision came from the national headquarters, and three trucking magnates actually travelled to Milan to sign the agreement in the company of their associates at the chamber of commerce there.[39] The knitwear workers conducted a remarkably disciplined campaign to force up wages, but they also received instructions from a central strike committee. Most disputes found their resolutions far beyond the boundaries of the province, and the Brescia Camera dutifully executed the directives of the regional Lombard council.

Important agitation broke out in public services. Again, post, telegraph, and railway employees looked to the CGL for co-ordination and conclusion.[40] Making blunders very difficult for the cadres at home, the federation bargained with government officials in Rome.[41] Only in those trades where labour had gone beyond the realm of local solidarity to discover collective, pressure-group strategies could real progress be seen.

Red and White Union Rivalries among Rural Workers

Agitation in the countryside increased bourgeois anxiety. The prestige and power of the Federterra leagues grew as a result of successful strikes and boycotts during the spring of 1919. In some western basin communes, even sharecroppers began to enrol in the red unions.[42] But the post-war agreement that strengthened the Camera's position with the peasantry of the plains also spurred rural elders into reaction. Hostile to the incorporation of casual workers into contractual relations, employers tried to ignore the winter labour quota stipulated by the May accord. Catholic organizers too, smarting from their

---

[37] ACS, Min. Interno, DGPS, AGR 1920, b. 48b, cat. D13, fasc. Brescia, 15 and 22 June 1920; *La Provincia di Brescia*, 22 June and 3 July 1920; *Brescia Nuova*, 29 June and 2 July 1920.

[38] *Brescia Nuova*, 13 December 1919; *Avanti!*, 12 and 13 December 1919.

[39] *La Provincia di Brescia*, 11 and 13 December 1919.

[40] ACS, Min. Interno, DGPS, AGR 1920, b. 70, cat. D2, fasc. Brescia, 17 January 1920.

[41] *Brescia Nuova*, 10 and 17 January 1920; *Avanti!*, 18 and 21 January 1920.

[42] ASB, GP, b. suppl. 33, fasc. disoccupazione agraria, diffide 1919.

humiliating exclusion from the last negotiations, hoped to undermine the monopoly enjoyed by the PSI in representing the rural proletariat. Thus, immediately after victory at the bargaining table and the following gains at the ballot box, activists of the left found themselves under attack and on the defensive. Confined to guarding concessions hastily granted the previous season, the maximalists watched as the opponents of socialism evened the score.

Already in January 1920, employers in agriculture attempted to develop a militant, co-ordinated response to the challenge of organized labour. Yet the rift between paternalistic proprietors and capitalist leaseholders deepened against the background of popular disorder, and the diversity of opinion remained considerable. The dispute crystallized out of a conflict of mentalities. Not unlike certain old-school businessmen in industry, some landowners felt isolated by the modern style of collective bargaining and longed for less competitive days.[43] These moderates, who tended to produce dairy goods in the western basin and had little use for casual help, continued to lose ground in the agrarian association, which was dominated by commercial farmers in the eastern plains.[44] Although a number of die-hards seceded to form a rival organization, the power of the splinter group had limits. Even after the detachment of established landed interests, large tenant growers remained the official spokesmen of the rural élite.[45]

The Associazione Conduttori di Fondi did not launch an attack on its own territory; there the Federterra enjoyed a large mass following among casual workers. The assault on the post-war ascendancy of the PSI began instead in the western flats, where salaried labourers and sharecroppers prevailed. Representatives of the employers' group refused to respect the pact they had signed in May but offered to serve as arbiters of a new accord between proprietors and the Catholic league.[46] The organizational weakness of the moderates compelled them to opportunism.[47] Despite a legacy of mistrust, landowners of the area did not hesitate to enrol the assistance of upstart tenants in the eastern basin to defeat the socialist federation. Sanctioning a boycott of the Pralboino employment exchange, the agrarian association encouraged growers to recruit cheaper help from peasant families.

[43] *La Sentinella Bresciana*, 4 January 1920.
[44] *La Provincia di Brescia*, 11 January 1920.
[45] *La Sentinella Bresciana*, 19 February 1920.
[46] *Il Cittadino di Brescia*, 2 and 4 January 1920.
[47] *La Sentinella Bresciana*, 4 and 11 January 1920.

On 12 January 1920 the red unionists brought out the landless to protest against the contractual infraction. The prefect engaged Professor Antonio Bianchi, who held a *cattedra ambulante* or 'touring lectureship' in agriculture, to settle the dispute, and the agronomist sided with the strikers.[48] State intervention contained violations of the pact, but the government decision on the side of the proletariat led undecided farmers to adopt a reactionary stance.

Throughout the zenith of structural unemployment, agrarians in most basin zones showed complete contempt for the contract written by the socialists. As talks for the 1920-1 peasant pact neared, the employer association insisted that the UCL participate in negotiations. Threatening boycott if the Catholics gained official recognition, the Federterra refused to acknowledge their competitors as legitimate delegates of the working class.[49] The prefect proceeded without representatives from the Camera del Lavoro and underestimated the strength of their organization in Brescia.

A 'mixed commission', appointed by the prefect, drafted a new pact which left little room for compromise. Based upon the loaded principle of class collaboration, the document extended contracts of share tenancy to casual workers in the basin.[50] The arrangement represented the inverse correlation of the socialist scheme for collectivization. By encouraging the revival of sharecropping as the most common form of tenure, rural strategists hoped to instil 'a more active peasant interest in cultivation without, however, diminishing the role of the *conduttore*, the guardian of technical expertise and high productivity'.[51] The conversion of wage labour, which preserved the authority of employers in management functions, would restore the spirit of economic advance through individual effort, at the expense of class solidarity. Turning back the clock, the official committee also abolished the eight-hour day, employment exchanges, and the labour quota imposed during winter months. In short, the proposed contract stood in open contravention of the Federterra accord.[52]

---

[48] *Brescia Nuova*, 17 January 1920; see also A. Bianchi, *Notizie su alcune delle principali attività della Cattedra Ambulante di Agricoltura per la provincia di Brescia dal 1915 al 1920* (Brescia, 1920).

[49] ACS, Min. Interno, DGPS, AGR 1920, b. 48b, cat. C1, fasc. Brescia, 22 February, 10 and 12 March 1920; *La Provincia di Brescia*, 22 February 1920; *Il Cittadino di Brescia*, 22 and 24 February 1920.

[50] *La Provincia di Brescia*, 17 and 18 March 1920.

[51] *La Sentinella Bresciana*, 4 and 11 January 1920.

[52] *Avanti!*, 18 March 1920.

When local civilian authorities endeavoured to mediate contractual relations in clear favour of management, official intervention provoked unrest among the masses. Excluded from the bargaining table and reluctant to accept an agreement that annulled the major conquests of the red leagues, the socialists could not capitulate. Already by 17 March enraged casual labourers had initiated agitation in the eastern basin.[53] The Camera mobilized all its resources for the struggle in the countryside and extended the work stoppage throughout the plains. Five days later, exactly one month after the Federterra first threatened action, a general strike in agriculture broke out.[54]

Employers' intransigence caused negotiations with the Catholics to founder too. At first the white unionists seemed eager to eliminate the perplexities of competition, and they unequivocally endorsed the commission's pact.[55] Still meeting with agrarian spokesmen to secure more favourable terms for small leaseholders as well as longer leases for sharecroppers, the UCL hoped to reach a satisfactory accord for all categories of agricultural labour.[56] The optimism of the league's leaders proved premature, however, since the day after they condemned the Federterra agitation, the agrarian association declared that what the *popolari* meant by class collaboration did not ensure sufficient social tranquillity on estates.[57] Not much later parish syndicalists in the foothills turned a somersault and urged the ranks to stop work.[58] The determination of growers to keep so tight a grasp on farm management and income left them vulnerable to strikes and boycotts launched at the provincial level just as the planting season got under way.

Relations between the PSI and the PPI labour organizations degenerated into bitter enmity during the spring of 1920, despite their common hostility to the machinations of the agrarian association. As the Federterra agitation spread through the central and eastern plains, the Catholic offensive penetrated the western basin and the foothills. Much like rural unrest in the Veneto, divisions between sharecroppers, small leaseholders, and landless farm employees widened when bloody conflicts erupted between members of the competing

---

[53] ACS, Min. Interno, DGPS, AGR 1920, b. 48b, cat. C1, fasc. Brescia, 18 March 1920.
[54] Ibid., 21 March 1920; ASB, GP, b. suppl. 33, fasc. disoccupazione agraria, sfasc. sciopero agrario, 20 and 21 March 1920; *Brescia Nuova*, 21 March 1920.
[55] *Il Cittadino di Brescia*, 16 and 19 March 1920.
[56] ACS, Min. Interno, DGPS, AGR 1920, b. 48b, cat. C1, fasc. Brescia, 20 March 1920.
[57] *La Sentinella Bresciana*, 21 March 1920.
[58] *Il Cittadino di Brescia*, 23 March 1920.

leagues.[59] Instructing strikers to 'influence their more timid comrades', the red activists preached the use of boycotts, intimidation, and physical assault against proprietors and UCL followers alike.[60] At Pralboino zealous wage-workers mortally wounded a milkmaid, who belonged to the white union, because she refused to leave an animal unattended, and they seriously injured another person.[61] Peasants with stable interests in land and livestock became alienated by the destruction of property that accompanied the strike. Socialist attempts to create a monolithic movement in a province where the party did not represent the majority of village dwellers meant combining persuasion with coercion, but such tactics ultimately served to undermine what little unity existed in the splintered rural world.[62]

Nor could farmers resist the appeal to violence. Unable to raise blackleg labour for fear of union reprisals, they looked again to state intervention for their defence. But, sensitive to the parliamentary instability in Rome and the social turbulence throughout the country that paralysed the Nitti cabinet during the spring of 1920, the prefect at Brescia declined to risk a confrontation with the left. While Bacchetti displayed a new reluctance to act as the obedient guardian of rural élites, he failed to prevent officials nominally under his command from deferring to outraged landed interests. Police complicity in the lesser ranks allowed employers to recapture the initiative. Taking his orders from a large proprietor in the eastern plains, the deputy at the village of Leno banned all public meetings in the zone and enforced a curfew days before the strike. By the second day of agitation, *carabinieri* had been dispatched to the dairy farms neighbouring Cremona to protect agricultural enterprises from vandalism. At three estates in the district of Verolanuova policemen actually milked cows, and military reinforcements on occasion served as vigilante units to combat strikers.[63] The harsh offensive of management, which fore-

---

[59] *La Provincia di Brescia*, 25, 26, and 28 March 1920; F. Piva, *Lotte contadine e origini del fascismo*, pp. 162–73.

[60] ACS, Min. Interno, DGPS, AGR 1920, b. 48b, cat. C1, fasc. Brescia, 10 and 24 March 1920 (especially enclosure 1, Federterra poster); *Brescia Nuova*, 28 March 1920.

[61] *La Sentinella Bresciana*, 24 March 1920; *La Provincia di Brescia*, 25 March 1920.

[62] ACS, Min. Interno, DGPS, AGR 1920, b. 48b, cat. C1, fasc. Brescia, 25 and 26 March 1920; *Il Cittadino di Brescia*, 24, 25, and 27 March 1920.

[63] ACS, Min. Interno, DGPS, AGR 1920, b. 48b, cat. C1, fasc. Brescia, 4 April 1920 (interrogazioni: D'Aragona, Bianchi, e Maestri).

shadowed agrarian fascism, perpetuated a climate of civil war by inviting socialist retaliation.[64]

The readiness of public servants to participate in private patrols confirmed the incapacity of central government to discipline and to control local agencies of state power. In the nervy atmosphere of the spring strike, the lower reaches of civilian authority did not hestitate to show where their primary loyalties lay. When the proprietor Migliorati, who also served as mayor of Isorella in the eastern basin, failed to obtain troops by a formal request to the prefect, the rural entrepreneur simply recruited a small army of drunken *carabinieri* to watch the lands he had purchased during the war.[65] The farmer and his business associate Costanzi took the more combative peasants prisoner, locking them up with animals in stalls. His son Giovanni, who had a criminal record, led punitive expeditions of armed police-men to break boycotts imposed by the Federterra.[66] One evening young Migliorati beat a disabled, fifty-seven-year-old employee to death as an intoxicated marshal stood guard.[67] At nearby Castenedolo soldiers gunned down two strikers attempting to hang a red flag from a farmhouse. Moderate landlords tried to detach themselves from intransigent employers after these savage episodes took place. Some attempted to negotiate individual agreements with the socialists, but the police prohibited all arbitration conducted independently of the agrarian association.[68]

Police intimidation proved no way to pursue collective bargaining on behalf of organized agrarian interests. Direct collaboration with bellicose employers exposed civilian authority as corrupt and incapable of preserving public order. The PSI deputies from Brescia filed official complaints in Rome, and the CGL secretary D'Aragona demanded a parliamentary inquiry into the gross partiality practised by the local keepers of the peace.[69] The prefect adamantly denied the

---

[64] *Brescia Nuova*, 28 March 1920; *La Provincia di Brescia*, 27 and 29 March 1920.

[65] ACS, Min. Interno, DGPS, AGR 1920, b. 48b, cat. C1, fasc. Brescia, 24 and 31 March 1920; *Brescia Nuova*, 3 April 1920.

[66] ACS, Min. Interno, DGPS, AGR 1920, b. 48b, cat. C1, fasc. Brescia, 23 and 25 March 1920.

[67] *La Provincia di Brescia*, 25 March 1920; account of Migliorati's trial, during which he was acquitted, in *Brescia Nuova*, 8 August 1920.

[68] ACS, Min. Interno, DGPS, AGR 1920, b. 48b, cat. C1, fasc. Brescia, 24 and 31 March 1920; *La Sentinella Bresciana*, 25 and 26 March 1920; *Brescia Nuova*, 28 March 1920.

[69] ACS, Min. Interno, DGPS, AGR 1920, b. 48b, cat. C1, fasc. Brescia, 31 March and 4 April 1920 (interrogazioni: D'Aragona, Bianchi, e Maestri).

charges of complicity levelled against him as well as the men under his control, and he sought to project an impartial image by giving some satisfaction to the left during negotiations. Bacchetti yielded to pressures from the Camera del Lavoro and excluded the *popolari* from the bargaining table.[70] The red unionists refused to recognize the UCL, which could accept the accord reached by the Federterra and the agrarian association but would play no part in the negotiation of the pact. The main objective of the socialists during contract discussions remained the annihilation of clerical competition.[71] The March settlement brought the Catholics to their knees at the cost of enfeebling the agricultural labour movement internally.

Landlords emerged as the unintended beneficiaries of the operation. Wage-workers as well as peasants with fixed salaries obtained significant pay increases, yet the leagues made concessions on more vital questions. The agreement obliged farmers to find casual help through employment exchanges staffed by union representatives. Since the agrarian association retained exclusive control over the management of such recruitment agencies, rural élites dictated the terms of the hiring system.[72] The labour quota for irrigated estates grew slightly from the previous year, but at the expense of abandoning the eight-hour day in agriculture.[73] Aware that their qualified success resulted from the tactical mistakes of proprietors during the strike, socialist organizers proceeded cautiously in negotiations. They intended to consolidate their political position in rural areas, to the discomfiture of the Catholic movement, even though the numerical strength of the *popolari* stayed the same. Above all, the imposition of a uniform contract throughout the province dealt a direct blow to the UCL, which now had to use Federterra machinery in order to gain advantages for its constituency.

The socialist monopoly over the most effective means of improving wages and conditions in agriculture left the white unionists without a practical programme to sell on an open market. The PPI ideal of class collaboration found no place in the settlement of the March dispute. The agrarian association eventually pursued centralized bargaining with the Federterra, and the exclusion of Catholics on the mixed committee caused them to transgress against the collective agreement.

---

[70] *Il Cittadino di Brescia*, 28 and 29 March 1920.
[71] *Brescia Nuova*, 28 March 1920.
[72] Ibid., 3 April 1920.
[73] P. Albertario, *I salari agricoli*, p. 212.

By April only the containment of its organizational rival came to matter to the UCL, which encouraged employers to repudiate the new peasant pact in return for greater freedom of action in estate management.[74] At Lonato, Longinotti sought to undermine the 1920-1 sharecropping contract by mobilizing tenants to accept less favourable terms with individual farmers.[75] When the parish following refused to co-operate, the provincial secretary of the Christian syndicates moved closer to the right and got the dissident Associazione Proprietari di Terra to impose insecure leases on the frightened flock. Although the red league leaders in the eastern high ground sabotaged the effort by threatening another strike, they seemed more intent on domesticating the competition than on defeating landlords. As recalcitrant employers violated the collective accord with greater frequency, the rural labour movement collapsed into a feud between its two component parts.[76]

The 'Sarezzo incidents' of 27 June 1920 disclosed the calamitous course of the labour war. Representatives from the town Camera del Lavoro led an incursion of hecklers to disrupt a religious festival in the central uplands. In the heightened tension, however, a teenage anarchist saw his chance to take the podium.[77] After PPI and PSI leaders shouted down nineteen-year-old Arturo Camossi, the youth allegedly pulled out a gun and shot a policeman dead. The crossfire that ensued killed three metalworkers. Soon after another died of his injuries.[78] Socialist demagoguery transformed this obscure vendetta into a nervous crusade against the church.

The maximalists completed the disaster by shifting responsibility for the hopeless outburst to a parish priest, in an attempt to gain political mileage from what appeared to be a libertarian deed. The chamber of labour leaked rumours that the 'unfortunate policeman' had been murdered by Don Galloni, a UCL activist in the textile industry.[79] In his drive to disgrace the PPI, Arturo Maestri pressured five Camera members at Sarezzo to perjure themselves, though a worker later revealed that the PSI deputy in parliament asked his

[74] *La Sentinella Bresciana*, 27 and 30 April 1920.

[75] *Brescia Nuova*, 8 May 1920; *Il Cittadino di Brescia*, 15 May 1920.

[76] Ibid., 28 May and 2 June 1920; ACS, Min. Interno, DGPS, AGR 1920, b. 64, fasc. Brescia, 3 June 1920.

[77] Ibid., b. 48b, cat. C1, fasc. Brescia, 28 June 1920; *La Provincia di Brescia*, 28 June 1920.

[78] *Il Cittadino di Brescia*, 28 and 29 June 1920.

[79] ACS, Min. Interno, DGPS, AGR 1920, b. 48b, cat. C1, fasc. Brescia, 12 July 1920; *La Sentinella Bresciana*, 28 June 1920; *Avanti!*, 2 July 1920.

comrades to sign blank sheets of paper in the name of the class struggle.[80] On 28 June agricultural strikes broke out at Castrezzato and Rudiano, in supposed solidarity with the dead victims of clerical and military violence miles away.[81] In both villages farmers ignored their binding agreement with the Federterra in March, but contractual infractions became a secondary issue in the agitation. The socialist party leadership in Brescia offered to protect peasants in the western basin from a backlash by landlords in return for popular support of the campaign against 'white terrorism'.[82] The anticlerical obsession distracted and discredited the left. While problems between rival organizations became more difficult than their relations with employers, political impetus swung to the right. Conservatives in the countryside began to forge alliances with new brokers of power.

Class Conflict at the Eclipse of the Biennio Rosso

The socialists proclaimed themselves the champions of proletarian solidarity. The tactics they pursued, however, left little room for compromise and alienated the most likely allies. At its national congress in 1919, the Federterra called for the collectivization of state, church, and uncultivated lands but, without a programme to deal with all classes of peasants, it made little progress outside districts where the underemployed casual labourer prevailed.[83] The PSI could attempt to win over those progressive Catholics for whom the conservatism of the provincial PPI provided an uncomfortable home, yet anticlerical reaction remained a conditioned reflex of the dechristianized party. Maximalists at Brescia also waged a bitter campaign against the combatants' association, despite the electoral results of November 1919, which placed the radical faction at the helm of the local organization.[84] While the moderate mutualism of the ANC presupposed co-operation with the liberal state rather than its abolition, the veterans deserted their *petit-bourgeois* reformism in those areas where they never expected to speak for the masses. Ghislandi,

[80] ASB, Corte d'Assise, b. 58, fasc. 3, procedimento penale contro Arturo Camossi; *La Sentinella Bresciana*, 8 August 1920. Camossi eventually won his freedom on an appeal.

[81] ACS, Min. Interno, DGPS, AGR 1920, b. 48b, cat. C1, fasc. Brescia, 28 and 29 June 1920.

[82] *La Provincia di Brescia*, 29 June 1920.

[83] R. Zangheri, *Lotte agrarie in Italia: La federazione nazionale dei lavoratori della terra, 1901–1926* (Milan, 1960), pp. 373-4; for the formulation of a more radical peasant platform in Bologna, see A. Cardoza, *Agrarian Elites and Italian Fascism*, pp. 275-8.

[84] *Il Combattente*, 8 January 1920.

the ANC deputy in parliament, promoted the cause of the red unions during the great agricultural strike, aware that his group had no hope of mobilizing casual labour independently of the leagues.[85] In return the political purists at the Camera del Lavoro denounced the support of such lower middle-class interests, unable to appreciate the social discontents the minority movement represented.[86]

The veterans continued to work for an understanding with leaders of the left, but all prospects of acceptance by the PSI vanished late in the summer. The local ANC extended membership to ex-servicemen enrolled in the Lega Proletaria, a CGL affiliate, and maximalists used this gesture as an opportunity to permeate the group with their own militants and capture the Brescia chapter for the Camera del Lavoro. In August the new adherents took advantage of low attendance at a routine meeting and voted to convert the association into a Marxist organization by a majority of five ballots. Although the executive combatants' council expelled the conspirators and overrode their mandate, the fiasco extinguished all future possibilities for agreement. Projected into September, when Ghislandi had shed his conservative allies in parliament, the petty plot did little to redeem the credit of the socialists as potential partners during the October administrative elections of 1920.[87]

The occupation of the factories confirmed the inadequacies of maximalism when it exposed the hestitations and limitations of revolutionary leaders in the province. Rather than firm political purpose, the representatives of labour displayed weakness and confusion. As always the forces of proletarian resentment remained divided, split between those who wished to better conditions immediately and those who refused to accept a favourable settlement negotiated by a third party. During the last year of Bacchetti's reign at Brescia, unity between both groups had been briefly attained, but the new civil liberties permitted by Malinverno after Giolitti's return to power resuscitated doctrinal disputes. The anarcho-syndicalists' desire to work alongside the Catholic metallurgical union increased hostility with the Camera del Lavoro. The dissidents, adhering to the Unione Sindacale Italiana, attacked their PSI associates for betraying the masses by bargaining with the bourgeois state at the expense of

[85] Ibid., 23 March 1920.
[86] *Brescia Nuova*, 3 and 10 April 1920.
[87] Ibid., 21 August 1920; *Il Combattente*, 5 and 12 September 1920; *La Provincia di Brescia*, 8 September 1920; G. Sabbatucci, *I combattenti*, pp. 321-2.

class solidarity.[88] According to the inspector-general, the CGL and the USI clashed on almost every issue. They differed on municipal socialism; they argued over electoral participation. More than anything else they could not agree on methods of working-class action, since the reformists at the FIOM put saving the organization above the violent overthrow of capitalist society.[89]

The slow-down of 21 August 1920, initiated nationally by the FIOM, brought tensions between the revolutionists and reformists to a climax. The dispute arose from the refusal of industry to discuss proposals for minimum wage scales and cost-of-living supplements. Reduced demand for labour and rising unemployment reduced union prerogatives, so the slump strengthened the position of management.[90] And since the metallurgical federation lacked financial reserves for prolonged agitation, a regular strike would have emptied its coffers. Though USI militants urged factory seizure, the UCL decided to observe the partial stoppage in the interests of common action and the syndicalists finally followed the Catholic lead. By 22 August the pace of production fell off, not only in firms belonging to the Lombard steel consortium but also in independent companies.

Once agitation spread to the Franchi concerns, the USI saw its chance to transform the slow-down, during which divisions within labour had been briefly overcome, into a general strike. Abandoning a formal truce made with the Camera del Lavoro days earlier, anarcho-syndicalists proceeded to mobilize Catholic workers at one isolated plant. Longinotti went along for the ride, delighted that he could flaunt his organization's militance in the face of the competition. Although jointly endorsed, the job action failed to bring out most metallurgists in sympathy. The FIOM came down hard on unruliness, and membership obeyed orders to continue the partial work stoppage.[91] Despite this show of solidarity, the episode embarrassed the socialist federation, for management had earlier ignored moderate unionists, on the grounds that their hold remained insecure. On 30 August 1920, at any rate, employers ended the stalemate and threatened a provincial lock-out.[92]

---

[88] *Guerra di Classe*, 7 August 1920.

[89] ACS, Min. Interno, DGPS, AGR 1920, b. 74, cat. D13, fasc. Brescia, 20 August 1920.

[90] ASB, GP, b. suppl. 33, fasc. disoccupazione, 18 August 1920; R. Bachi, *L'Italia economica nel 1920*, pp. vii-viii.

[91] ACS, Min. Interno, DGPS, AGR 1920, b. 74, cat. D13, fasc. Brescia, 23 August 1920.

[92] ACS, Min. Interno, DGPS, AGR 1920, b. 74, cat. D13, fasc. Brescia, 30 August 1920.

The determination of organized industry to precipitate a show-down caused union moderates to lose ground. The maximalist directorate of the Camera del Lavoro seemed eager to stage a factory occupation, but the metallurgical federation showed reluctance to sanction the course of seizure, which its reformist leaders had condemned just a week before. The loose radical enthusiasms of militants on the shop floor confirmed that the left could not command obedience. At the Züst automobile plant, anarchist operatives sabotaged production and took to physical violence against the instructions of the USI.[93] The ransacking of the administrative offices at three other combines scared the conservative classes, who began to believe the myth of proletarian insurrection and that the government had lost its nerve.[94] The socialists triumphantly reported that management had been shorn of the privileges of property and that employers found it difficult to deflect the drift towards revolutionary action.[95]

If the workers acted with confusion and indecision during the dispute, their masters reacted with unity and resolution.[96] The situation escaped socialist control when Milan's Romeo car works closed its gates late on the afternoon of 30 August, and the city's FIOM branch had no alternative but to announce plans for a factory seizure.[97] Soon the occupation extended to all the metallurgical and engineering shops of the Lombard capital. Operatives at Brescia and other industrial centres, however, received orders to continue their still partial stoppage. The FIOM intended to contain the revolutionary repercussions of the take-over movement by regionalizing it, yet employers escalated the attack and declared a national lock-out. In the face of maximalist pressures to make the sit-down strike general and the renewed provocations of organized industry, the metalworkers' federation could only endorse the legendary occupation of the factories.

The post-war deflation exposed the shaky foundation of the local union movement. Falling prices and unemployment predetermined the strategies of the left. Unable to defeat employers or to assail the state, provincial working-class politics remained absorbed in old, familiar priorities. Despite its internationalist creed, the PSI would

[93] Ibid.; F. Porta and R. Rovetta, *L'occupazione delle fabbriche a Brescia: Settembre 1920* (Brescia, 1971), pp. 18-19.
[94] *La Provincia di Brescia*, 29-31 August 1920.
[95] *Brescia Nuova*, 28 August 1920.
[96] M. Abrate, *La lotta sindacale*, pp. 289-94.
[97] *Avanti!*, 2 September 1920.

not foresake stale obsessions at home. The party subdued its anti-feminism, yet anticlericalism and antipatriotism continued to isolate many a new voter. Although the Camera laid bare the uncertainties of social Catholicism, at the same time it spurred on the process of peasant fragmentation. The anarcho-syndicalists eloquently uncovered the pretensions of maximalism, but at the cost of weakening organized labour as a whole. By the eve of the occupation of the factories, Brescian trade unionism was a spent force.

The internecine competition of labour revived the latent isolationism of rural notables. Eager for the protection of state authority in trade disputes, employers in agriculture none the less refused to accept the other side of the coin. They disliked the government's mediating role in collective bargaining, and disunity within the union ranks encouraged agrarian intransigents to go it alone. The failure of their private assaults, however, did not teach farmers the virtues of corporatist compromise. Notwithstanding the incoherence and disarray of the working-class community, the belligerent tone of proletarian protest made industrialists think too. Quietly, they retaliated.

5
Conservative Revival in the Search for Order

WITH the change of government early in the summer of 1920, the old political establishment scored its first victory of the post-war period. The ousting of Nitti, whose rule came to represent economic austerity, social unrest, and the ambiguous status of Fiume, meant that liberal élites no longer intended to watch the country descend into violence while the authorities in Rome slept. Support for the prime minister withered during his third cabinet crisis, when the constitutional parties looked to an ageing figure from the past to restore law and order. Denounced as a traitor over the issue of intervention, Giolitti suddenly found acceptance in public opinion. Determination to secure parliamentary consensus, bureaucratic control, and domestic peace drove conservatives to court the politician they had rejected five years before. Even nationalists entrusted the return to normality and the salvation of the state to the former premier, now nearing eighty. The consolidation of industrial pressure groups in the autumn and the municipal election returns of November gave further testimony to the regeneration of the right.[1]

The occupation of the factories during September 1920 revealed the limits of Giolittian liberalism, as more than 400,000 metallurgists seized hold of plants and workshops throughout the peninsula. The labour cause began with wage claims but widened to include demands for workers' control. Industrialists left little room for manœuvre and closed off lines of communication by calling a lock-out, so no complications over bourgeois collaboration existed for the reformists of the CGL. Union leaders felt compelled to endorse the spontaneous sit-in strike, expecting a united socialist front to force state arbitration and settle the dispute. The premier did intervene later to arrange a compromise scheme, in the interests of ending the PSI's intransigence in parliament, but the failure of the left to realize the myth of

[1] C. Maier, *Recasting Bourgeois Europe*, pp. 180-2; C. Seton-Watson, *Italy from Liberalism to Fascism*, pp. 561-70.

proletarian revolution disillusioned activists without making government the beneficiary. Party moderates stayed alongside maximalists as the opposition in the chamber, and the communists seceded to form their own organization during the national congress at Livorno in January 1921.[2]

The sight of the most educated and mature of the Italian proletariat banded together in a single strike effort, coupled with the absence of police protection on the side of management, alienated members of the business community.[3] Designed to exhaust the left, the conspicuous neutrality of the prime minister during the factory occupations also infuriated the right. Though they were ready to tolerate discussion about revision of war contracts and registration of bearer bonds when Giolitti assumed the premiership, conservatives showed latent hostility to both measures once they recognized that his powers as the 'old magician' were waning on the domestic front. Employers vociferously opposed factory council legislation, and while the onset of recession troubled the capital goods sector, the slump did enable industrialists to undermine and retract concessions without the aid of the liberal state.[4]

The Occupation of the Factories at Brescia

Two days after the Milan seizures, the FIOM instructed its members in Turin and Rome to stay put in the factories as local employers attempted to close their gates. Agitation extended to Brescia on the evening of 2 September 1920, but during the first week of the sit-in strike there, only 1200 operatives took part in the job action.[5] Local businessmen had hoped to circumvent a show-down with the left by abandoning plans for a general lock-out, and as a result less than an eighth of the metalworkers in the province initially organized production at the plants. Most industrialists still refused to meet union representatives and two militant manufacturers, acting independently of the Lombard consortium, even sacked socialist trouble-makers on the

---

[2] *Avanti!*, 11 and 24 October 1920; P. Spriano, *L'occupazione delle fabbriche* (Turin, 1964), pp. 108-24; M. Clark, *Antonio Gramsci and the Revolution that Failed*, pp. 157-80; G. Bosio, *La grande paura: Settembre 1920* (Rome, 1970), pp. 61-75; T. Detti, *Serrati e la formazione del Partito Comunista Italiano* (Rome, 1972), pp. 47-55.

[3] G. Neppi Modona, *Sciopero, potere politico e magistratura 1870/1922* (Bari, 1973), pp. 236-43.

[4] M. Abrate, *La lotta sindacale*, pp. 297-306; E. Conti, *Dal taccuino di un borghese* (Milan, 1946), pp. 239-51; A. Lyttelton, *The Seizure of Power*, p. 209.

[5] ACS, Min. Interno, DGPS, AGR 1920, b. 74, cat. D13, fasc. Brescia, 2 and 7 September 1920; *La Provincia di Brescia*, 9 September 1920.

shop floor.[6] Yet employers in the town and throughout the uplands avoided open confrontation, presumably for fear that without government intervention the dispute might end unfavourably for them. People of property saw the occupations in six of the region's twenty-seven steel and engineering concerns as a veritable onslaught on the capitalist system. And if the state refused to restore discipline in labour, then a threatened bourgeoisie vowed 'to strangle bolshevik bestiality' alone.[7]

The strike of municipal employees, staged by the Camera del Lavoro just days after the metallurgical plant seizures in an effort to bring down the town council, created almost as serious an impression of socialist insurrection.[8] The inspector-general at the prefecture reported that the national occupations had influenced all members of the provincial proletariat, encouraging radicalism in other sectors by spontaneous imitation.[9] Middle-class observers, however, chose to draw much more than a casual connection between the dual labour assaults, since soviet flags flown from factories in Brescia as well as socialist talk of expropriation troubled the bourgeois mind.[10] The urban councillors contemplated mass resignation, but the clerical-moderate administration insisted that they resist pressures from the left and crush the revolutionary conspiracy. Industrialists demanded military assistance to deter 'the warlike spirit of the excited workers'.[11] Obsession with 'the infantile excesses of maximalism' became an emotional reality that would temporarily unite outraged employers in the capital with conservatives in the countryside.[12]

Despite maximalist hopes and liberal apprehensions, the occupation of the factories never went beyond the capacity of capitalism. At Brescia the agitation first fizzled out because the FIOM came to an early agreement with Attilio Franchi. On the edge of financial ruin, the intransigent employer apparently lost his nerve and promised wage supplements to all his workers in an effort to thwart the impending seizures.[13] Against the objections of the Camera del Lavoro, the

---

[6] *Avanti!*, 5 September 1920.

[7] *La Sentinella Bresciana*, 5 September 1920.

[8] *Brescia Nuova*, 7 and 14 September 1920.

[9] ACS, Min. Interno, DGPS, AGR 1920, b. 48b, cat. C1, fasc. Brescia, sfasc. agitazioni varie, 5 and 9 September 1920.

[10] *La Sentinella Bresciana*, 7 September 1920.

[11] ACS, Min. Interno, DGPS, AGR 1920, b. 74, cat. D13, fasc. Brescia, 3 and 18 September 1920.

[12] *La Provincia di Brescia*, 14 September 1920.

[13] *La Sentinella Bresciana*, 3 and 7 September 1920.

metallurgical federation thus eliminated 43 per cent of the provincial labour force in heavy industry from the dispute. A prelude to the dissensions and divisions that would split the socialist movement at Livorno, the makeshift truce with management left the relative role of the unions and the party unresolved.[14]

Maximalists at Brescia got a second chance to transform the limited occupation into an all-out seizure after Franchi displayed complete contempt for the document he had just signed. The FIOM's inability to make the industrialist stick to his agreements reduced the prestige of local union representatives, and the initiative passed to PSI revolutionaries, who rejected the obstructionist tactics of the reformist labour leaders. By 15 September 1920 agitation enveloped almost every metallurgical and engineering concern of the zone. Determined to make the strike general, party purists over-rode the metallurgical federation's directive two days later. The Camera del Lavoro, under orders from Arturo Maestri, issued a mimeographed manifesto, instructing metalworkers at the Franchi Gregorini and the Metallurgica Bresciana plants to assume control of production.[15]

Franchi now refused to deal with FIOM representatives under any circumstances, since the hold of union moderates seemed so insecure. He shifted the locus of action by declaring his intention to shut down operations. A betrayal of provincial industry's collective pact to abstain from provocation, the threat of a lock-out found an unfriendly reception among members of the manufacturing community.[16] Abandoned by his business associates and reluctant to proceed unaided, the employer asked for police to guard the factory gates, but Malinverno ignored the request.[17] In order to press his demands on indifferent civilian authority, the industrialist leaked rumours of a mysterious machine-gun, guaranteed by its inventor to revolutionize European field warfare. He claimed that the fancy firearm ran the risk of capture and misuse at the hands of the workers if they invaded the Metallurgica Bresciania plant, yet no troops arrived from the garrison to protect the secret weapon. Instead, armed forces barricaded the

---

[14] *La Provincia di Brescia*, 9 September 1920.

[15] ACS, Min. Interno, DGPS, AGR 1920, b. 74, cat. D13, fasc. Brescia, 16-18 September 1920.

[16] *La Sentinella Bresciana*, 17 September 1920; *La Provincia di Bresciana*, 17 and 18 September 1920; *Avanti!*, 19 September 1920.

[17] ACS, Min. Interno, DGPS, AGR 1920, b. 74, cat. D13, fasc. Brescia, 18 September 1920.

Camera del Lavoro, after Maestri attempted to coerce urban shop-keepers into providing strikers with free food.[18]

By the time the Camera del Lavoro finally got around to enacting its controversial occupation, the Confindustria had already agreed to accept a compromise settlement dictated by Giolitti.[19] But Franchi, expecting the presence of Catholic metalworkers on his premises to foil socialist agitation, stuck to his guns and defied the decree. The strike committee mobilized labour from other companies to join in the battle and seize the industrialist's factories. Ignoring the advice of CGL unionists and party moderates, Maestri warned that the local railwaymen would paralyse the province in revolutionary solidarity. Management still refused to budge.[20] Now the PSI deputy in parliament resorted to more direct methods and kidnapped the employer. Franchi became a prisoner of the 'red guards', with payment of a generous 'donation' to the Camera del Lavoro as the condition for his release.[21] According to his captors, the hostage owed roughly 15,000 lire to FIOM members in arrears of pay, so the money 'morally belonged to the proletariat'.[22]

The intimidation and improvisation that accompanied the Franchi Gregorini seizure, calculated by the strike committee to force the employer's hand, compelled state authority to intervene. The occupation petered out when the police arrested Arturo Maestri, together with the other principal culprits in the abduction. Even though Franchi returned home hours later to find the national FIOM settlement hastily imposed upon him by Malinverno, and the wages of his employees increased by 20 per cent, the provincial workers' movement suffered because of the episode.[23] Far from signifying success for the metallurgical federation or the Camera del Lavoro, the pathetic plot exposed the inability of union officials to keep their extremists in line and compromised the credibility of the maximalist party leadership. A PSI member of parliament had inspired a campaign of individualist terrorism that only the arm of the law could hold down. Reformists at Brescia used the September crisis to oust Maestri and

---

[18] Ibid., 19 and 20 September 1920; *Il Combattente*, 23 September 1920.

[19] *Avanti!*, 21 and 22 September 1920.

[20] ACS, Min. Interno, DGPS, AGR 1920, b. 74, cat. D13, fasc. Brescia, 21 September 1920.

[21] Ibid., 22 September 1920.

[22] *La Provincia di Brescia*, 23 September 1920.

[23] ASIG, Società Anonima Franchi Gregorini, Consiglio di Amministrazione, verbale, 4 November 1920.

his friends from positions of authority.[24] Yet, with all his faults, the socialist deputy alone had enough prestige among the proletariat to command popular support. The hold of this revolutionary over the masses continued as a permanent source of tension for those who wished to preserve what little organizational strength remained of the left.[25]

For Brescian businessmen, worried about civil war just weeks before, the September occupations produced more conclusive results. The outmoded tactics pursued by Franchi brought about a crisis in labour relations that the crusty entrepreneur could not turn to his advantage. After the agitation he remained the only major supplier of producer goods to resist membership of the Lombard consortium, which belonged to the Confindustria, and such detachment enabled other employers in iron and steel to break his influence in the province.[26] Franchi, aware that his stubborn independence during the strike could cost him further estrangement from corporate capitalists, tried to appease the Consorzio leadership. Too stingy to pay the ransom demanded by the 'red guards', he preferred to declare that 'in a moment of struggle, I cannot play the blackleg to my colleagues.'[27]

Few found his conversion to the collective cause convincing. Franchi had always opposed the tyranny of pressure-group tactics in the name of private entrepreneurial autonomy, and he confirmed the fatuity of claims made under the duress of detention. The industrialist disowned the employers' movement and denounced the FIOM accord within a day of his release.[28] These retractions did little to redeem his credit in the conservative camp. Both the clerical and the liberal press teamed up with Giulio Togni and Filippo Carli at the chamber of commerce to cast slurs upon the 'deranged' magnate.[29] Joined together in an effort to fight labour and close ranks, organized business interests used the obstinate outsider as a scapegoat for their

[24] ACS, Min. Interno, DGPS, AGR 1920, b. 74, cat. D13, fasc. Brescia, 26 September 1920.

[25] *La Provincia di Brescia*, 24 and 25 September 1920; *Il Cittadino di Brescia*, 24 and 27 September 1920.

[26] *La Provincia di Brescia*, 23 and 27 September 1920.

[27] *La Sentinella Bresciana*, 23 September 1920.

[28] ACS, Min. Interno, DGPS, AGR 1920, b. 74, cat. D13, fasc. Brescia, 24 September 1920.

[29] *La Provincia di Brescia*, 24 and 25 September 1920; *La Sentinella Bresciana*, 24 September 1920.

technical defeat. Even Malinverno spoke openly of his contempt for the man who 'behaved like a real clown and bungled the talks'.[30]

Capitalists felt injured and indignant about giving way to the Giolittian compromise.[31] Preoccupied with the containment of left-wing unionism, businessmen in iron and steel failed to appreciate that working-class radicalism had been effectively diluted. The September agreement, which entrusted factory council legislation to a mixed commission, represented a nominal victory for the FIOM. However, maximalist inability to transform the revolutionary moment illustrated the limitations of subversive strategies. The true triumph belonged to the employers, who progressed in their struggle for internal cohesion. Italian industry showed its power to drive a hard bargain, and the solidarity of organized labour cracked under the strain. Hardly justifying the fears of the right, negotiations proceeded in an orderly manner with state supervision. The occupations provided a decisive impulse to the movement of association. The seizures stimulated adherents of the Lombard consortium to react collectively both to the militancy of the proletariat and to indiscipline within the managerial class.

Throughout the remainder of the year, when recession began to afflict metallurgical and engineering concerns, organized labour continued to suffer serious set-backs. The slump deepened during the winter of 1920-1, and the mood of industry soured as a result. Unemployment grew, heightening the demoralization of the provincial proletariat. Union leaders restricted agitation to a defence of their new contract. This policy of restraint encountered many obstacles. Already on 8 October militants at the Togni tubing plant left their positions on the shop floor because management refused to pay for services rendered during the September troubles. The internal commission threatened another seizure, though the FIOM ordered its members to end the stoppage, after the company agreed to give cash advances to a quarter of the amount owed to each striker.[32] That same afternoon workers at Franchi Gregorini laid down their tools to

[30] ACS, Min. Interno, DGPS, AGR 1920, b. 74, cat. D13, fasc. Brescia, registrazione telefonica, 24 September 1920.

[31] *Avanti!*, 30 September and 1 October 1920; although the promised bill for workers' participation was never passed in parliament, the FIOM did secure a daily pay rise of 4 lire for the membership; see P. Spriano, *L'occupazione delle fabbriche*, pp. 112-15; G. Maione, *Il biennio rosso*, pp. 269-76.

[32] ACS, Min. Interno, DGPS, AGR 1920, b. 74, cat. D13, fasc. Brescia, 8 October 1920.

protest against repeated violations of the Rome settlement, but they resumed production within a few hours.[33] A group of activists at the Società Nazionale Radiatori defied their federation's orders and reoccupied part of the factory for a day, to no avail. Participants in a walk-out at the Belemotti steel firm took down their red banner from the factory gates, once the boss gave his word to respect the collective accord signed less than a month before.[34]

Thirty men, against the will of the local FIOM section, abstained from production in protest over the failure of the Cavagna arms manufactory to apply the wage scales negotiated nationally.[35] Eager to come to terms peacefully at a time when job action had little chance of success, the metallurgical federation refused to take up the cause of impatient members until the company dismissed a leading militant. The wildcat strike then received official endorsement, but the employer intended to regain territory lost in September and ignored union demands.[36] Ten days later socialist leaders finally enrolled the assistance of Luigi Marcialis, the new prefect, who called both parties to his office and laid down the law.[37] Although management mistook governmental conciliation as liberal weakness, the state never lost its mediating function in industry.

Moderate trade unionists again came to blows with anarcho-syndicalists, in the atmosphere of economic downturn and employer toughness. Internal discord grew during the aftermath of the September crisis, and another labour war broke out. On 19 November USI militants tried to 'liberate' the two Togni concerns in town by setting off explosives on the shop floor, evacuating all operatives, and then making the workers stay outside the factory gates.[38] The FIOM instructed its members to resume production, only to find that many of them supported the surprise strike. The leaders of the federation fought desperately for a truce, yet their recruits sided with the competition. The prefect needed a few truck-loads of troops to end the agitation, a move which left the socialist organization open to charges of police collaboration. That afternoon about a hundred

[33] Ibid., 9 October 1920; *La Provincia di Brescia*, 9 October 1920.

[34] ACS, Min. Interno, DGPS, AGR 1920, b. 74, cat. D13, fasc. Brescia, 11 October 1920.

[35] Ibid., 10 November 1920.

[36] *Brescia Nuova*, 13 November 1920.

[37] Ibid., 20 and 27 November 1920; *La Provincia di Brescia*, 21 November 1920.

[38] ACS, Min. Interno, DGPS, AGR 1920, b. 74, cat. D. 13, fasc. Brescia, 19 November 1920.

revolutionists attempted to incite an insurrection at the Metallurgica Bresciana plant, but the majority on the assembly line had felt the pinch of repression and declined to participate in the plot.[39]

If internal divisions and external conditions weakened the labour movement during the autumn of 1920, the right did not seem to notice. The administrative elections of October and November revealed that at Brescia, just as throughout the whole of Italy, conservative forces combined in their antisocialism. The occupation of the factories proved especially instructive for the urban middle classes, who grumbled about the absence of police protection against 'an obscene internationalism'.[40] Abandoned by state authority in the midst of the dramatic strike, they based their campaign slogans on the civilian defence of municipalities threatened by the red menace. A sense of social isolation and political disarray worked to transform ideological rifts between Christian democrats, clerical-moderates, and Masonic liberals into an alliance called the Blocco Nazionale. Unprepared to bequeath local power to the maximalists, provincial notables quickly shelved old rancours and presented a united front for the first time since radiant May.[41]

The Municipal Elections and the Rise of the Local Fascio

The provincial parties of order sprang into action during the autumn of 1920 to deny the largest elected body in Italy a share of municipal power at Brescia. The alliance against the left used doomsday rhetoric in its propaganda and platform. A new political weekly surfaced, bankrolled by the conservative press to serve the purposes of the Blocco Nazionale. *La Riscossa* played on fears of imminent revolution and harped on the violent nature of the struggle ahead. Most bourgeois spokesmen came to believe that even a broad centrist coalition might lose the battle for the town council. Determination to save the country's civic heritage from 'bolshevik disfigurement' drove constitutional forces to underwrite a movement that had started as a reaction to the traditional governing class.[42] Thus began the strange pact of collaboration between the liberal establishment and the local *fascio*.

[39] Ibid., 20 November 1920; *La Sentinella Bresciana*, 20 November 1920; *Brescia Nuova*, 27 November 1920.

[40] *La Sentinella Bresciana*, 17 November 1920.

[41] *La Provincia di Brescia*, 11 and 13 October 1920; *Il Cittadino di Brescia*, 15 October 1920.

[42] *La Sentinella Bresciana*, 9 and 10 October 1920; *La Riscossa*, 16 October 1920.

Limited in effectiveness and expansion, fascism at Brescia stayed on the fringes of the provincial political scene until the October municipal campaign. Benito Mussolini had founded the first *fascio di combattimento* in Milan at a small meeting of war veterans, revolutionary syndicalists, and former socialists during March 1919. Although its initial programme contained radical demands, including the expropriation of all church lands and the confiscation of most war profits, the group failed to win over lower-class recruits and the mass of infantrymen. After the November general elections, the marginal movement rejected the workings of popular democracy and rushed into the torrents of the right. Ideology became vague and pragmatic, but aimed always against the parliamentary caste. A romantic sense of nationalism combined with a pervasive mood of revolt to attract the support of university students and young officers in urban centres throughout the North.[43]

Students comprised the organizational core of fascism in Brescia when the movement made its first provincial appearance. Born with the 'impetus of a rifleman', Alessandro Melchiori contacted the central committee in Milan, on the advice of his father. The eighteen-year-old professed to be against the church, but only after his classmates refused him membership of the Catholic youth association. As a democrat, he formed the Roberto Ardigò circle with three friends, who also resented the clerical oligarchs in their secondary school. These four boys came together in 'patriotic indignation' and made up the nucleus of the local *fascio*, inaugurated on 5 April 1919.[44]

Melchiori flunked a class at school and almost failed a second time, so he limited his activities to staging demonstrations and distributing *Popolo d'Italia* in town until he passed his supplementary exams in July. By August the group boasted about fifty supporters, yet, as the newcomers soon realized, the future of the *fascio* seemed unpromising with the young graduate at the helm. The older spirits of the extreme right complained of his 'adolescent incompetence', while the cadets disliked the absence of military service.[45] Revolutionary interventionists became alienated from the cause, and the conservative servicemen

[43] A. Lyttelton, *The Seizure of Power*, pp. 42-60; R. De Felice, *Mussolini il rivoluzionario, 1883-1920* (Turin, 1965), pp. 419-544.

[44] *La Sentinella Bresciana*, 2 May 1924; P. A. Vecchia, *Storia del fascismo bresciano 1919-1922* (Brescia, 1929), pp. 29-31; *Il Cittadino di Brescia*, 10 November 1919.

[45] ACS, MRF, CC dei Fasci, b. 100, fasc. Brescia, cartella 1, n. 4, 5 August 1919; n. 5, 7 July 1919; n. 9, 12 August 1919; n. 10, 19 August 1919; n. 14, 27 August 1919.

withdrew their support after a quarrel with him.[46] All wanted a political secretary with more brains and authority, but Melchiori refused to resign. The combatants' association offered to run three feature stories on the Blocco Fascista in return for an endorsement of the ANC ticket. This ploy for a little publicity nearly cost the teenager his job, since the articles never appeared, once the fascists had backed the radical Ghislandi slate. The local movement steadily declined after the 1919 electoral blunder, and only a handful of students, republicans, and officers remained as members.[47]

Although the November fiasco discredited Melchiori, for six months he resisted the attempts of older associates to depose him.[48] Finally the youth took off to fight in Fiume, giving the republicans and the cadets a chance to expose the peculations of the secretariat.[49] Huge stacks of *Il Fascio* came to light in the group's headquarters at the Caffè Maffio, where the student members had plunged the association into debt for drinks. Not a single copy of the Milan weekly had been sold during the boy's tenure, 'not even for pulp'.[50] Vincenzo Mancini presided over the *fascio*, but within three weeks of assuming office, he too left for the Adriatic. Lieutenant Giuseppe Vitale held the post for a fortnight, and then the leadership passed to Innocente Dugani, a shock trooper who resigned after one month.[51] By the autumn of 1920 the fascist central committee had tired of carnival capers and piazza parades staged by the motley crew at Brescia, especially since no wealthy patron from the constitutional right would support the escapades of these bohemians operating on an overdrawn account. Umberto Pasella, secretary of the national movement, appointed an engineer as temporary head of the local group while he looked around for someone more permanent. During the occupation of the factories, the fascists made contact with Augusto Turati, a former legionary and current editor-in-chief of *La Provincia di Brescia*. .

A native of Parma, Turati came from lower middle-class stock. He struggled to get an education, working part-time, but never managed

[46] Ibid., n. 32, 13 October 1919; n. 33, 18 October 1919.

[47] Ibid., no. 36, 5 November 1919; n. 38, 19 November 1919; n. 42, 25 November 1919; n. 41, 29 November 1919; n. 43, 11 December 1919.

[48] Ibid., n. 72, 7 April 1920; n. 73, 8 April 1920; n. 76, 16 April 1920.

[49] Melchiori, a member of the national PNF directorate in 1924, became a publicist for the fascist militia; see A. Melchiori, *Milizia Fascista* (Rome, 1929).

[50] ACS, MRF, CC dei Fasci, b. 100, fasc. Brescia, cartella 1, n. 98, 18 June 1920.

[51] Ibid., n. 101, 30 June 1920; n. 102, 13 July 1920; n. 104, 14 July 1920; n. 106, 14 July 1920; n. 113, 7 August 1920; n. 125, 20 August 1920.

to finish his university course in law. Deeply influenced by the writings of Georges Sorel, the college drop-out entered politics as a follower of the syndicalist Alceste De Ambris.[52] He got his first break when *La Provincia* advertised a position for a staff writer. Soon after taking the job, the talented outsider ingratiated himself with town democrats to become the press spokesman for the Zanardellian left; before the year's end he received promotion to an editorship, as well as an invitation to join the Freemasons' lodge. A month after Italy's entry into the war Turati enlisted, and he departed from the front lines a bemedalled hero.[53] The discharged legionary assumed direction of the influential newspaper on his return to Brescia and married into a prominent family of local fame. But despite all attempts to climb his way up the social ladder, Turati could not break down the barriers which restricted access to institutional power in the province. The stagnation and inflexibility that characterized the traditional governing establishment forced this venturesome young man to seek opportunities for office through less conventional party affiliations.[54]

Turati deserted the democrats soon after an envoy from Pasella approached him. Far too ambitious ever to stay content as an editor, he resigned from *La Provincia* late in September 1920, ostensibly to try his luck as a free-lance writer.[55] He joined the *fascio* four days later, seized its leadership, and installed friends in the reconstituted directorate.[56] The central committee in Milan, hoping to tap the financial resources and influence of liberal élites, intended this conversion to give the movement at Brescia an air of bourgeois respectability. But the new *ras* or provincial boss, derived popularity from his very failure to assimilate into the local ruling class.[57] The '*giovanotto*' represented the self-made man, an incarnation of social mobility. And fascism gave him the chance to make politics his profession.[58]

A change in the fascist line of attack became apparent almost

---

[52] A. Turati, *Fuori dell'ombra della mia vita: Dieci anni nel solco del fascismo* (Brescia, 1973), pp. 8-9.

[53] G. A. Chiurco, *Storia della Rivoluzione fascista*, vol. v (Florence, 1929), pp. 232-3.

[54] G. Nozzoli, *I ras del regime: Gli uomini che disfecero gli italiani* (Milan, 1972), pp. 50-65.

[55] *La Provincia di Brescia*, 25 September 1920.

[56] ACS, MRF, CC dei Fasci, b. 100, fasc. Brescia, cartella 2, n. 140, 29 October 1920.

[57] Fascists used the term *ras*, which derives from the Ethiopian title for feudal overlord and tribal chieftain, as their appellation for a local political secretary; see G. Salvemini, *The Fascist Dictatorship in Italy* (New York, 1967), pp. 172-9.

[58] P. Morgan, 'Augusto Turati', in F. Cordova (ed.), *Uomini e volti del fascismo* (Rome, 1980), pp. 475-519.

immediately after Turati's accession to power. No longer would the leadership cater to the small minority of students, syndicalists, and servicemen hostile to the old parties of order. Instead, he wished to develop a broad-based nationalist association 'with a strong bourgeois numerical presence'.[59] The fresh accent on social variety followed the guide-lines of the national leadership, which wanted the support of wealthy business interests. Turati took the tactic one step further, for he insisted on enrolling members of the proletariat. He sought to exploit reaction to socialism, but this meant as much exposing the failures of maximalism to the workers as it did playing on conservative fears of bolshevik revolution. At its first meeting the new directorate unanimously approved the proposal to recruit at the steel mills, but when metallurgists chased the blackshirts from the factory gates, the propaganda stopped. Since the very rich and very poor still kept their distance from the Brescia *fascio*, the appeal of the local movement had yet to go beyond the urban middle class.[60]

Turati refurbished the image of the *fascio*, now packaged as an association of 'producer classes' brought together by antisocialism. Offering to reinforce the lethargic constitutional parties with wilder spirits, his group acted as a patriotic rather than a political organization during the municipal elections. He harboured few illusions about the struggle for power. Aversion to clericalism stayed concealed in the October campaign, while contempt for certain moderate liberals never surfaced. Turati became the most vigorous orator of the 'bloc of fear'. His commentaries in *La Riscossa* demonstrated a real talent for scare tactics, such as listing the names and addresses of non-voters, so that conservatives could identify 'traitors' among the provincial bourgeoisie.[61] The aggressive rhetoric was accompanied by reticence at the polls. No fascist candidates appeared on the slate, as the central committee preferred to avoid the disaster of November 1919, but the local movement finally established ties to wider circles of Brescian society.

The municipal elections proved the undoing of maximalism. The Blocco Nazionale, formed under the sponsorship of civilian authority, used all possible means to keep provincial administration from red control. The polling proceeded with prefectural intervention, and

[59] *La Riscossa*, 16 October 1920.
[60] *La Sentinella Bresciana*, 12 November 1920; P. A. Vecchia, *Storia del fascismo bresciano*, pp. 50-2.
[61] *La Sentinella Bresciana*, 31 October 1920.

constituents long dead cast votes.[62] At the Federterra stronghold of Leno, patients from a lunatic asylum allegedly participated in the balloting and deprived the left of an expected victory.[63] And the socialists themselves made plenty of mistakes. After the ANC offered to back the PSI ticket in three communes dominated by the PPI, the Camera del Lavoro threatened to sue *Il Combattente* for slandering a comrade whose reputation was already frayed. Petty intrigue tainted the platform of the proletarian party. Denying that he had tied the nuptial knot in church, Maestri turned his Catholic wedding to a former nun into an untimely scandal. At a debate of some importance, police arrested the groom for physical violence against a prominent democrat, who had produced the marriage certificate for public viewing.[64] The '*promessi sposi*' affair became a major campaign issue. Anticlericalism remained the fixation of the provincial workers' movement, and the outrageous behaviour of the deputy elected to parliament continued as a liability.

The revolutionary pretensions of the PSI programme confirmed the worst suspicions of the right. The maximalists proposed to replace the town council with a 'people's soviet', since they intended to defend only the interests of the proletariat. The provincial party leadership declared its hostility to the retail distribution of food and announced plans to ration supplies after the seizure of the municipal palace. Although the agrarian platform put forward did not abolish private property, the local revolutionaries vowed to subject landlords to new administrative controls, including the maintenance of full employment in the countryside, even during the winter. Socialists abandoned the threat of collectivization because peasants must first acquire technical expertise by participating in farm management. Shorn of its radical embellishments, however, this last plank bore a striking resemblance to the demands of Catholic co-operatives in the central basin.[65]

The pragmatic reformism of the veterans met with greater success at the polls. They aimed to destroy neither religion nor property, only to tame both politically. Limiting attacks on the church to corruption and clientelism, the ANC had a sense of mission. Professor Monti, troubled by the dealings of the *cattedra ambulante di agricoltura*,

[62] *Brescia Nuova*, 21 October 1920.
[63] Ibid., 14 October 1920; see also letter to the editor in *La Provincia di Brescia*, 24 October 1920.
[64] *Il Cittadino di Brescia*, 23 October 1920.
[65] *Brescia Nuova*, 9 October 1920.

publicly exposed Antonio Bianchi for administrative mismanagement and fraud. *Il Combattente* charged the clerical-moderate government of the Brescia municipality with financial incompetence and published itemized accounts of the communal budget to substantiate the allegation. It condemned the negativism of conservative bloc politics. The newspaper chided the nationalists for their 'aggressive ardour', the democrats for forgetting anticlericalism 'in the refuge of the Masonic lodge', the *popolari* for acting in the interests of ecclesiastical authority.[66] The socialists found themselves conspicuously excluded from the servicemen's polemic, which never foreclosed conciliation. This co-operative policy allowed the association to benefit from divisions in other parties. When the PPI in the important town of Chiari split over the question of collaboration with the right, the combatants enlisted the support of the larger, radical faction, and the electoral coalition in the Catholic stronghold delivered the ANC its sweetest victory.[67]

The October and November returns represented a triumph for the former servicemen. The ANC ticket polled outright majorities in over fifty upland constituencies. Other contenders saw less conclusive results during the autumn vote. Though the provincial and city administrations did not escape from clerical-moderate control, participation in the Blocco Nazionale provoked serious divisions within the Catholic camp. The very vagueness of the PPI programme, due in part to the social diversity of its flock, already doomed the Christian party, but the conservative electoral alliance hastened its decline. Church notables justified their common slate with the right liberals by way of the red threat theme. While the 'united front' argument made some sense in the city, where the socialists drew their numerical strength, it had little appeal among peasants of the foothills and mountains. The urban ecclesiastical leadership backed an alliance that alienated the mass following of the white union movement throughout the countryside simply to please old friends and past patrons in local government.[68]

Moderate liberals reaped the rewards of co-operation with the PPI. They polled the least ballots of any group yet retained the mayoralty of the city, not to mention key posts in provincial administration.[69]

[66] *Il Combattente*, 31 October 1920.
[67] Ibid., 24 October 1920; *Il Cittadino di Brescia*, 21 October 1920.
[68] Ibid., 4, 10, 12, and 30 October 1920.
[69] *La Sentinella Bresciana*, 2 November 1920.

Better still for the forces of order, the Blocco Nazionale managed to circumscribe the political influence of the left. The PSI may have obtained 40 per cent of the total vote, but the party found its main support confined within the town limits. The maximalists returned only 556 councillors, while 314 conservatives, 424 democrats, 433 combatants, and 1,940 *popolari* got seats.[70] Electoral laws disguised the numerical strength of the socialists, who had actually gained support in the industrialized zones since 1919. As far as the terms of battle in the countryside went, the autumn return of 1920 showed the power of the pulpit to prevail over the peasantry of Brescia.

The *fascio* benefited from a good deal of publicity. Since its members became the most energetic propagandists of the antisocialist coalition, often acting as armed guards outside precincts, the standing of the group increased greatly in the wake of the PSI defeat. Turati received compensation for his role in the campaign through contacts. With the confidence of local politicians and the friendship of the prefect behind him, he entered the clientele world of provincial government. And the fascist movement grew remarkably. On the eve of the elections, the local section claimed less than forty adherents, but by December almost 200 men had enrolled.[71]

The fivefold increase transformed the *fascio*, for the new members differed greatly from the original supporters. No longer the exclusive domain of republican students, former officers, and Fiume volunteers, the group also turned into a sanctuary for tough men of few inhibitions. Ferruccio Migliorati, whose brother had allegedly clubbed an old peasant to death during the great agricultural strike of March, became active in the local squad.[72] Arrigo Arrighi, a big tenant farmer in the plains, joined. Turati's sidekick, Luigi Begnotti, drifted through Brescia after losing some shady business deals in his native Brazil. Giuseppe Cirielli and Giovanni Campagnoni both boasted prison records. While the early *petit-bourgeois* enthusiasts in town resented the dominance of the rural and criminal converts, the boldness of the recent recruits increased the prestige and influence of the local movement. *La Provincia* gave tacit approval to the 'illegitimate

---

[70] *La Provincia di Brescia*, 26 October and 1 November 1920; *Il Cittadino di Brescia*, 1-3 November 1920.

[71] ACS, MRF, CC dei Fasci, b. 100, fasc. Brescia, cartella 3, n. 142, 28 October 1920; P. A. Vecchia, *Storia del fascismo bresciano*, pp. 53-4; *La Sentinella Bresciana*, 11 December 1920.

[72] ASB, Corte d'Assise, b. 77, fasc. 9, procedimento penale contro Giovanni Migliorati (see sfasc. 3).

but justified' conduct of these thugs, who pushed the mystique of violence towards gang warfare against the socialists.[73] *La Sentinella* applauded their paramilitary 'reprisals', which included disrupting PSI rallies and patrolling streets during strikes.[74] After the municipal elections and factory occupations, propertied interests began to take the blackshirts seriously as a means to combat perceived enemies on the left. Had it not been for the political opportunism and social insecurity of the liberal establishment, together with the partiality of state authority, fascism might have stayed on the periphery of civic life.

Political Fragmentation in the Countryside

The rapid expansion of Mussolini's movement in neighbouring rural centres accelerated the fascist penetration of Brescia. Punitive expeditions, sparked off by the Palazzo D'Accursio incidents at Bologna late in November 1920, radiated throughout the Po valley and the Lombard lowlands. This massive onslaught brought notoriety to the local *fascio*, for middle-class citizens looked to Turati's association to restore order by terrorist means in their province too.[75] Armed squads from the town soon began to infiltrate the villages of the central and eastern plains, provoking clashes with union militants and launching assaults against Catholic as well as socialist leagues. Gangs of toughs patrolled the countryside to the applause of basin farmers, who regarded the action of the squads as the political complement of their own economic reaction. Employers seemed bent on the destruction of all peasant organizations before the renegotiation of agricultural contracts in the spring.

The Catholics refused to acknowledge the alignment of forces in the basin zones, where the mediating apparatus of the state broke down. The white leagues continued to focus their attention on undermining the red competition, inadvertently modifying the balance of power to the advantage of employers. Political strife appeared particularly intense in the countryside, whence the PPI derived electoral strength. And because the Federterra had subverted the Christian labour movement in the 1920 negotiations for a peasant pact, the antisocialist polemic became the major preoccupation of

---

[73] *La Provincia di Brescia*, 22 November 1920.

[74] *La Sentinella Bresciana*, 6 January 1921.

[75] *La Provincia di Brescia*, 22 November 1920; *La Sentinella Bresciana*, 22 November 1920 and 29 January 1921.

Longinotti's syndicates.[76] Obsession with the PSI obscured better intentions. Throughout the winter of 1921, a time during which agricultural unemployment reached a seasonal high, UCL unionists played into the hands of the agrarian association in a desperate attempt to regain lost ground. Promises of preferential treatment from above encouraged them to let landlords violate the terms of the March agreement right across the board. The equivocal tactics pursued by the *popolari* disclosed the spiritual poverty and the organizational limitations of the amorphous church party. The provincial leadership aimed only to cement the interests of local notables with those of the masses it professed to represent. Yet farmers did not hesitate to support Turati's rival movement in return for discipline by action, while workers adhered to the group that negotiated more favourable contracts.[77]

The PPI's pragmatic disregard of the fascist challenge best demonstrated the political *naïveté* of the local *popolari*. During the administrative campaign of 1920, the provincial leadership chose not to notice the *fascio*'s presence in the electoral bloc. This policy of benign neglect facilitated clerical collaboration with old liberal allies, for official recognition would have ensured great opposition from the church left. The blackshirts, however, made themselves difficult to ignore. At the third Lombard congress of Mussolini's movement in February 1921, Turati announced a new offensive. Popular Catholicism, fascism's most 'obstinate enemy' at Brescia, would be energetically annihilated during the coming months. White socialism, as he called the UCL, was just as repugnant as the red variety, but more pernicious since it contained treacherous bourgeois elements.[78]

At first the provincial PPI did not take the *fascio*'s death sentence seriously. Party moderates expected some protection from local conservatives, but the right liberals stood by their new friends.[79] Action began to accompany Turati's threats. After the Brescia squads led reprisals against UCL organizers at Chiari, the *popolari* attempted to unite.[80] The crisis led to a decline in the influence of clerical reactionaries, yet the timid directorate which remained took a fort-

[76] *Il Cittadino di Brescia*, 6 January 1920.
[77] Ibid., 15 February and 1 March 1921; *La Sentinella Bresciana*, 17 February 1921; *La Voce del Popolo*, 18 February 1921.
[78] P. A. Vecchia, *Storia del fascismo bresciano*, pp. 61-2.
[79] *La Voce del Popolo*, 5 March 1921.
[80] *Bandiera Bianca*, 6 March 1921.

night to respond to fascist provocation.[81] The jolt, though, finally purged many Catholics of their antisocialism. Abandoned and isolated, they now looked to the left for possible allies.

The prominence of the fascist movement throughout the peninsula and in the province created tension within the ANC too. Although the veterans enjoyed control of numerous municipalities, along with a strong mass following, their leaders recognized that popularity came from the able defence of local issues. Since the group could never hope for widespread support outside the uplands, many members wished to use their key position at the administrative level to aid more powerful and established political affiliations. Some adherents sought to strengthen the traditional governing class and eliminate its dependence upon the *fascio*.[82] The small, conservative faction led by Cirillo Bonardi advocated this policy of bourgeois reinforcement, but the vast majority of mountaineers took fright at the thought of aiding 'old and corrupt parliamentarians'.[83] Radicals on the governing body urged co-operation with the socialists, a merger which would precipitate desertion by the right and the eclipse of the combatants as an independent movement.

On the eve of the parliamentary elections of 1921, the working-class challenge had disintegrated in Brescia. As the forces of conservative resentment moved further to the right, the socialist party leadership remained hopelessly divided against itself, and the contraction of the European market caused union militancy to flag even further. The economic recession, most pronounced in the machine and steel sectors, allowed employers in industry to tighten the screws on activists. For about 150 PSI activists at Brescia, secession to the newly formed Partito Comunista Italiano represented a way out of this deadlock, yet the immediate effect of the January split increased the vulnerability of an already languishing labour movement.

Class conflict became far more acute in the hinterland, where the harsh labour offensive revived the chronic xenophobia of rural notables. They disliked the government's insistence on collective bargaining with labour, and disunity among the peasantry encouraged agrarian intransigents to renege on concessions. Although the Brescia fascists claimed to protect middling folk in the town, the rapid expansion of the local movement in the conservative periphery

[81] *Il Cittadino di Brescia*, 20 March 1921.
[82] *La Provincia di Brescia*, 28 January 1921.
[83] *Il Combattente*, 30 January 1921.

precluded a drift to the left. Farmers, who felt sandwiched between the contagious radicalism of the Po valley leagues and the social repercussions of industrialization in the zone, began to look to the *fascio* as an agency of resistance. The provincial federation would turn into a refuge for rural employers, isolated in a changing countryside.

6

Lamentations and Recriminations

BENITO Mussolini conceived fascism as a minority creed of *petit-bourgeois* patriots in towns, but the clandestine advance of the action squads at the beginning of 1921 turned it into an organ for generalized reaction in the countryside.[1] The temperament and magnitude of the national movement changed as a consequence of the agrarian offensive. New sympathy and support resulted from each punitive expedition against the socialist leagues. First at Ferrara, where inside one month the number of sections jumped from five to forty with over 6,000 adherents, then at Bologna, which saw membership grow to more than 5,000 recruits by March, the rural as well as the urban middle classes rallied behind the blackshirts and provided the basis for a mass following.[2] The reconnaissance campaigns spread from Emilia to Tuscany, Umbria, Lombardy, Apulia, and the Veneto. Paramilitary extremism gathered strength. The perpetuation of gang warfare gave the political secretaries in the provinces some autonomy from the central committee in Milan. Major landlords, big tenant farmers, and small-town professionals rewarded the men of violence by way of donation and protection.

Mussolini welcomed the flood of rural recruits to fascism, but hoped to transform their terrorist course into a political and semi-juridical approach to power. The local bosses, though, saw little future in operating by the rules of the parliamentary system. Imperfectly bridged in antisocialist opposition, the conflict that split the central leadership from the provincial chieftains surfaced once the threat of bolshevik revolution loomed no longer. Divisions arose between the bureaucrats from Milan who wished to conciliate moderate liberal opinion and those activists in the countryside bent on maintaining a state of siege. The dominance of agrarian interests also caused early republican supporters in the cities of the North to despair. Crude

[1] A. Tasca, *The Rise of Fascism in Italy 1918–1922* (London, 1938), pp. 37, 90-1.
[2] P. Corner, *Fascism in Ferrara*, pp. 120-2; A. Cardoza, *Agrarian Elites and Italian Fascism*, pp. 315-17.

class reaction throughout the lowlands had obscured the 1919 mission of national redemption.[3]

The power struggle between urban and rural enthusiasts plunged the movement as a whole into deep crisis, especially when the national leadership tried to limit vigilante operations. Police complicity and public opinion made governmental repression of fascist assaults difficult, adding to the image of invincibility enjoyed by the agrarian wing. The success of the Po valley squads during the electoral campaign of May 1921 awakened Mussolini to the dangers of excessive growth and anarchic violence in the countryside. Later that year he clarified uncertainty about political definition and central direction by advocating republicanism, moderation, and a new organizational structure. A pact of pacification, signed on 2 August, ended offences against the socialist unions. While the Duce had to abandon this temporary truce in return for internal discipline at the November congress, the constitution of a formal party machine ensured his personal authority over the provincial fiefs and confirmed the logic of a parliamentary strategy.[4]

Schisms and Discontents in the Fascio

Fascism developed slowly in Brescia, for the social heterogeneity of the province engendered crisis and complicated consolidation. Augusto Turati hoped that industry would play a central role in the local movement, yet managers and workers alike kept their distance from the *ras* during 1921. Most businessmen sympathetic to the cause promoted moderate national leadership. Blackshirt organizers had been spotted at the Franchi Gregorini factory in town, but the owner declined to let them set up shop.[5] The recession reduced the need for squad violence and company unions in the machine and steel sectors; manufacturers saw their bargaining power over the FIOM increase once unemployment set in. Agriculture offered even fewer opportunities for the formation of a strong mass following. The political hold of the clergy remained over much of the peasantry in the foothills and uplands. Socialist loyalties stayed strong among the rural proletariat of the basin flats and the high ground.

The elections of May 1921 gave the *fascio* exposure around town.

---

[3] A. Lyttelton, *The Seizure of Power*, pp. 54-6.

[4] A. Tasca, *The Rise of Fascism in Italy*, pp. 133-67; R. De Felice, *Mussolini il fascista. I. La conquista del potere 1921–1925* (Turin, 1966), pp. 100-89.

[5] *Brescia Nuova*, 21 May 1921.

Designed to isolate the PSI and the PPI nationally, Giolitti's crass decision to include Mussolini and his supporters on a list with the constitutional parties strengthened the position of the blackshirts in the provincial capital. Ghislandi and his veterans reinforced the socialist vote, which stood firm, but the National Bloc emerged with a significant percentage gain in relation to the last parliamentary returns. Its numbers moved from the November 1919 low of 3,200 to 4,950 a year and a half later.[6] Rightist liberals, who deserted their clerical friends to join the slate, represented part of that accretion. The coalition, however, derived most new support from the increased turnout of voters. At Brescia, as in Genoa, Milan, Florence, and Mantua, fascist participation on the ticket appears to have prompted an influx of voters who had hitherto abstained from the polls.[7] Turati's group became a major asset to the conservative campaign by bringing out a number of previously uneasy or apathetic constituents, and neither democrats nor moderates could reject the artificial implant of popularity.[8]

The election results encouraged the Brescia *fascio* to venture beyond the antisocialist platform. During the first months of his tenure, Turati had concentrated efforts on exploiting middle-class reaction to the left and on winning acceptance from the liberal establishment of the province. May 1921 signified a triumph as far as these initial objectives went, but eagerness to serve the purposes of the rich in the countryside laid the group open to charges of conservative contamination. Membership among townspeople had climbed from 675 in March to 941 during May, not a spectacular increase on the eve of a poll, whereas rural support almost doubled over the same period and the number of village *nuclei* grew from five to ten.[9] The *ras* intended to keep the agrarians in check by creating an independent power base among the neutral masses. The balance of incompatible forces in provincial politics compelled him to pursue two alternative lines of development for the local movement. He continued to harp on

[6] *La Provincia di Brescia*, 16-18 May 1921; the Catholics received 44,545 votes in the provincial returns, while the Unione Nazionale polled 25,453. The PSI obtained 35,585 votes. The PPI candidates elected were Longinotti, Salvadori, Montini, and Bresciani. Bonardi and Ducos went to Rome as representatives of the constitutional bloc, and the socialists returned Viotto, Maestri, and Bianchi.

[7] U. Giusti, *Le correnti politiche italiane*, p. 109; A. Lyttelton, *The Seizure of Power*, pp. 67-8.

[8] *La Provincia di Brescia*, 17 May 1921; *La Sentinella Bresciana*, 17 May 1921.

[9] ACS, Min. Interno, DGPS, AGR 1925, b. 96a, cat. G1, Costituzione dei Fasci, sfasc. Brescia, 14 March and 6 May 1921.

the theme of revolutionary subversion in the basin zones and reserved his radical trappings to sway the urban crowd. The monarchists in the city section contested both directions, but Turati did little to pour balm on their discontents. The split by the moderate right component in early June marked the first bout in a series of domestic feuds, over which the '*giovanotto*' would prevail.[10]

The *fascio* showed new concern for practical issues in an attempt to exploit electoral publicity and to widen public support. After Giolitti's elimination of the bread subsidy, the socialists had tried to negotiate municipal controls on food costs, but the civilian authorities refused to co-operate. Turati decided to embarrass the PSI militants by fulfilling his own pledge to ease the pinch of the budget on the urban dweller. Inviting shopkeepers and salesmen to help tame inflation, he announced plans to slash the retail rates of non-dairy produce by 20 to 30 per cent, and the wholesale outlets of the province promised to drop prices for as long as stocks lasted. On 18 June shoppers swamped the communal market-place, where the reductions first went into effect. Soon panic struck the retailers of the countryside, and the Camera del Lavoro complained of foul play.[11] Three days later, much to the dismay of the townspeople, the city council lifted the ceiling. Hoping to attract a constituency which cut across class lines, the leader of Brescian fascism vociferously frowned on the unleashing of the speculative forces 'that so plague our citizens'.[12]

The *fascio*'s bid to win over the proletariat had little chance of success. The blackshirts again tried to recruit metallurgists at the Franchi Gregorini company and failed a third time. Only a handful of municipal cafeteria employees joined the local movement.[13] Turati had even less luck in cementing a following among agricultural workers, since his propertied backers showed no interest in catering to the rural poor. The *ras* agreed with agrarian strategists that wage labour should be abolished, but he expressed disapproval of developments in Emilia and the dominance enjoyed by 'reactionary landlords' there;[14] at Brescia, by contrast, the masses needed to know that fascism stood 'against the parasitic establishment'.[15] He once

[10] *Fiamma*, 28 May and 6 June 1921.

[11] ACS, Min. Interno, DGPS, AGR 1921, b. 57a, cat. C1, fasc. Brescia, sfasc. 4, 18 and 21 June 1921.

[12] *La Provincia di Brescia*, 21 June 1921.

[13] *Fiamma*, 30 July 1921; *La Sentinella Bresciana*, 28 July 1921.

[14] ACS, MRF, CC dei Fasci, b. 100, fasc. Brescia, cartella, 4, n. 171, 16 August 1921.

[15] *Fiamma*, 9 July 1921.

suggested distributing marginal plots of land to sympathetic peasants for the sake of social stability, but the demagogic implications of the proposal scared away some farmers. Reluctant to give the ambitious outsider parcels of property with which to build an autonomous core of support, a group of suspicious estate owners threatened secession. The central committee in Milan thwarted a formal break.[16]

The pact of pacification opened another round of fighting within the *fascio*. Touted as an olive branch to the socialists, the proposal that sought to demobilize the squads also aimed to curb the freedom of action enjoyed by the provincial bosses and to give Mussolini more room for manœuvre in Rome. All components of the movement at Brescia united in hostility to the truce, but their political secretary followed the path of least resistance and refused to condemn any initiative launched by the national leadership.[17] Instead of attacking the idea of a peace treaty, Turati simply questioned its timing for his own territory where, he claimed, the red menace seemed to be show-ing signs of revival. Such tactical ambivalence and timid hesitation exacerbated tensions between the feuding factions and the local directorate. Agrarians in the eastern basin, who disliked the sub-ordination of paramilitarism to parliamentarianism, announced plans to join the intransigents in Mantua. Unwilling to sacrifice revolution-ary purity for the constitutional machinery of the old ruling class, the town radicals took umbrage too and voted to leave the official group.[18]

Turati endured these provocations. When the dissidents proposed a change in the secretariat, he dissolved the directorate. Then they sent an envoy to Milan who, mysteriously, never arrived.[19] Denounc-ing the betrayal of fascism's redemptive spirit, the secessionists plastered Brescia with posters and leaflets. Again Turati foiled the opposition and dismissed the propaganda as a socialist ploy to dis-credit the *fascio*.[20] His professed loyalty to Mussolini paid off in the end. The central committee instructed him to restore order in the local organization and to reconcile the feuding parties. Unification proceeded with difficulty. The *ras* engineered a compromise settle-ment by strengthening the position of the republican faction in the urban executive, but the locus of power shifted away from the town

[16] ACS, MRF, CC dei Fasci, b. 100, fasc. Brescia, cartella 3, 5 July 1921.
[17] *Popolo d'Italia*, 10 August 1921.
[18] *Fiamma*, 6 August 1921.
[19] ACS, MRF, CC dei Fasci, b. 100, fasc. Brescia, cartella 4, n. 167, 18 August 1921.
[20] *La Provincia di Brescia*, 20 August 1921.

section. The formation of a provincial federation freed Turati from control by the early city fascists, and his network of influence in the rural districts widened. The existence of an organizational structure that could suppress general assembly and crush internal opposition made leadership more hierarchical and authoritarian.[21]

At first old polemics failed to disappear. The redistribution of key posts left a legacy of distrust between the city executive and the provincial leadership. Personal incompatibility and mutual suspicion envenomed all attempts at conciliation. The 'first hour' fascists set off another crisis within weeks of the administrative reshuffle, forcing Turati to abnegate the secretariat.[22] The central committee designated some unknown from Voghera to replace him at the helm, but the bankrupt *fascio* at Brescia had difficulty raising the salary requested. Turati, who lived off his earnings as a journalist and propagandist, suddenly seemed less expendable.[23] He withdrew his resignation days later, while the men in Milan tried to cow the opposition of the left. Despite Pasella's intervention, the republicans' bid for autonomy grew as their influence in the movement declined.[24] The dissidents announced a mass resignation, which Turati refused to accept. The deadlock continued for almost a fortnight, until finally the dissatisfied members broke with the official group in disgust at its centralist and cliental tendencies.[25]

Turati emerged from this episode with uncontested power. Embarrassed by the erratic deviations and the angry resignations of his republican rivals in the old executive, he assumed full responsibility for policy and extinguished all pockets of resistance. Three of his acolytes filled the vacancies created in the directorate. The *ras* hoped to consolidate a mass following through the expansion of squads in the lowlands. Because he intended to stamp the region with his own brand of provincial intransigence, events in the Po delta served as portents for fascism in the Bresciano. The 1921 clash shifted the balance of power to the disadvantage of the city *fascio* and paved the way for the conquest of the countryside.

Late in the summer of 1921, the terrorist offensive intensified

[21] ACS, MRF, CC dei Fasci, b. 100, fasc. Brescia, cartella 4, n. 174, 16 September 1921.

[22] *La Provincia di Brescia*, 2 and 9 October 1921.

[23] ACS, MRF, CC dei Fasci, b. 100, fasc. Brescia, cartella 4, n. 179, 8 October 1921.

[24] Ibid., n. 181, 17 October 1921.

[25] Ibid., n. 196 (n.d. but late October 1921).

throughout the provincial basin area. The action of the squads underwent a dramatic transformation, especially after the abandonment of
pacification. Incidents provoked by undisciplined thugs months
before had evolved into planned surveillance expeditions by early
1922. No longer confined to intimidating militants or breaking
Federterra boycotts, assaults became less haphazard.[26] The company
commanders set out to destroy systematically the socialist and
Catholic labour organizations, adopting the belligerent tactics
employed by the Po valley fascists. Turati welcomed and even
encouraged the militarization of the movement, for the armed
auxiliaries would form the base of his power. But stimulus and
instruction came from outside. Bands from the Mantua and Cremona
plains played a vital role in 'training' the amateurs of Brescia.[27] The
equipment used by the local blackshirts seemed more sophisticated.
They travelled in motor cars and war-surplus lorries instead of by
bicycle. Ordinary members of squads as well as militia bosses now
carried revolvers.

The partisan justice of the prefect and the magistrates compounded
the assault on legality. As the focal points of fascist activity moved
from metropolitan Brescia to the backwaters of the province, collusion
by the local agencies of military and civilian authority accelerated the
descent into violence. Police stationed in rural outposts drifted
towards the shock troopers of the extreme right and volunteered their
services during raids into the countryside.[28] At the village of Seniga on
the Cremona border, one officer of the peace oversaw the murder of a
radical PPI organizer. The inspector on duty chose not to detain the
three squad members responsible for the shooting. He preferred to
press charges against the remaining Catholic unionists, who had gone
unarmed.[29] In the hamlet of Pisogne near Bergamo, a hundred blackshirts fell upon a socialist gathering to punish the leftists for holding a
demonstration on the day of the Lovere *fascio*'s inauguration. A bomb
went off, wounding several people, two of them fatally. The explosive
had been planted by a *carabiniere*.[30] Such sedition by the immediate

[26] P. A. Vecchia, *Storia del fascismo bresciano*, pp. 151-8.

[27] ACS, Min. Interno, DGPS, AGR 1921, b. 76b, cat. G1, fasc. Brescia, 9 August and
8 November 1921.

[28] *Brescia Nuova*, 1 and 15 October 1921.

[29] ACS, Min. Interno, DGPS, AGR 1921, b. 76b, cat. G1, fasc. Brescia, sfasc. Seniga,
28 October 1921; *Il Cittadino di Brescia*, 24 and 29 October 1921.

[30] ACS, Min. Interno, DGPS, AGR 1921, b. 76b, cat. G1, fasc. Brescia, sfasc. Pisogne,
27 September and 31 October 1921.

representatives of the law in the hinterland doomed officialdom to destruction there.

Fascist Inroads in Agriculture

The accent on agrarian, vigilante tactics in a major industrial zone reflected circumstances, not design. Unlike urban businessmen, who hesitated to enlist the help of the *fascio* in the conversion of the proletariat, rural employers jumped at the chance to fight organized labour with the aid of a bold ally. The readiness of entrepreneurs in agriculture to accept armed protection made them fall easy prey to the will of Turati. Fascism thus found its first foothold in the province. Casual collaboration between basin farmers and the Brescian squads began early, during the spring of 1921, when growers in the central flats repudiated the existing peasant pact and banned the Federterra from contract renewal talks. Counting on police partiality and terrorist activity to tame the opposition, the Associazione Conduttori di Fondi concluded exclusive negotiations with the UCL. Marcialis, the prefect in town, 'cordially asked' the socialists to sign the document, which lightened the winter labour quota and overlooked the eight-hour day. Although PSI militants denounced the settlement as rigged and retrograde, landlords refused to entertain changes, in the interests of 'collective discipline'.[31]

Determination to return the blow dealt by the Camera del Lavoro the previous year drove the UCL into an alliance with employers, but the Federterra would not play second fiddle to the white competition. Socialist organizers suggested state mediation for the renewal of agricultural contracts. They hoped that all parties could abide by the arbitration decision on the Soresina conflict in the Cremona plain, where the Catholic leagues of Guido Miglioli had put forth demands for peasant partnership in rural enterprises.[32] Antonio Bianchi had yet to deliberate on the dispute, and the agrarian association of Brescia saw no need to wait for his findings.[33] The red leagues threatened job action in a last-ditch effort to gain recognition. Almost one month after the warning, they finally held a strike, with the aim of bringing the basin economy to a halt. The May agitation lasted less than three days,

---

[31] *Il Cittadino di Brescia*, 11 March 1921; P. Albertario, *I salari agricoli*, p. 213.

[32] *Il Contadino Rosso*, 20 April 1921; *La Provincia di Brescia*, 24 April 1921.

[33] On Bianchi's decision in the Cremona dispute see A. Zanibelli, *Le leghe 'bianche' nel Cremonese*, pp. 110-26; A. Fappani, *Guido Miglioli e il movimento contadino* (Rome, 1978), pp. 169-93.

for armletted patrols quickly brought militant peasants to their knees.[34] Fascist intervention had a double thrust. The offensive of the blackshirts enabled employers to avoid both conciliation by government and co-operation with labour. A local squad led an attack on the family of Professor Bianchi. The company commander spoke of mayhem should the non-partisan agronomist attempt to settle the affairs of private property. Farmers at last found themselves freed from the pressures of trade unionism. In early June the Federterra capitulated and came to an agreement virtually dictated by the Associazione Conduttori di Fondi.[35]

Tomaso Nember's group managed to hold the red leagues in check, but failed to discipline its own ranks. Far from buttressing the collective strength of farmers, the squads' protection served as a crutch for agrarian individualism. Within days employers began to violate the terms of the pact drafted by their association. Unofficially stripped of contractual guarantees, the Federterra as well as the UCL issued formal protests. The complaints of socialist and Catholic organizers fell on deaf ears, even in the prefecture. Attempts to co-ordinate joint labour action degenerated, so on 22 June two separate strikes broke out.[36] The concurrent strike assaults pitted the peasants against one another and accentuated the divisions among them. The agitation which activists had intended as a show-down with landlords became, in the words of Marcialis, a contest 'to see which party could attract the greater number of adherents'.[37] Fascist reprisals, along with police repression, kept participation low in both basin disputes and almost broke the rural union movement.

With collective bargaining in abeyance, individual employers continued to abuse contractual agreements during the summer and autumn of 1921. Most growers in the eastern basin ignored the labour quota for union help, and some imported cheap migrant workers through the offices of middlemen in black shirts.[38] At a time when jobless members crammed the ledgers of the socialist labour exchanges, those in estate management looked elsewhere to hire hands. Mutual

[34] ACS, Min. Interno, DGPS, AGR 1921, b. 76b, cat. G1, fasc. Brescia, 20, 23, and 24 May 1921.
[35] *Il Contadino Rosso*, 4 and 11 June 1921; *La Provincia di Brescia*, 8 June 1921.
[36] *Il Contadino Rosso*, 18 June 1921; *Il Cittadino di Brescia*, 19 June 1921.
[37] ACS, Min. Interno, DGPS, AGR 1921, b. 57a, cat. G1, fasc. Brescia, sfasc. 7, 23 June 1921.
[38] ASB, GP, b. suppl. 33, fasc. disoccupazione agraria, sfratti 1921; *Brescia Nuova*, 23 July, 13 August, and 3 September 1921.

assistance between fascists and farmers not only damaged the position of the peasant leagues, but also came close to destroying the viability of the Associazione Conduttori di Fondi. Punitive expeditions and scab recruits reduced the need for a political pressure group. With the protective reaction of the squads, many landlords retreated to organizational complacency. The agrarian association suffered in popularity and prestige.[39]

The fascists waged the decisive battle in the eastern basin, which had suffered from an autumn drought. Federterra representatives put forth demands for a new peasant pact as the hardships of winter approached, but local growers chose to disregard the agenda of the leagues. Against the directives of the agrarian association, the dissentient employers revised contracts on their own terms: labourers could either accept a 35 per cent reduction in wages or find another place to work.[40] Although the majority of landlords from the more prosperous central plains still paid allegiance to Nember's group, they too intended to retract earlier concessions.[41] Beginning in September, when proprietors refused to respect the old labour quota, harvesters at Rudiano staged a partial work stoppage. Threatened with dismissal, however, the agitators yielded after a few days. Then during October, the mayor of Longhena informed his dependents that they must accept an agreement of his making. The UCL brought out its followers in protest, yet the strikers returned to the estate less than twenty-four hours later.[42] Intimidation by the squads forced 120 farm hands at Corzano to forsake their Catholic co-operative and to accept the conditions imposed by two recalcitrant landlords there.[43]

Political fragmentation in the countryside damaged all attempts at conciliation. By November 1921 the situation on the periphery had degenerated beyond repair, as struggles over contract renewal raged in the basin estates. The socialists sought the assistance of the state to circumvent prolonged agitation during the harsh winter months. The Associazione Conduttori di Fondi also favoured government intervention in the hope of containing landlords' indiscipline. But many employers wanted liberty in labour relations, opposing any interference from Rome in farm management matters. The UCL disliked

[39] *La Provincia di Brescia*, 2 September 1921.

[40] *La Sentinella Bresciana*, 17 November 1921.

[41] ACS, Min. Interno, DGPS, AGR 1921, b. 57a, cat. G1, fasc. Brescia, sfasc. 7, 16 November 1921.

[42] Ibid., 24 October 1921.

[43] Ibid., 25 October 1921.

the monopoly of representation enjoyed by the Federterra among casual workers and would not entrust the dispute to a mixed committee either.[44] Catholic hesitations and agrarian deviations, then, pushed the Camera del Lavoro to risk a show-down by calling a general strike of the agricultural proletariat.[45]

The socialists demanded no new concessions, only asking that landlords respect previous ones. None the less, farmers resisted the pressures of the union movement. With the help of the *fascio*, they fought to restore discipline and deference in labour. Turati extracted, as the price for services rendered by his squads during the strike, the imposition of fascist-inspired sharecropping contracts for casual help. Although Mussolini's national agrarian programme appeared in June, the *ras* himself made no mention of land policy for the Bresciano until early December. The provincial federation intended to exploit the success of similar campaigns in the Po delta, where the movement had cemented a strong rural following with promises to wage-earners, and emphasized the stabilizing effect of giving peasants a fixed interest in the soil they tilled.[46] Employers amended the proposal, couched originally in radical terms, to meet their specifications: they dropped the clause providing the eventual passage of the plot to its cultivator; they reserved the right to revoke leases at four months' notice and to dismiss workers found drunk on private property; and they curtailed security of tenure by stipulating yearly amortization of payments.

If the land programme of the local Partito Nazionale Fascista now seemed tailor-made for them, then not all employers in agriculture cared to wear this coat of many colours. Turati encountered the independent attitude of Nember's group in addition to hostility from the red and white leagues. The agrarian association issued a communiqué denouncing the 'technical and social implications' of the PNF pact. The *fascio* responded by founding a rival federation, the farmers' syndicate.[47] The agronomists Achille Marangoni and Giuseppe Presti, both members of the rising rural bourgeoisie, became chief patrons of the organizational development that paralleled employer initiatives in Cremona and Bologna.[48] These two commercial growers in the eastern plains endeavoured to break the

[44] *Il Cittadino di Brescia*, 28 November 1921.
[45] *Brescia Nuova*, 2 December 1921.
[46] *Fiamma*, 10 December 1921.
[47] *La Provincia di Brescia*, 11 December 1921.
[48] *Fiamma*, 24 December 1921; A. Lyttelton, *The Seizure of Power*, p. 221; A. Cardoza, *Agrarian Elites and Italian Fascism*, pp. 395-401.

influence of the Associazione Conduttori di Fondi through the enforcement of 'collective sharecropping' on basin estates.[49] Their appeal to national interest and disciplined compliance glossed over a conflict of mentalities within the propertied élite. The fascists exploited the call for unity as a weapon against the 'selfishness' of breakaway landlords.

While the formation of a farmer's syndicate took the attack against the liberal agrarian leadership one step further, Marangoni did not hesitate to enlist the help of absentee landlords in the campaign against Nember's association. He offered to underwrite the interest on small-scale investments for irrigation and other betterments, in order to get the old guard's support behind the new organization.[50] The scheme was meant to alleviate structural unemployment, or so the agronomist claimed, and to work in tandem with government efforts at national reconstruction. But proprietors could not be persuaded to foot the bill for improvements on land cultivated by their prosperous tenants, even in the name of social stability. Neither would they submit to fascist preferences about whom to hire or the terms of employment. The owners refused to deal with the PNF organization and sign its special pact. Instead they granted exclusive recognition to the Catholic leagues.[51]

Some early advocates of the fascist land programme wanted their old independence back once socialist defeat seemed imminent. Ready to contest the PNF's authority in dictating employment policy, one tenant farmer at Gottolengo ignored the contractual guarantees of the *fascio* and attempted to impose his own terms. Party activists took no punitive measures against the large leaseholder, though the coercive might of the prefecture and the provincial federation caused him to yield.[52] Gang violence played a more active role in forcing compliance from below. Late in December 1921, two squad members founded a peasant syndicate that relied on intimidation and terrorism to recruit a mass following.[53] The black union movement, based upon manipulation of the rural labour market, threatened the proportional representation of other groups. The Federterra leaders tried to forestall the

---

[49] *Fiamma*, 31 December 1921. *Compartecipazione collettivo* involved leasing land on a yearly basis to 'teams' of peasants. The arrangement would eliminate wage labour without affecting property distribution.

[50] ASB, GP, b. suppl. 33, fasc. disoccupazione agraria, n. 93, 11 January 1922.

[51] *Il Cittadino di Brescia*, 15 January 1922.

[52] *Fiamma*, 17 December 1921; *La Sentinella Bresciana*, 23 December 1921.

[53] *Fiamma*, 31 December 1921.

advance of their new rivals by negotiating a settlement with the Associazione Conduttori di Fondi. Like socialist militants, moderate employers found regimentation under the fascist banner difficult to accept. The agrarian association reached a hasty accord with the Camera del Lavoro on 27 January 1922, so 'collective sharecropping' touched only estates on the eastern plain.[54]

The destruction of the red and white leagues continued throughout the winter months. *Squadristi* arriving by the truck-load from Mantua and Cremona would swamp the basin at night to help the Brescia commandos beat up union activists and raid employment exchanges. During these desperate days, the rural labour world offered no unified response to the growing violence of the right. Militant anticlericalism among socialists did more harm than good. The Catholics, as always, worked against the Camera's monopoly over collective bargaining. They refused to sign the January settlement, preferring to accept lower wages in return for better leaseholder and sharecropper terms.[55] Disparities in social position and political affiliation thus defeated all prospects for a bipartisan front among villagers. The Federterra concentrated on the agricultural proletariat, whereas the UCL again appealed to the intermediate categories farming the land. Agrarians demonstrated a sound appreciation of the incoherence that beset the provincial peasant community when they insisted on a single pact which could exclude neither organization. By deflecting conflict in the countryside towards the two groups in competition for the allegiance of the masses, individual employers also moved on to the attack.

In April 1922 employers and fascists launched a joint assault. Growers at Verolavecchia repudiated the January accord, disowned the agrarian association, and cut already miserable wages by another 13 per cent. The Federterra countered by calling a regional strike, limited to three villages on the Cremona border. Although the socialists racked every nerve to avoid a more extensive clash, violations of the pact soon spread beyond the frontier, as farmers in the central and western plains began to desert the Associazione Conduttori di Fondi.[56] Taught by the troubles of Soresinese white leagues that same spring, the UCL radicals had learned to expect provocation by the black cudgel, and they urged a united work

---

[54] *La Provincia di Brescia*, 28 and 29 January 1922.

[55] ACS, Min. Interno, DGPS, AGR 1922, b. 43, cat. C1, fasc. Brescia, 10 April 1922; *Il Cittadino di Brescia*, 20 March and 11 April 1922.

[56] ACS, Min. Interno, DGPS, AGR 1922, b. 43, cat. C1, fasc. Brescia, 22 April 1922.

stoppage with their red rivals.[57] The Camera del Lavoro misjudged the moment by printing attacks on the *popolari* as conspirators with landlords.[58] Armed bands from neighbouring provinces infiltrated the flatlands of Brescia and ravaged the Catholic co-operatives on orders from Roberto Farinacci, while lorries full of scab labourers came up from Ferrara. A policy of restraint no longer made sense. By the time the PSI and the PPI announced joint job action in retaliation, the squads had crushed the basin cadres of both organizations.[59]

Membership of the farmers' syndicate soared. The new adherents joined with unanimous support for the terrorism which had pushed the peasant leagues out of the picture, but enthusiasm faded once the blackshirts proposed infringements on the prerogatives of private property. Most agrarian spokesmen preferred to shelve the *fascio*'s 'collective sharecropping' scheme in favour of existing tenurial systems; they wanted to lower production costs, not to destroy wage labour. Basin growers also pressed for the abolition of the seasonal employment quota; the 1921 slump in agriculture had caused many to cut back cultivation, and demand for hired help consequently dropped. Turati dismissed these deflationary nostrums as 'absurd, unfair, and immoral', chiding critics for not having captured the true spirit of class collaboration. He did, however, give hesitant landlords some satisfaction by adding that the PNF would draft *compartecipazione* contracts 'according to the fascist norm, that is with the maximum degree of interpretation by proprietors'.[60]

Turati drifted amid conflicting currents as the head of fascism in the Brescian basin. There, agrarians watched while paramilitary forces killed all prospects of rural revolution. Impotent to turn back the post-war advance of the peasant leagues, they expected the provincial federation to reverse the damage done by three years of labour troubles, and to go no further. The local PNF leader helped growers to disarm the union movement and revise costly contracts, but he knew enough from developments in the Po valley not to barter away his position among the masses in agriculture. When a number of moderate landlords started to stipulate terms individually with the UCL, they threatened Turati's coign of vantage among estate

[57] Ibid., 25 April 1922.

[58] *Il Contadino Rosso*, 27 April 1922.

[59] ACS, Min. Interno, DGPS, AGR 1922, b. 43, cat. C1, fasc. Brescia, 5 and 11 May 1922.

[60] *Fiamma*, 6 May 1922.

workers.[61] To the discomfiture of the *fascio* as well as the Federterra, negotiations proceeded between farmers and Catholics in six villages.[62] For their participation at the bargaining table, proprietors and the new prefect earned the animus of the *ras*, who removed any doubts about which syndicate would receive preferential treatment from employers.

Turati placed the foundation of organized strength above the preservation of entrepreneurial freedom. As militiamen from Verona reinforced the Brescia, Cremona, and Mantua regiments, the PNF offensive expanded to include dissident landlords. The basin district soon contained no fewer than 1,500 blackshirts, far outnumbering the 567 troops which stood behind civilian authority. Squad members occupied the estates of those neglecting to use the PNF employment roster for hired hands. From the prefecture, Achille De Martino reported that the owners 'have found their concerns taken over by fascists, from whom they would like to free themselves but cannot'.[63] The rural proletariat likewise felt the impact of such coercion, and the new peasants' syndicate flourished immediately. Now threatened with dismissal, farm workers in the plains capitulated to the *fascio* and deserted their old leagues. Already on 2 June 1922 about 150 wage labourers of Calvisano circumvented the boycott imposed by the *ras* by signing up with his union. That same day at Pralboino, Gottolengo, Visano, and Isorella, all villages in the eastern flats, the landless left the Federterra to become 'sharecroppers' after a fashion.[64] By the next morning, the syndicate had enrolled nearly 2,000, most of them stolen from the socialist competition.[65] The provincial federation could soon boast that it had undone in the short space of two weeks what had taken the Camera del Lavoro ten years to build up.[66]

What began as an attempt to broaden the social base of agrarian fascism turned into a comprehensive campaign against the independence of propertied interests and public agencies in the basin. The first blow fell upon the municipalities under PSI administration. The conversion of the Federterra leagues into PNF syndicates allowed violence and coercion to play a secondary role during the conquest of the bolshevik town governments. The deposed mayor of Bagnolo

---

[61] ACS, Min. Interno, DGPS, AGR 1922, b. 43, cat. C1, fasc. Brescia, 17 May 1922.
[62] Ibid., 29 May 1922.
[63] Ibid., 30 May 1922.
[64] Ibid., 2 June 1922.
[65] Ibid., 3 June 1922; *La Provincia di Brescia*, 2–5 June 1922.
[66] *Fiamma*, 17 June 1922.

Mella described the line of attack as he lamented the passage of agricultural workers to the black unions: 'The majority on the council . . . has become automatically deprived of the mandate given by their constituents, namely these formerly socialist peasants.'[67] Early in July civilian authority appointed a prefectural commission, stacked with fascist sympathizers, to replace the elected representatives of the people in the eastern plains commune.[68] Catholic elders resisted when the provincial federation used similar tactics to depose the PPI junta at Verolanuova. Unlike the socialists, the *popolari* based their power on a patronage network, representing commercial and banking interests, that Turati found tough to crack. Two more fruitless attempts to sap the vitality of the church in civic life compelled the Brescian boss to postpone the capture of clerical strongholds in the countryside until after the national seizure of power.[69]

Throughout the summer of 1922, the squads concentrated on fulfilling the syndicate's pledge of preference in employment to members. In this endeavour landlords proved lukewarm allies. Although basin farmers eagerly used the services of the provincial federation to domesticate peasant radicalism, they resented any interference in the recruitment of hired help. And some attempted to play off the socialist, Catholic, and fascist unions in order to weaken all three. When at Calvisano proprietors attached to the PNF turned away workers of the same affiliation, Turati threatened physical violence to force the unco-operative to abide by the new rules. He deplored the 'reactionary and independent postures of certain agrarians', spurred by the gospel of private profit to forsake the principles of class collaboration, and warned that 'those who do not obey will be chased from the ranks without pity'.[70] Not long after the *fascio*'s ill-fated plot to capture their municipal council, the growers of Verolanuova concluded an agreement with the UCL. In Pavone Mella, Milzano, Gambara, and Leno, rebellious owners carried out secret negotiations with PPI leaders to encourage the entrenchment of white leagues.[71] Turati, moreover, managed to offend even the most compliant entrepreneurs in agriculture after mention of a 'fascist labour quota', determined by land productivity rather than by estate size.[72] Soon the

[67] ASB, GP, b. 21, fasc. Bagnolo Mella, 29 June 1922.
[68] Ibid., 6 July 1922; *La Provincia di Brescia*, 7 July 1922.
[69] ASB, GP, b. suppl. 32, n. 1005, 12 July 1922; ACS, Min. Interno, DGPS, AGR 1922, b. 43, cat. C1, fasc. Brescia, 19 July 1922; *Fiamma*, 22 July 1922.
[70] *Fiamma*, 1 July 1922.
[71] ASB, GP, b. suppl. 32, n. 1005, 6 June, 12 and 16 July 1922.

defiant attitude of rural notables to such talk and action brought his syndical movement to an abrupt halt.

Friction between competing chieftains on the Lombard plain exacerbated tensions. The provincial federation had betrayed the hopes of its propertied backers, who fought to stay an independent force. Turati tried to weather the storm and disband the employers' syndicate. But the members stuck together and chose to bypass him by urging secession to the aggressive Cremona *fascio*. The Brescian blackshirts, complained the farmers to the prefect, 'want to impose conditions harsher than those stipulated by the red and white leagues to consolidate their popular following'.[73] By late August the dispute had so degenerated that the *ras* assaulted the spokesman for the basin growers in public.[74] The landlords waged a timid campaign against the local PNF leader, writing letters to the *Sentinella* and calling upon Michele Bianchi to intervene. The national party secretary, albeit reluctant to encourage Turati, meant to curb the power base of Farinacci, the imperious boss next door.[75] After squads arrived at estates where observance of the fascist hiring policy seemed slow, the 'agrarian revolt' again ran out of steam.[76]

Employers and Unions in Industry before the March on Rome

The recession of 1921 brought bad times to local industry. During this difficult year the chronic malaise that had plagued local steel producers since the armistice became acute. Many independent valley operators survived the crisis by laying off workers, but the grand old man of the Brescian business community saw his provincial empire collapse. Attilio Franchi, with so many debts left to settle from the war, hoped to ward off the worst. He met with Giolitti's minister of commerce in search of state subsidies, he borrowed 3 million lire from the Bergamo cement king Cesare Pesenti to pay out dividends, he even wanted to lease back two plants when the Banca Commerciale chose to foreclose.[77] In November, at the age of 61, the owner of the

---

[72] *Fiamma*, 19 July and 12 August 1922.

[73] ACS, Min. Interno, DGPS, AGR 1922, b. 43, cat. C1, fasc. Brescia, 24 August 1922.

[74] *Fiamma*, 26 August 1922.

[75] On the career of Roberto Farinacci, a former railwayman, see G. Prezzolini, *Fascism* (New York, 1927), pp. 70-2; H. Fornari, *Mussolini's Gadfly: Roberto Farinacci* (Nashville, 1971), pp. 31-65.

[76] *Fiamma*, 2 September 1922; *La Sentinella Bresciana*, 2 September 1922.

[77] ASIG, Società Anonima Franchi Gregorini, Consiglio di Amministrazione, verbali, 4 and 22 November 1920, 12 September 1921.

firm bearing his family name finally stepped down as managing director. Ten months later the COMIT group agreed to let the petulant entrepreneur keep the dolomite extraction works at Marone, in exchange for his resignation from the supervisory board of the parent company.[78] Two years in the red ended with the sexagenarian's departure from the steel dynasty he had spent three and a half decades creating.

Before surrendering control of the steelworks to his Milanese creditors, Franchi gave the work-force a taste of company troubles. Defying the Lombard consortium yet again, he denounced the pay agreement that the association had signed in the aftermath of the factory occupations. When he proceeded to reduce wages by 25 per cent, the FIOM urged labour action, but the rank and file delayed lest participants be fired. On 7 June 1921, the metallurgical federation at last mobilized 5,000 operatives in a disciplined strike, to which the employer responded by declaring a lock-out.[79] Seven weeks later the agitation collapsed. Unable to prevent the slip in salary, union members voted to resume production.[80] Seven hundred militants on the shop floor lost their jobs in the process.[81]

The situation looked even gloomier in the textile sector, where all employers tended to pursue the same deflationary policy towards labour. Dependent on keeping production costs at home low to stimulate sales abroad, these export businessmen stubbornly opposed any economic concessions to *hoi polloi* on the payroll. Three firms simply sacked unionized help as a cushion against falling prices for their wares. Montanari e Studer, one of the largest hosiery concerns in Lombardy, systematically laid off members of the socialist federation and hired peasant girls to replace them at almost half the standard rate.[82] Following a walk-out by a hundred women at a nearby cotton shop, which also expected to use scabs, police came to the owner's defence and pushed the ladies back inside the factory gates. The bellicose behaviour of the provincial manufacturers bothered not only leaders of the FIOT, but also missionaries for the UCL, who feared the loss of their most valuable asset, co-operation from above. At

[78] Ibid., 15 November 1921 and 30 September 1922.

[79] ACS, Min. Interno, DGPS, AGR 1921, b. 71, cat. D13, fasc. Brescia, 8 June 1921.

[80] *Brescia Nuova*, 11 and 18 June, 9 and 23 July 1921; *La Provincia di Brescia*, 21 and 22 July 1921.

[81] ASIG, Società Anonima Franchi Gregorini, Consiglio di Amministrazione, verbale, 12 September 1921.

[82] *Il Cittadino di Brescia*, 12 and 17 June 1921; *Brescia Nuova*, 18 June 1921.

Verolanuova Catholic organizers had little recourse but to strike. They tried to stir up sympathizers at the local mill, yet the partial stoppage proved a total disaster. After the national accord of August 1921 left wages slashed by nearly 20 per cent, workers began to disown their unions.[83]

September 1921 witnessed scenes of struggle in the wool branch of textiles. As the European market continued to contract, conditions of work and terms of employment deteriorated too. In open defiance of a national agreement, provincial manufacturers of the fabric more than matched the example of their associates in cotton, for pay scales underwent a 28 per cent reduction.[84] *Brescia Nuova* reported that two companies proposed a reversion to the twelve-hour day.[85] According to the *Cittadino*, four firms brought back the pre-war six-day working week.[86] At first the harsh policy of management seemed to encourage a united labour front. When fascist bullies from the town broke a socialist strike, the Catholic workers abstained from production in solidarity with their comrades at the Camera del Lavoro. Within a few days, however, the UCL organizers again lost their nerve and settled on a 20 per cent wage cut, while the FIOT resumed agitation to protest against the clerical compromise.

The general secretary of the Confindustria saw state intervention as the logical next step. Since the Catholic flock had capitulated to their masters, the remaining socialist participants should return to the factories under force in the interests of 'harmonious class collaboration'. A curious defence of contractual freedom led Gino Olivetti to urge official repression of the partial job action so that government could protect 'liberty to work' against 'the contrary desires of some competing unions'.[87] The FIOT still instructed its followers to stay out, but police collusion with management made agitation difficult. Hours after civilian authority detained the first militants, a hundred members crossed the picket lines. One day and five arrests later, the textile federation called off its strike. The defeat shattered the cadres of the Camera del Lavoro in light industry, but employers pugnaciously pressed home their advantage. During this ebb tide of

[83] *La Provincia di Brescia*, 22 August 1922.

[84] ACS, Min. Interno, DGPS, AGR 1921, b. 57a, cat. C1, fasc. Brescia, sfasc. 5, 12 September 1921.

[85] *Brescia Nuova*, 17 September 1921.

[86] *Il Cittadino di Brescia*, 14 September 1921.

[87] ACS, Min. Interno, DGPS, AGR 1921, b. 57a, cat. C1, fasc. Brescia, sfasc. 5, 24 September 1921.

organized labour, two cotton manufacturers instituted a ten-hour day, and another returned to a six-day schedule.[88] The Cotonificio Turati quietly dismissed those who complained of conditions on the shop floor, since fascist blacklegs from Bergamo offered to fill in for less pay.[89]

The provision of strike-breaking services did not count for much among industrial leaders at Brescia. Financial support for local fascism never went beyond some textile and paper mills scattered throughout the countryside. When the FIOM called a regional walk-out in June 1922, Turati took the occasion to found a PNF metal-lurgists' union, with which he hoped to win the sympathy of manufacturers. But employers in the steel and machine concerns saw no need to promote the coercive recruitment of labour that entre-preneurs in agriculture had seemed willing to underwrite. Given the caution of big business and the resistance of most operatives, syndicalists kept a low profile outside the yard gates as well as on the shop floor. 'Agitation' took the form of pushing workers across the picket line. Squad members would accompany blacklegs into the factory and invite them to join the party organization, hinting at special terms from company bosses.[90] Few actually abandoned the socialist federation for the *fascio*'s affiliate, and management stayed indifferent. The scab escort service stopped after three days.[91]

Those businessmen sympathetic to the PNF tended to identify with the national leadership. Their belief in order and hierarchy stood as a direct antithesis to the local *fascio*'s use of violence and claims to power. The steel and arms producers, along with the rising hosiery manufacturers, circumvented the provincial federation in making contributions. Although Togni donated 3,000 lire, Glisenti 1,500, Beretta 1,000, Montanari e Studer 5,000, and Ambrosi 5,500 to the central committee's fund-raising drive, all kept their distance from the movement at home.[92] Turati did maintain close contact with Alfredo Giarratana, an engineer at the Edison electrical subsidiary, who had

[88] Ibid., 7 and 8 October 1921; *La Provincia di Brescia*, 8 October 1921.

[89] *Brescia Nuova*, 22 October 1921; *Il Cittadino di Brescia*, 3 November 1921.

[90] ACS, Min. Interno, DGPS, AGR 1922, b. 56, cat. D13, fasc. Brescia, 10 June 1922.

[91] *La Provincia di Brescia*, 12 June 1922; *Brescia Nuova*, 17 June 1922.

[92] ACS, MRF, b. 70, fasc. distinte oblazioni, cartella 2, Brescia, 14 January 1922 and 14 February 1923; the most generous provincial sponsor of the national organization, the Cartiera Maffizzoli (30,000 lire), also seems to have been the only major company to finance the local squads. On industrial contributions to the central fund, see R. De Felice, 'Primi elementi sul finanziamento del fascismo dalle origini al 1924', in *Rivista Storica del Socialismo*, vol. viii (1964), pp. 223-51, and A. Lyttelton, *The Seizure of Power*, pp. 210-11.

collaborated on the Blocco Nazionale's *La Riscossa* during the November 1920 campaign. But when both propagandists made a premature play for control of the Brescia city council, just two weeks after Farinacci had municipal government suspended in Cremona, the respectability of their partnership faded.[93] The fiasco of July 1922 isolated Giarratana from others in management and forced his resignation from communal administration. Turati, for his part, incurred the displeasure of the old guard in enterprise and never found a pool of patronage among urban employers.

Industry preferred to continue unaided in its offensive against labour. In September hosiery manufacturers cut wages to just above the bare minimum for consumption in the countryside, and the white textile league threatened retaliatory action. Although Domenico Viotto at the Camera del Lavoro condemned the Catholic initiative on principle, FIOT leaders overrode his objection and agreed to collaborate with the rival union. The fascist bombing of the Casa del Popolo late in the summer, not to mention the collapse of the Federterra cadres, had apparently purged some maximalists of their anticlericalism. The strike, also called to equalize pay scales in rural factories and those of the town, represented the first joint undertaking of the PPI and the PSI. The socialists showed unusual magnanimity by accepting the leadership of the UCL, which claimed the majority of workers in the sector.

The strike that lasted a little over a month halved the UCL textile membership. Foiled by the indiscipline of the white rank and file, the bold front fell apart within weeks. The *popolari* proved unable to co-ordinate proletarian protest of regional proportions. Because previous agitation had taught the Catholic masses to content themselves with advantages negotiated on a local basis, those unaffected by the wage cuts declined to join the picket. The four largest firms sought to exploit past organizational techniques by refusing to discuss the issue of collective bargaining. Before long rural labourers defied the directives of the provincial leadership and settled grievances with individual employers.[94] Such deviations infuriated the socialists, who withdrew their support before final disaster hit.[95] Management in

---

[93] On the fascist seizure of the Cremona town council, see R. Farinacci, *Squadrismo: Dal mio diario della vigilia 1919–1922* (Rome, 1933), pp. 125-38; C. Maier, *Recasting Bourgeois Europe*, pp. 318-19.

[94] ASB, GP, b. suppl. 32, fasc. sciopero calzificio, 23 September 1922.

[95] Ibid., 29 September 1922; *Brescia Nuova*, 7 and 14 October 1922.

every shop took the opportunity to slash salaries below the level originally proposed. At Borgo San Giacomo one manufacturer required a written statement disowning any trade affiliation before he would reinstall a worker. In Botticino Sera a Catholic unionist publicly apologized to an industrialist about the walk-out so that recruits could stay on the payroll. Only where the militant priest Don Bissolotti had intervened did workers get their old wages back.[96]

The catastrophic strike in hosiery and knitwear represented a double disillusionment for the Catholic workers' movement. The friction generated in the wake of defeat prevented united action on any other front. The embarrassed UCL blamed the socialists for deserting the common cause.[97] Frustrated FIOT leaders countered by accusing their competition of 'systematic scab activity'.[98] The slanders of the Camera del Lavoro against white unionism weakened the position of lay reformers, and the search for culpability by church conservatives made matters worse. Using the labour alliance as a scapegoat for defeat, the city directorate confirmed the 'moderate tendencies' of the Brescia Partito Popolare. Carlo Bresciani of the clerical right now had the last word on collaboration with the PSI. Oblivious to the political situation of October 1922, when the deputy in parliament still thought the PPI could be fussy about friends and ignore certain enemies, he condemned a sodality with the ungodly.[99]

The march on Rome brought the *popolari* back to reality. The fascist festivities at Brescia culminated on 28 October with the occupation of the Palazzo San Paolo, headquarters of the PPI.[100] During the dramatic events, socialists slipped increasingly into the background. Having lost key municipalities in July, the PSI ceased to exist as a significant force in local government. And because the protracted strike in agriculture had impoverished the Camera del Lavoro, expenditure on propaganda became difficult to sustain. Limited resources caused *Brescia Nuova* to fold, though the maximalist deputies in parliament pooled enough funds to publish a last issue on the Mussolini premiership.[101] The Casa del Popolo received its share of armed action, but the PNF commandos focused most of their attentions on eliminating the Partito Popolare, which still wielded institu-

---

[96] *Il Cittadino di Brescia*, 7 and 8 October 1922.
[97] Ibid., 12 October 1922.
[98] *Brescia Nuova*, 14 October 1922.
[99] *Il Cittadino di Brescia*, 10 October 1922.
[100] *La Sentinella Bresciana*, 2 November 1922.
[101] *Brescia Nuova*, 11 November 1922.

tional power in the province. The indiscriminate persecution of 'bolshevik conspirators' now turned into a fervent crusade against the clerical keepers of administrative authority. Squads charged into the offices of eight Catholic communes, obtaining mass resignations from the village councillors.[102] While the street warfare did damage to the party of the proletariat, the blackshirts made the Catholic lay organization their primary target.

The old constitutional forces, regrouped as the Partito Liberale Italiano, overlooked the piecemeal disintegration of government at the local level. In composition the Mussolini ministry excluded only the socialists, and to many it appeared as a broad conservative coalition. Provincial democrats saw no cause for complaint, since their favourite son became under-secretary of state in the new cabinet. The appointment of Carlo Bonardi appeased both left and right liberals, making the regime in Rome more palatable to them.[103] Quick to denounce the brutal tactics pursued by the blackshirts at Brescia, none the less they gave the national leader of the partisan militia 'a free hand for this bold experiment'.[104] The orchestrations of the *fascio* did not escape notice, but legalists seemed sure that the moderating power of the premier would subdue the more combative members of the armed movement.

The local fascists derided the formation of the ministry. The march on Rome revealed the strength of the national movement, yet underscored the price that the provincials would have to pay. Turati had pressed for a pedigree PNF cabinet. The intransigent chieftain already distrusted the Duce's flirtation with parliamentary intrigue, and rumour implicated the Brescia *ras* in a D'Annunzian plot against Mussolini's leadership.[105] Party militants found the inclusion of three democrats and two Catholics in the government excessive, but news of the Bonardi nomination came as a complete surprise. Turati made no secret of his displeasure. The snubbed boss felt cheated, 'rigorously cast aside'. He had little intention of steering the bullies back home away from their parochial extremism just because of compromise in the capital. 'We proceed', he trumpeted, 'down our road as before'.[106]

Turati often professed to defend, first and foremost, the interests of the labouring masses. After breaking the basis of revolutionary

[102] *Il Cittadino di Brescia*, 3 November 1922.
[103] *La Provincia di Brescia*, 3 and 4 November 1922; *La Sentinella Bresciana*, 3 November 1922.
[104] *La Provincia di Brescia*, 2 November 1922.
[105] St Antony's Documents, J. 330, 113307-10, 3 March 1927.
[106] *Fiamma*, 4 November 1922.

solidarity, he would have liked to use the organized strength of the urban working class for his own political ends. Instead, the balance of forces in the periphery, as well as the success of paramilitary expeditions throughout the country, made him assert power in the name of outraged conservatism. The *ras* managed to manipulate a fragmented rural community by trading on its regionalism and anxiety. The impact of national developments in provincial affairs threatened to destroy the independence of this ambitious boss. Taunted by the moderate tendencies of the Mussolini government, in addition to the agrarian reaction of neighbouring federations, Turati embarked upon an uncharted course of radical intransigence in order to preserve the autonomy of the local movement.

7

The Brescian Road to Fascism

WHEN Mussolini journeyed from Milan to Rome by wagon-lit, he had yet to formulate his ultimate political aims. The Duce met the king to accept the premiership inside an hour of arriving in the capital.[1] PNF militants looked forward to purging the old gang and to calling new elections. They saw no need for the co-operation of Catholics or the look of legality. The choice of a mixed ministry disappointed these purists, even though decisive posts in the state machinery came under their control. Acting independently of the party, the prime minister showed himself conciliatory to conservative as well as church opinion. He went far on the basis of tactical skill. The confidence of the chamber won him a year's plenary powers for financial and administrative reform. Royal appointment and parliamentary endorsement gave the cabinet some semblance of constitutional rectitude, but ambiguity persisted about the form fascist governance would take.

Between the march on Rome in October 1922 and the murder of Matteotti in June 1924, the Duce faced contrary imperatives as leader of a mass movement and head of a coalition cabinet. He widened the sphere of the executive soon after taking office. He consolidated the PNF's institutional power by creating the Grand Council and the militia.[2] Police repression forced the communists underground, and electoral reform ensured a permanent majority in the chamber for the government list. The political establishment saw the premier as a natural ally, despite measures which represented advances towards

---

[1] A. Répaci, *La marcia su Roma, mito e realtà*, vol. i (Rome, 1963), pp. 571-8.
[2] The Grand Council, made up of the party executive and fascist officialdom, co-ordinated PNF activities with those of the state; this organ displaced the cabinet as the deliberative body on high policy. The Milizia Volontaria per la Sicurezza Nazionale centralized control over the squads and maintained them at public expense; the MVSN served as Mussolini's armed police reserve. See C. Seton-Watson, *Italy from Liberalism to Fascism*, p. 634; A. De Grand, *Italian Fascism: Its Origins and Development* (Lincoln, 1982), pp. 43-4; A. Aquarone, 'La milizia volontaria nello stato fascista', in A. Aquarone and M. Vernassa (eds.), *Il regime fascista* (Bologna, 1974), pp. 85-111.

dictatorship. The stalemate in parliament during the post-war period convinced paternalistic élites that proportional representation must end. Hatred of opposition in the legislature drove conservative apologists to support rule by decree. Mussolini actively courted the liberal party, although plans for a federation failed. Fusion with the Italian Nationalist Association met with greater success, but this 1923 merger with monarchists alienated many blackshirts. Provincial extremists distrusted the spirit of compromise that surrounded the inception of the ministry, and they feared the loss of official influence to fascism's fair-weather friends. The local *ras*, who maintained a climate of crisis and disorder to justify the exercise of power, found the play for respectable opinion especially insidious.

Political secretaries and party syndicalists understood the necessary expedients of mass organization, using influence and intimidation to conquer public indifference. But those back-room boys who delivered safe constituencies to the government regarded the centralization of power as an intolerable evil. Behind the defence of local liberties lay the fear that the new regime in Rome would wrench paramilitary muscle in the provinces. The movement's rural understrappers had acquired position by perpetuating violence and illegality, and respect for the authority of the state continued to elude them even with the Duce as premier. The exigencies of fascist operations on the periphery subverted most attempts to reform the intransigent wing. PNF moderates that deprecated the bastard populism of the agrarian bloc lacked institutional channels for change. Since they never went for the numbers or the large clienteles, this vocal élite could establish their claim to legitimacy only through the person of the prime minister. The polemic against the rule of the *ras* occupied revisionists, most of whom hoped to substitute the bald fanaticism of the country caciques with a conciliatory programme for national reconstruction. Mussolini himself sympathized with the cry to control the extremists. His attitude infuriated squad members and gave insecure bosses reason for reproach.[3]

Grievances against Government: The Revival of White Unionism

The campaign to supplant the provincial *popolari* stepped up after the march on Rome. The fascist preoccupation with the church presence in civic life dated back to the summer of 1922, when the Federterra

[3] A. Lyttelton, *The Seizure of Power*, pp. 150-4; R. De Felice, *Mussolini il fascista, I*, pp. 404-9, 412-60.

finally collapsed as a result of boycotts and persecution. Following the example set by the Cremonese squads in early July, the local black-shirts began a relentless assault on clerical strongholds in the foothills and the western plains.[4] Twice Turati warned the city government that the PNF would force its demise, but both attempts to suspend the town council failed. He tried to weaken the white union movement internally by intriguing against the UCL organizer, Francesco Castagna. This plot backfired too. An inspector at the prefecture called the new course of reaction the 'Catholic phase', for the *ras* now threatened to 'undermine the Partito Popolare by violence'.[5] Shock tactics acquired particular urgency after October 1922. Not only did the Brescia intransigents mean to crush ecclesiastical authority in lay politics, but they also intended to reaffirm their own autonomy and counteract the centripetal tendencies of the Mussolini government.

Again a decisive struggle took place in the countryside, where the UCL attempted to renew leasehold contracts.[6] The reappearance of Catholic competition caused problems for Turati. He had eliminated both the old agrarian association and the dissident employers' move-ment, and reconstituted the PNF growers' organization along different lines. In contrast with the previous spring, the fascists did not lure members by promising vigilante protection. The accent now fell on class collaboration, which meant recognition of the black peasant league as the sole representative of labour. Terror squads, at first reserved for 'subversives', aimed also at 'reactionary landlords'.[7] The *ras* 'cordially invited' men of property to join his syndicate, inaugurated early in October. In characteristic hectoring tone, he added that refusal to enrol would result in disciplinary action, 'harm-ful to the farmer'.[8]

Under such circumstances even liberal stalwarts in the western plains found Turati's rhetorical posturing difficult to resist. Soon the syndicate boasted the unanimous support of provincial growers. Some agrarians, concentrated in the eastern basin, joined with genuine sympathy. According to the agronomist Marangoni, president of the

[4] ACS, Min. Grazia e Giustizia, Affari Penali, 1922, b. 131, fasc. 84, sfasc. Brescia, 26 September 1922.

[5] ACS, Min. Interno, DGPS, AGR 1922, b. 68, cat. G1, fasc. Brescia, 5 September 1922.

[6] ASB, GP, b. suppl. 33, fasc. disoccupazione agraria, n. 1487, 23 August 1922 (Federazione Provinciale Lavoratori Agricoli).

[7] *Fiamma*, 23 September 1922.

[8] Ibid., 4 October 1922.

new organization, anarchic individualism undermined the advance of techniques and production. The free play of agricultural enterprise, he declaimed, gave way to poverty and confusion. Constancy in contractual relations, moreover, required the regimentation of employers as well as workers, and the fascists alone intended to discipline both sides in the interests of efficient estate management.[9] But just when local party officials thought that they had brought all farmers to heel, many proprietors became nervous about giving the PNF complete control. These landlords left the door wide open for the UCL.

Determined to undercut the Catholics in the foothills, fascist organizers hit back hard. Landlords received instructions to dismiss peasants enrolled in the UCL in favour of those affiliated with the PNF. Unemployment threatened virtually thousands of share-croppers, small leaseholders, and dependent labourers. Pietro Bulloni, a white union lawyer, took their case to a higher authority.[10] The minister of agriculture urged conciliation, and the prefect endeavoured to follow government guide-lines. At first black syndicalists appeared uncommonly magnanimous to church and civilian officialdom. The mass evictions stopped, which gave the impression of an implied truce.[11] Days after the march on Rome, however, the Brescia federation reverted to more conventional means and tried to steer the flock away from the *popolari* by offering better terms.[12] *Compartecipazione* was shelved in favour of wage work; Turati did not deign to explain his volte-face. The reversal proved a bitter disillusionment to the agrarian backers of the movement, for the new scheme brought back the eight-hour day in agriculture and returned the basin labour quota to its 1919-20 level.[13] The party demanded that its accord stand as the only one applied in the province, but dropped the old clause requiring membership in a syndicate. This way tenants could stay tied to the co-operatives even though they had signed an agreement with the corporations.[14]

Castigation of the UCL had most immediate importance in five basin municipalities, where administrative elections were approaching.[15] But the PNF plan to discredit the Catholics in labour organiza-

[9] Ibid.
[10] ASB, GP, b. suppl. 33, fasc. disoccupazione agraria, n. 27, 25 September 1922.
[11] Ibid., 24 October 1922.
[12] *Il Cittadino di Brescia*, 5 November 1922.
[13] *La Sentinella Bresciana*, 16 November 1922.
[14] *Il Cittadino di Brescia*, 20 November 1922.
[15] *Fiamma*, 20 November 1922.

tion just about failed, through the indiscipline of some landlords. Employers who still felt hesitant about allowing the fascists a clean sweep paid lip-service to the directives of the growers' syndicate. Proprietors in the foothills began talks with the white league for small leaseholders. Antonio Bianchi, Castagna's close friend, offered to oversee negotiations with the help of De Martino.[16] Already in early November a rebellious Turati had informed the government of his reluctance to disband the squads;[17] complicity between the professor and the prefect on behalf of the *popolari* gave him a pretext for a show-down with the central state.

Armed blackshirts descended upon Catholic centres throughout the western part of the province a fortnight after Turati's initial warning to Rome. Founding satellite *fasci* where none existed, the platoon commanders proceeded to 'intervene energetically when necessary'.[18] This unofficial mobilization widened as more agrarians tried to collaborate with the UCL. By late November the fascists had extended their campaign to include the central basin. They reconstituted the PNF in three municipalities dominated by the PPI, since employers there seemed particularly perfidious to the syndicate.[19] Squad leaders used the new puppet sections to co-ordinate reprisals against clerical notables in positions of administrative authority. On 2 December 1922 tensions heightened in the hillside hamlet of Capriolo. Arriving by war-surplus lorry, fourteen thugs ravaged the church club and rummaged through the parish safe. They ransacked the quarters of the curate and the priest as a punishment for railing against the regime during mass.[20] While Catholic laity had suffered the slings and arrows of such fortune before, Don Martinazzoli and Don Libretti became the first clergymen in the area to fall victims to paramilitary violence. PPI politicians appealed to the government, and the bishop of Brescia pursued the issue with General De Bono, director of public security.[21] When *Popolo d'Italia* published a statement critical of the expedition, Turati threw down the gauntlet.[22] The

[16] *Il Cittadino di Brescia*, 22 and 27 November 1922; *La Provincia di Brescia*, 29 November 1922.

[17] ACS, Min. Interno, GF, OP, b. 4, fasc. 35, sfasc. 12.4, 8 November 1922.

[18] *Fiamma*, 25 November 1922.

[19] Ibid., 29 November 1922.

[20] ACS, Min. Interno, DGPS, AGR 1922, b. 68, cat. G1, fasc. Brescia, sfasc. Capriolo, 5 and 13 December 1922; Misc. affari penali 1922, b. 31, n. 84/9193, 11 December 1922.

[21] Ibid., 6 and 7 December 1922.

[22] *Popolo d'Italia*, 8 December 1922.

local party transmitted a communiqué to the national leadership in remonstrance. The provincial federation assumed full responsibility 'for any further measures its leaders may be forced to take if the present protest does not have the just and intended result'.[23]

The necessities of the situation made Turati unleash a frightful campaign to vindicate the vandals. With the Duce away in London, the incident provided ample opportunity to defy state bureaucracy and to remove the prefect. Under normal circumstances the December expedition, which included stealing the silver watch of the parish priest and beating his ill, sixty-five-year-old sister, might have seemed too sordid to publicize.[24] But the *ras* used the Capriolo reprisal to reanimate the polemic with the Mussolini government. He refused to apologize to the episcopacy, ordering instead a full mobilization of the provincial squads.[25] The enemies of fascism 'attacked on two fronts: Brescia and Rome', so the intransigents vowed to follow suit. The authorities in the capital also received final notice that Professor Bianchi must leave the travelling lectureship in agriculture. The local blackshirts stood 'ready once again to break the treacherous web of hostile forces'.[26]

The government faced a real dilemma. De Martino at the prefecture urged that the ministry of the interior should follow normal administrative procedure in the *cattedra ambulante* affair.[27] But Cesare Forni, captain of the north-west legions, attempted to expedite the professor's dismissal by threatening to mobilize fourteen provinces. In an open letter from 'slimy Rome', this agrarian extremist applauded the armed struggle against 'the ignoble class of deserters and disbelievers' and gave the Brescians 'affectionate solidarity'.[28] The appeal to squad violence ended the indecision of the authorities.

---

[23] ACS, MRF, CC dei Fasci, b. 100, fasc. Brescia, cartella 4, n. 220, 8 December 1922; see also n. 205 (Minniti to Bianchi), 4 December 1922.

[24] Ibid., n. 202, 7 December 1922; *Il Cittadino di Brescia*, 4-9 December 1922; *La Provincia di Brescia*, 9 December 1922.

[25] ACS, Min. Interno, GF, OP, b. 4, fasc. 35, sfasc. 12.4, 11 December 1922 (Sansanelli's letter to the provincial federation also in CC dei Fasci, b. 100, fasc. Brescia, cartella 4, n. 218) and 16 December; *Corriere della Sera*, 12 and 14 December 1922; A. Lyttelton, *The Seizure of Power*, pp. 160-2.

[26] *Fiamma*, 16 December 1922; see also S. Jacini, *Storia del partito popolare italiano* (Milan, 1951), pp. 180-2.

[27] ACS, Min. Interno, GF, OP, b. 4, fasc. 35, sfasc. 12.4, 12 December 1922; DGPS, AGR 1922, b. 68, cat. G1, fasc. Brescia, sfasc. Capriolo, 13 December 1922; *La Provincia di Brescia*, 12 December 1922.

[28] *Corriere della Sera*, 12 December 1922; *Il Mondo*, 13 December 1922.

Within two days the local party got its way. De Bono moved fast, summoning Farinacci to serve as a trouble-shooter in the dispute. The Cremona *ras* detested the author of the *lodo Bianchi*, which had incorporated the co-operative farming schemes of Guido Miglioli on estates in his own territory, and sided with the fellow fascists of the neighbouring province.

Turati did more than simply show that 'one collaborates with the *popolari* in Rome, not Brescia'.[29] Complaints from the local *fascio* brought about a change in civilian administration. Because De Martino refused to act as a party hack during the incidents, he found himself transferred from the province for truculent interpretation of the law. Arturo Bocchini, whose services included surveillance activities for Farinacci, replaced the outgoing prefect.[30] The December troubles also got rid of Antonio Bianchi, weakening the power of liberal élites in agriculture. An investigative team, headed by the president of the Cremona employers' association, at first suspended and then finally dismissed the professor for abusing his office. It also dissolved the supervisory board of the *cattedra ambulante* and charged the standing committee for rural improvement with neglect of statutory duties. Such notables as Count Vincenzo Bettoni Cazzago, Senator Ugo Da Como, and Tomaso Nember, all traditional spokesmen for propertied interests, figured prominently in both bodies. The position of the PNF farmers' syndicate strengthened, once the fascists forced open that 'closed caste' of oligarchs who controlled patronage in the countryside.[31]

The local fascists tried to implicate Carlo Bonardi in the shady administration of the travelling lectureship, but innuendo took them nowhere. 'It's a matter of jealousies, of competition for power in a milieu yet to be defined,' reported the prefect. 'Turati still thinks he's in the running.'[32] The combatants had charged Bianchi with corruption before, although these reformers lacked means of redress. Friends of the agronomist then managed to delay an official inquiry indefinitely, and the professor stayed on as a syndic for the Credito

[29] L. Salvatorelli and G. Mira, *Storia del fascismo: L'Italia dal 1919 al 1945* (Rome, 1952), p. 172.

[30] ACS, Carte Farinacci, b. 1, fasc. 2, Bocchini, 23 February 1923.

[31] ACS, Min. Interno, GF, OP, b. 4, fasc. 35, sfasc. 12.4, 21 June, 30 July, and 17 August 1923; SPCR, b. 39, fasc. 242/R, sfasc. Farinacci, 4 August 1923; Presidenza del Consiglio, 1923, fasc. 3/1.2, 5 May and 23 August 1923.

[32] ACS, Min. Interno, DGPS, AGR 1922, b. 68, cat. G1, fasc. Brescia, 29 December 1922.

Agrario Bresciano bank. Adding little to the original accusations, the *fascio* essentially plagiarized the ANC's findings. Conservative liberals behaved with deceptive detachment during the whole episode. The evidence of jobbery may have remained the same since 1920, yet moderates made little effort to cover their controversial associate now. Careful not to offend the Brescian blackshirts, the *Sentinella* placed part of the blame on a party man in the capital. Aldo Finzi at the ministry of the interior wanted to divert the waters of the Chiesa river to the dry Mantua plain and Bianchi stood in his way, or so the story went. Disguising the political motivation behind the purge, the old right set the scenario for collaboration with provincial fascism.[33]

The democrats identified with the central government against the provincials. Annoyed by Turati's attempt to sully the Bonardi name in the Bianchi affair, left liberals at first kept their distance from the *ras*.[34] By January 1923, however, the under-secretary from Brescia wished to settle his differences with the local *fascio* and obtain his PNF card. The town section refused him membership in the party, but dangled the possibility of a truce. Jealous of the fellow-traveller's position in the capital, intransigents in the provincial federation also feared encroachment upon their dominion at home. When *La Provincia* published an article condemning a squad mission in the village of Piancamuno, Turati jumped at the chance to break off relations. 'Let's talk no longer of philofascism,' he wrote Bonardi. 'Such a thing would be absurd.'[35]

The day after Bianchi's 'liquidation', Turati called a mammoth meeting of the farmers' syndicate. Some 2,000 basin growers and squad members attended the mandatory session. With all alternatives closed to them, agrarians unanimously approved the PNF pact.[36] Party propagandists hailed the 1922-3 accord as the ultimate in class collaboration: its uncontested acceptance by both employers and workers represented 'a clear understanding of certain necessities in agricultural economy'.[37] Except for a fall in hourly wages, the fascist contract differed very little from the one negotiated by the Federterra the year before. Yet the real victory of the black unions lay not in labour economics but in municipal politics. The syndical conquest of

[33] *La Sentinella Bresciana*, 13 and 16 December 1922.
[34] *La Provincia di Brescia*, 13-15 December 1922.
[35] Bonardi Papers, Turati to Bonardi, 10 February 1923; see also 19 February 1923.
[36] *Fiamma*, 23 December 1922.
[37] *Fiamma*, 30 December 1922.

the countryside paved the way for the siege of five more town councils during special administrative elections in the plains. By eliminating the role of the UCL in peasant organization, Turati came finally to a position from which to assail the voting strength of popular Catholicism.

Municipal Fascism and the Attrition of Clerical Control

The drive for administrative power entered a new phase after the removal of De Martino. Since patronage and corruption began at the local level, only through control of the communes could the black-shirts use political influence for electoral purposes as well as divert economic resources for party ends. Catholics still held most muni-cipalities in the province. With prefectural help, fascists aimed to bring about a change of custody. Early in the spring of 1923, they revived the campaign against city hall, which faced bankruptcy. When the Brescia town government failed to pay employees cost-of-living supplements, the *fascio* immediately assumed the defence of the 'exploited intellectual proletariat'.[38] Although white-collar support of the movement presumably stemmed from genuine causes, political opportunism led PNF recruiters to engage it. Making wage demands that exceeded the capacities of the treasury, the syndicalists used labour action as a tool to 'break the parasitic grasp' of the *popolari* over civic life.[39]

Spurred by designs upon city hall, Turati threatened a strike of all municipal employees should they fail to receive wage increases. His bluff almost worked. Constitutionalists on the right had concluded an alliance with the *fascio* days earlier, and spokesmen for *La Sentinella* considered a merger with the new PNF daily.[40] When moderate liberals stalemated town government by sticking up for their fascist friends, the isolated Catholic councillors offered mass resignations.[41] Yet however brilliant the scheme, its timing was wrong. Given the premier's priority to dissolve parliamentary opposition during the electoral reform campaign, not to mention government coolness towards the provincial federation after the December incidents, Turati misjudged the moment. Mussolini vehemently condemned the local party's attempt to subvert clerical authority through union

---

[38] *Popolo di Brescia*, 22 March 1922.
[39] Ibid., 23 March 1923.
[40] Bonardi Papers, Ducos to Bonardi, 21 March 1923.
[41] *La Sentinella Bresciana*, 23 and 24 March 1923.

action. The Duce promised to 'strangle' the PNF agitation, which 'reproduced bolshevik tactics to perfection'.[42]

Turati bowed to his master's wishes as far as they concerned the proposed labour offensive. He withdrew the threat of a municipal strike, but not before plunging the PPI city delegation into crisis.[43] Forty-three councillors caved in to pressures for their removal, and a special commission undertook the supervision of urban government. But the new prefect had no intention of bequeathing the town's administration to the local intransigents. At the Duce's request, Bocchini ignored some *fascio* favourites and instead selected one clerical reactionary in addition to several liberals as appointees.

Again, the goals of the Brescia federation conflicted with those of the central state. Turati responded to the restrictions placed on manœuvres in the metropolis by widening the attack on smaller communes in the countryside, where he exercised tighter control. The diverted assault had a double thrust. It weakened the nexus of church authority throughout the province and purged the democratic *popolari* from municipal power. Since the local PNF staged its seizures in the villages least protected by clerical conservatives and the episcopacy, the radical minority within the PPI went into forced retirement. At Cortenedolo in the uplands, blackshirts from neighbouring Breno issued an ultimatum to the pious councillors, who resigned immediately.[44] Ten Catholic councillors of Campoverde near Salò surrendered their seats when the liberal right connived with the fascists against them.[45] At Carpenedolo, where the UCL had based its peasant operations, doctored charges of corruption relieved church representatives of their administrative duties.[46]

The local Partito Popolare fell to pieces slowly, and its rump body drifted further towards the right. In the basin commune of Calcinato, clerical councillors actually formed an alliance with PNF candidates in a stumbling attempt to penetrate old socialist territory.[47] The PPI's national congress bore witness to the fundamental ambivalence of the town leadership. Before the April meeting provincial delegates

[42] ASB, GP, b. 21, fasc. crisi comunale-Brescia città, 22 March 1923.

[43] *Il Cittadino di Brescia*, 30 March and 4 April 1923.

[44] ASB, GP, b. 21, fasc. crisi comunale-Cortenedolo, 2 April 1923.

[45] Ibid., fasc. crisi comunale-Campoverde, 2 April 1923.

[46] Ibid., fasc. crisi comunale-Carpenedolo, 8 April 1923; *Popolo di Brescia*, 9 and 10 April 1923.

[47] ASB, GP, b. 21, fasc. crisi comunale-Calcinato, 25 March 1923.

seemed dead set on participation in the Mussolini ministry.[48] They pushed collaboration with the government coalition in the spirit of patriotic discipline.[49] But soon after the audience in Turin booed the conservative wing and applauded Don Sturzo's antifascist motion, the indecisive Brescians speedily switched sides.[50] The inconsistency and incoherence of popular Catholicism doomed the evangelical impulse in the Lombard *isola bianca*. Drained of political vitality, the party with greatest electoral support condemned itself to a passive, defensive role in municipal affairs. The 'Christian coming' never materialized, not even at Brescia. Church officialdom declined to organize competing camps within the lay movement. The *popolari*, unable to guide, failed to take advantage of their massive and well-dispersed following.

Through no effort of church activists, the expansion of Turati's dominion nevertheless came to a temporary halt. The October conquest of the capital brought new adherents to the local *fascio*. The PNF now represented the party of consensus to the recent disciples, who looked to Mussolini for a return to normality.[51] The Brescia section swelled with converts of the 'thirteenth hour' after the march on Rome, and enthusiasts from an earlier time reacted violently against the flood of such conformists. From all his radical rhetoric, Turati went out of his way to accommodate members from the old political establishment. By January 1923 he had renounced 'official intransigence' in respect for the Duce's coalition. One week later Alfredo Giarratana took over the federation's daily newspaper;[52] the engineer, who had made amends to alienated friends in high finance, got his PNF card just months before assuming the editorship.[53] Such clerical-moderates as the arms manufacturer Vincenzo Bernardelli and the hosiery magnate Ambrogio Ambrosi became neighbourly with their home-town *ras*. Giuseppe Bertelli, a commercial farmer elected mayor of Irma as a conservative liberal, joined the party early in 1923,

---

[48] A. C. Jemolo, *Chiesa e Stato in Italia negli ultimi cento anni* (Turin, 1948), p. 603 (Livio Tovini of Brescia spearheaded the national campaign to 'amputate' the PPI left at the fourth party congress); on the Tovini family in local politics, see F. Fonzi, 'Giuseppe Tovini e i cattolici bresciani del suo tempo', in *Rivista di storia della Chiesa in Italia*, vol. ix (1955), pp. 233-48.

[49] *Il Cittadino di Brescia*, 11 April 1923.

[50] Ibid., 14 and 15 April 1923.

[51] G. Lumbroso, *La crisi del fascismo* (Florence, 1925), pp. 61-9.

[52] *Fiamma*, 6 and 9 January 1923; *La Sentinella Bresciana*, 16 January 1923.

[53] Interview with Alfredo Giarratana in Rome, 9 January 1976; G. A. Chiurco erroneously dates membership back to 1920 in *Storia della Rivoluzione fascista*, vol. ii, p. 407.

and the owner of the Rocco chemical company pledged his support then too.[54] Representatives of the business community, who never had time for the gang warfare or the rhetorical violence of the revolutionary right, now understood the need to conquer provincial fascism from within.

During the spring and the summer of 1923, Turati made conciliatory overtures to members of the liberal establishment. With the Acerbo bill under parliamentary review, the Brescia blackshirts had every reason to respect political realities in Rome. Although he remained the provincial intransigent when attacking the Partito Popolare, the local chieftain even developed some tolerance towards the Honourable Carlo Bonardi. In July the under-secretary himself superintended negotiations to merge *La Provincia* with the fascist daily.[55] Other democrats on the newspaper's board finally rejected the proposed fusion, but Bonardi did receive his PNF card as a reward for services rendered in the take-over bid.[56] Turati courted a few clerical reactionaries too. Angelo Passerini, an influential Catholic senator who deviated from the party line during the Partito Popolare's congress in Turin, waited until August to resign from the PPI. The *popolari* never managed to recover from his defection.

Revisionism had its repercussions. The fact that the provincial movement welcomed conservative recruits from other parties infuriated old-timers in the PNF. Initially pacified by the persecution of the *popolari*, the fascist dissidents from the Iseo uplands threatened secession. This faction, led by the instigators of the Capriolo reprisal, accused the local federation of 'false intransigence'.[57] The radical polemic of the parochial mountaineers disguised personal rivalry between the Brescia boss and the squad commanders in the hills. Reluctant to recognize the authority of an outsider over the subalpine zone, these backwoods militiamen remained jealous of their tyrannical rule and refused to demobilize after the Bianchi affair. They exhibited an independence designed to undermine Turati's drive to win over respectable opinion in town. Official expulsion from the *fascio* in April 1923 made the seditious stronghold to the north more difficult to dismantle.[58]

[54] ASB, b. 26, n. 1276, 28 August 1923; b. 27, n. 1044, 27 December 1923.

[55] *La Provincia di Brescia*, 30 July 1923.

[56] *Popolo di Brescia*, 8 August 1923. Turati, however, refused to conduct the initiation ceremony; Farinacci arrived from Cremona to make Bonardi a PNF member.

[57] Bonardi Papers, Relazione sui combattenti, May 1923.

[58] *Popolo di Brescia*, 3 and 4 April 1923.

The ground swell of dissidence that shook *fasci* all over Italy during the spring of 1923 released tensions hitherto suppressed within the local movement.[59] Not only in the mountains but also in the plains, bad blood between the party leadership and its rural following subverted efforts at consolidation. Prominent propertied interests at Bagnolo Mella attempted to form an autonomous association, again under the patronage of Farinacci.[60] Such unruly behaviour placed Turati in a combative frame of mind, and he put the threat of competition from a neighbour to the test. Against the advice of Bocchini, who owed his position as prefect to the Cremona boss, the Brescia federation forced anxious agrarians to endure steep fines and some beatings 'as punishment for indiscipline'.[61] The influence of the secessionists grew as a result of the vendetta, for employers in nearby villages soon became restive. Dissatisfaction with one-man rule in the province began to undermine the syndicalist activities of the PNF throughout the countryside. Many farmers attempted to weaken the fascist unions by negotiating secret agreements with individual labourers.

By the end of March nineteen basin sections had repudiated the provincial directorate. At that time, a fortnight before the federation's annual congress, the fall of Turati seemed inevitable. However, ambiguous relations among the local party, civilian authority, and the central state left room for manœuvre. Hoping to disarm the feuding factions, the Brescian leader roused interest in Rome over the rising tide of agrarian intransigence from Cremona. His play on the Duce's fears of furthering the domination of Farinacci proved successful. Mussolini suspended the April meeting, giving Turati 'full powers to resolve the syndical and political situation'.[62] Three weeks later, the more plebeian plotters in the hills found themselves eliminated from the contest too. When squad members of the Gavardo and Villanuova sections went rampaging through the PPI territory of Volciano, the boss in the capital city responded by dissolving both chapters.[63]

Turati's position as potentate became firmly established in the aftermath of the dissident crisis. Moreover, the expulsion of the PPI from Mussolini's coalition meant an end to government controls on

---

[59] See R. De Felice, *Mussolini il fascista. I*, pp. 413-18; A. Lyttelton, *The Seizure of Power*, pp. 176-8.

[60] *La Provincia di Brescia*, 16 March 1923.

[61] *Popolo di Brescia*, 18 March 1923.

[62] ACS, Min. Interno, DGPS, AGR 1923, b. 50, cat. G1, fasc. Brescia, 8 April 1923 (Mussolini to Turati).

[63] Ibid., sfasc. Volciano, 27 April 1923; *Il Cittadino di Brescia*, 28 and 29 April 1923.

violence against the *popolari*. While Don Sturzo's relations with the premier degenerated during the summer of 1923, the campaign to break the church's local network of influence gathered fresh momentum. In June the PNF penetrated the western flats district of Rovato, where police placed the mayor and two councillors under house arrest for having attended the congress of Turin.[64] Charges were dropped days later when a prefectural commission, nominated by the provincial federation, assumed control of the municipality.[65] At S. Gervasio Bresciano, the blackshirts seized the town hall and refused to demobilize until representatives of the Partito Popolare agreed to abdicate their seats.[66] The fascists also engineered a peasant march on the piazza of Bassano, using the rural syndicates to obtain the resignation of the Catholic minority on the local council.[67] The combination of political blackmail, brute force, and demagogic tactics uprooted clerical authority in the countryside.

The exuberance of militiamen scared the councillors of Alfianello who, once exposed to physical assault, offered a mass resignation.[68] The PNF seized control of nine municipalities in the Valcamonica over the course of one week, and a crisis was imminent in four other up-country towns.[69] The PPI bastion of Chiari collapsed after PNF representatives withdrew their support of the governing coalition. At Bedizzole, Cavagese, Cividate Camuno, Capriolo, Cizzago, Corzago, and Farfengo, Catholic administrations succumbed to pressure from Turati during July and August. Defeat at the village level forged unity of purpose among *popolari* in Brescia. The fall of communes throughout the western foothills forced clerical politicians at Brescia to abandon their customary moderation. Apart from the notable defection of Passerini to the fascist camp, even church conservatives stayed in the party when the provincial leadership began to drift towards the left.[70]

Although the Brescia *ras* pretended to make peace with prominent

[64] ACS, Min. Interno, GF, OP, b. 12, fasc. 4, 28 June 1923 (Longinotti to ministry); *Il Cittadino di Brescia*, 28 and 29 June 1923.

[65] ACS, Min. Interno, DGPS, AGR 1923, b. 50, cat. G1, fasc. Brescia, sfasc. Rovato, 2 July 1923.

[66] ASB, GP, b. 12, fasc. S. Gervasio Bresciano, 14 June 1923.

[67] Ibid., fasc. Bassano Bresciano, 4 June 1923; *La Sentinella Bresciana*, 5 June 1923.

[68] ASB, GP, b. 12, fasc. Alfianello, 28 July 1923; *Popolo di Brescia*, 27 and 28 July 1923.

[69] ASB, GP, b. suppl. 42, n. 1152, 12 July 1923 (Dr Forini); *Popolo di Brescia*, 11-18 July 1923.

[70] R. Webster, *Christian Democracy in Italy*, p. 89; *Il Cittadino di Brescia*, 17 and 14 August, 19 and 25 September 1923.

clericals and constitutionalists, the party continued its offensive against the guardians of local government. In September and October, five more Catholic communes in the western foothills fell. The use of organized terror and street warfare became less necessary during the acquisition of municipal control. Turati had simply to announce the intended dissolution, and the PPI councillors would dutifully resign. Raids still occurred, but in the main they affected church circles and village parishes. These reprisals did not further the administrative grasp of the PNF. Rather, the haphazard attacks gave the intransigent wing within the provincial federation some degree of relief and averted squad dissension.[71]

The conquest of the provincial deputation, an elected chamber which regulated municipal administration, followed. Challenging the distribution of public subsidies to confessional clubs, the local black-shirts aimed to oust the PPI majority on the executive board.[72] The 'stately abstention' of Zanardellian democrats isolated the clerical delegates, and right liberals sided with their fascist friends.[73] The suspension of the council ensued without further intrigue. Catholic politicians, in the end, found themselves defeated by their own brand of patronage. Since four of their representatives stood condemned in the shady operations of the Comizio Agrario, which came under prefectural jurisdiction as a result of the Bianchi affair, the prospects for legal recourse seemed uncertain. On 23 December 1923 the *popolari* yielded to Turati's demands, and the local organs of state authority thus devolved upon the PNF.[74]

Towards a Mass Movement: Fascist Trade Unionism

The expansion of Turati's influence over Brescia government co-incided with an increase of PNF militancy in trade disputes. Gino Zucarelli, provincial secretary, maintained that the march on Rome augured well for labour. 'We have witnessed in these days the gradual destruction of the world created by the proletariat under the aegis of

---

[71] ASB, GP, b. 22, fasc. Crisi comunali, 11 September, 6 and 30 October, 29 November 1923.

[72] *Popolo di Brescia*, 6 December 1923.

[73] *La Provincia di Brescia*, 8 December 1923.

[74] Ibid., 13 and 24 December 1923; *Popolo di Brescia*, 23 and 24 December 1923. On 13 January 1924 the prefect appointed a provisional council, and Turati chose three of its five members; the *ras* expelled Tomaso Nember from the board in September, taking the agrarian's place. See Consiglio Provinciale di Brescia, *L'Attività della Reale Commissione nel 1924* (Brescia, 1925).

the socialists,' he conceded, 'yet woe betide if this means the downfall of the working class.'[75] The CGL ranks, however, remembered the violence and intimidation practised by the squads. Black syndicalists might boast about 'the means to co-operate' at their disposal, but such insidious propaganda brought few converts from the old unions. The refusal of most industrialists to patronize the corporations also limited recruitment. In contrast with commercial farmers, arms manufacturers and steel producers showed little interest in restricting, by blackleg terrorism, the right to association. Wage cuts assumed lower priority in the capital goods sector, where considerations of efficiency, discipline, and continuity on the shop floor remained uppermost. The independent attitude of urban businessmen meant that the fascists could not offer preference in employment, a promise which had cemented the mass following of the syndicates in the provincial basin.

At Brescia, as elsewhere in Italy, metalworkers stayed tenaciously faithful to the FIOM. Turati continued to wrestle with the problem of union recruitment in heavy industry, even though membership among those engaged in the sector seemed impossible to obtain. The *ras* ornamented propaganda with empty radical slogans. He spoke of 'productive' strike action; employers' stupidity as well as avid profiteering disgusted him.[76] But mere rhetoric did not suffice. The corporations needed more than words to compete with organized labour. They had to demonstrate the combative course of fascist syndicalism without alienating the business community. This entailed directing PNF militancy against isolated manufacturers.

The bargaining power of the fascist unions increased as a result of the economic slump of 1921-2. The recession hit the metallurgical and machine shops with particular severity. Although real wages in heavy industry at Brescia kept up during the first half of 1923, the number of jobless reached its highest level since 1913. Whereas the FIOM stood powerless in face of the reduced demand for labour, PNF syndicalists managed to connive with local industry at the public expense. In collusion with Turati, management at the Metallurgica Bresciana announced its intention to slash salaries by 15 per cent unless the government cancelled claims on war profits.[77] The state first refused to save the ailing steelworks from crisis, so the company countered by threatening to dismiss all 1,040 operatives. Here the *fascio* stepped in.

[75] *Fiamma*, 4 November 1922.
[76] *Popolo di Brescia*, 23 April and 5 May 1923.
[77] ACS, Min. Interno, DGPS, AGR 1923, b. 40, cat. D13, fasc. Brescia, 26 April 1923.

Proposing to avert factory closure, the party and the prefect petitioned the ministry of finance for a special subsidy, while the corporations got shop stewards to write a formal letter of protest.[78] Within a month of reducing the tax arrears, Turati established an unemployment fund, financed by Gabriele D'Annunzio, for the benefit of all, even socialists, on the payroll at the plant.[79]

Acute crisis at one company enabled Turati to exploit a situation of genuine proletarian discontent in Brescia. Recession produced the opposite result for the socialist movement. The slump made union leadership circumspect in industrial disputes while increasing the discouragement of the rank and file. The Mussolini government magnified the repercussions of economic malaise. The regime eliminated the ministry of labour during its first year in power, which also saw the cancellation of state subsidies to unemployment insurance.[80] A psychological defeat, the suppression of May Day, heightened the disillusionment of the left. Against this sombre scene must be set the *fascio*'s limited penetration of the working class. As the Camera del Lavoro showed new caution, the local fascist syndicates became more vigorous. In isolated circumstances the PNF promised to provide the protection and the security that the old associations could no longer offer.[81]

In light industry the corporations received some assistance from rural entrepreneurs. At the Cartiera Maffizzoli, the Turati cotton company, the Gavardo wool manufacturers, and the Montanari e Studer hosiery firms, each of which employed over 1,000 workers, PNF organizers converted the devastated white leagues into black unions.[82] Ambrogio Ambrosi, an early backer of the national movement, helped the syndicate in his knitwear shop get off the ground.[83] Gigi Begnotti had attempted to mobilize working-class support for the Brescia federation independently of employers. In March 1923 he canvassed five button companies bordering the Bergamo frontier, but the *fascio*

[78] *Popolo di Brescia*, 27 April 1923.

[79] ACS, Min. Interno, DGPS, AGR 1923, b. 40, cat. D13, fasc. Brescia, 25 May 1923. In 1923 the administrative board at Franchi Gregorini moved to sell holdings of Metallurgica Bresciana stock; by 1925 the local steelworks founded by Giovanni Tempini fell fully under the control of the Orlando shipbuilders at Livorno.

[80] *Avanti!*, 1 April 1923; G. Salvemini, *Under the Axe of Fascism* (London, 1936), pp. 302-4; C. Seton-Watson, *Italy from Liberalism to Fascism*, p. 636.

[81] B. Buozzi, *Le condizioni della classe lavoratrice in Italia 1922-1943* (Milan, 1973), pp. 68-9.

[82] *Popolo di Brescia*, 3 September 1923.

[83] Ibid., 8 September 1923.

abandoned the project weeks later. The local party had to contend not only with the hostility of labour and management, both loyal to the Christian social movement, but also with PNF competition from the neighbouring province.[84]

The syndicates witnessed difficulties developing again in agriculture. Conflict between the provincial federation and basin farmers widened when employers began to violate the PNF's peasant pact. As before, agrarians at Bagnolo Mella launched the seasonal offensive against the fascist labour organization. Employers in that rich plains district tried to reduce hourly wages, arguing that grain prices had dropped 20 per cent from the previous year. Turati reminded them that productivity had just about doubled, and his unions responded by increasing the rates charged by landless hired hands.[85] Squads occupied the estates of unco-operative landlords, who also got fined for disobedience.[86]

Moving on direct orders from Turati, the militiamen forced landlords, 'by all means at our disposal, to give labourers arrears in pay'.[87] When four farmers, all early members of the *fascio*, continued to resist, two PNF syndicalists arrived on the basin estates to bring pressure on 'the stingy tyrants'. Alessandro Arenghi, an active entrepreneur in agriculture, still refused to comply with party guide-lines, and the black unionists murdered him in 'the name of class collaboration'.[88] The incident put a damper on further unrest. Understandably, employers hesitated to circumvent the corporations after the killing, so conditions favoured the adoption of a new accord, drawn up a month before schedule. At Quinzano d'Oglio, fascist organizers even called two more partial strikes to caution the undecided.[89]

Since wages fell by 7 per cent, restive agrarians did receive some satisfaction from the 1923-4 peasant pact, which otherwise represented a victory for the local party. The new PNF accord abolished contracts for casual farm hands. While the authors of the new scheme claimed

[84] Archivio Comunale di Palazzolo sull'Oglio, b. 1923, cat. 11a, n. 380, trattative, March-April 1923; Pietro Capoferri, future head of the Milan corporations, was the PNF claimant from Bergamo.

[85] *Popolo di Brescia*, 15 September 1923; ASB, GP, b. suppl. 41, n. 1055, raccolto granario, 25 June 1923; Sindacato Nazionale Fascista Tecnici Agricoli, *Il frumento*, p. 44.

[86] *Il Cittadino di Brescia*, 20 September 1923.

[87] ASB, Corte d'Assise, b. 72, fasc. 2, procedimento penale contro Libera Baviera e Vitale Domenghini, sfasc. 2, letter of A. Turati (25 December 1923).

[88] *Popolo di Brescia*, 25 September 1923.

[89] ACS, Min. Interno, DGPS, Atti Diversi 1903-1949, b. 3, fasc. 26, agitazione agraria (Soldi to Mussolini), 9 November 1923.

that their policy simply sought to give sympathetic peasants some protection against 'certain miserly employers', the transformation of the agricultural proletariat had important political implications.[90] The extension of salaried worker status strengthened the position of the corporations in the basin by making the dismissal of surplus labour difficult during slack periods.

Such energetic attempts to draw a working-class audience showed the shape of things to come. Arturo Bocchini's transfer to the province of Bologna came through on 16 December 1923. When, one week later, Augusto Marri replaced the informant for Farinacci as prefect of Brescia, civilian authority acted with new alacrity to further the development of the corporations in heavy industry. Soon after the change of guard, Turati delivered an ultimatum to the Franchi Gregorini steelworks. Threatened with an immediate strike, not to mention the cancellation of government subsidies, management gave in and granted wage increases to those enrolled in the PNF organization.[91] The accord of 23 January 1924 conspicuously excluded FIOM members, whose union's national agreement provided no protection to recruits in non-syndicated firms. During the winter unemployment in the metallurgical and engineering concerns of the province jumped again. Subject to the fluctuations of such a capricious labour market, the socialist federation soon lost its ability to control the conduct of the rank and file.[92] Many operatives cast off the old leadership to sign the new contract, and within three weeks the fascists claimed some 1,000 converts in the capital goods sector.[93]

The search for a following in the factories occupied the local party to the full, and the intransigence of management at one troubled company gave blackshirts their first foothold among metalworkers. For Turati and his entourage, January 1924 marked 'the dawn of a new epoch'.[94] The *ras* used demagogic tactics to create an independent power base, and he blocked all avenues through which individual employers could bully public authority away from policies of concession. The Brescia *fascio*, which had established itself in civic life by

[90] *La Sentinella Bresciana*, 10 November 1923; *Popolo di Brescia*, 10 November 1923.

[91] Marri, however, still touched base with Farinacci after the Franchi Gregorini settlement; see ACS, Carte Farinacci, b. 1, fasc. 3, 24 January 1924.

[92] Ibid., Presidenza del Consiglio, 1924, fasc. 7/1.1, n. 73, sfasc. disoccupazione: Lombardia.

[93] *Popolo di Brescia*, 23-25 January 1924; *La Provincia di Brescia*, 25 January and 12 February 1924.

[94] *Popolo di Brescia*, 25 January 1924.

exploiting the primitive nature of agrarian protest, returned to the industrial zones of the province. Victory at the Franchi Gregorini steelworks thus completed fascism's first migration from country to town. As the centre of gravity within the movement shifted from rural outposts back to the capital city, the onus of syndical activities would fall upon the urban proletariat.

8

Strike and Stabilization

Revolutionary syndicalists had figured prominently in the higher echelons of the fascist movement up to the seizure of power, and Mussolini continued to call upon their services after the formation of his cabinet.[1] Cesare Rossi and Giovanni Marinelli did much of the Duce's dirty work in administrative matters after October 1922.[2] Michele Bianchi, the national party boss during the march on Rome, watched over the new ministry of the interior. Edmondo Rossoni, who made his name in New York City before the war as a Wobbly, headed the regime's trade union federation until 1928.[3] The premier feigned concern for the material claims of the proletariat, but he went out of his way to curb the independence of worker organizations, including the corporations which came under PNF tutelage. Despite the presence of former labour activists within the inner circles of civilian bureaucracy, government took special care to accommodate the interests of big business.

Rossoni sought to include both workers and employers in integral syndicates, but business spokesmen ably averted the threat of forced fusion.[4] Apprehensive that fascist militants might challenge managerial prerogatives on the shop floor, the captains of industry affirmed their own organizational autonomy. In return for recognizing the monopoly of party unions, they also received assurances that the PNF would forego the use of factory cadres as tools for the class struggle. The pact of Palazzo Chigi, concluded on 19 December 1923, thus signified success for the urban entrepreneurial community. The agreement compromised the totalitarian aims of the corporations,

---

[1] C. Rossi, *Mussolini com'era* (Rome, 1947), pp. 132-3; see also R. De Felice, *Sindacalismo rivoluzionario e fiumanesimo nel carteggio De Ambris–D'Annunzio (1919–1922)* (Brescia, 1966).

[2] A. Lyttelton, *The Seizure of Power*, pp. 46-7.

[3] D. Roberts, *The Syndicalist Tradition and Italian Fascism* (Chapel Hill, 1979), pp. 14-15.

[4] On 'integral syndicalism', see F. Cordova, *Le origini dei sindacati fascisti 1918–1926* (Bari, 1974), pp. 132-53.

which simply received a pledge of mutual support from the Confindustria, and dealt a blow to the socialist competition.[5]

If the Palazzo Chigi accords confirmed the superiority of organized industry over the delegates of labour, then the December pact also undermined the political autonomy of bourgeois parliamentarians. The Grand Council's co-operative attitude towards the Confindustria made good sense with an electoral contest only months away. The manœuvres of Mussolini for business support helped to legitimize his ministry in the eyes of manufacturers, who seemed anxious for signs of appeasement before they backed any ticket. Marked by a certain intensification of the abuses that had traditionally characterized Italian suffrage, the 1924 campaign represented the premier's final attempt to employ the outward forms of democratic procedure. The Duce did his best to silence petty party interests, especially those of the PNF, before the polling on 6 April. He sponsored a national list on which liberals and clericals appeared alongside fascists. Again, provincial intransigents found themselves isolated in the attempt to widen the government's mandate with respectable constituencies.

Fascist electoral reform guaranteed two-thirds of the chamber seats to the leading ticket, should that slate claim at least a quarter of the vote. Changes in proportional representation helped the opposition explain away the political realities of the April results. In fact, the Acerbo provisions appeared to parallel opinion at the polls. Albeit through low-level manipulations to procure a majority, the 'big list' scored a significant victory by receiving 60 per cent of all ballots cast. Some 374 backers of Mussolini won places in parliament, and 275 of these deputies belonged to the PNF. Popular endorsement of the coalition candidates, however, concealed divergent aims among government supporters, as well as significant regional deviations. Party moderates and liberal legalists expected the returns to give the regime constitutional legitimacy. Extremists within the movement, on the other hand, grew apprehensive about the revivification of democratic ways. The full consequences of their ambivalence became evident soon after the new legislature met.

The murder of Giacomo Matteotti in June 1924 caused the whole

[5] F. Guarneri, *Battaglie economiche tra le due grandi guerre*, vol. i (Milan, 1953), pp. 65-6; *La Stirpe*, May 1924; L. Rosenstock-Franck, *L'économie corporative fasciste en doctrine et en fait: Ses origines historiques et son évolution* (Paris, 1934), pp. 36-7; E. Rossi, *Padroni del vapore e fascismo* (Bari, 1966), pp. 149-51; M. Abrate, *La lotta sindacale*, pp. 387-90; P. Melograni, *Gli industriali e Mussolini: Rapporti tra Confindustria e fascismo dal 1919 al 1929* (Milan, 1972), pp 59-68.

electoral edifice to come tumbling down. Blackshirts kidnapped the socialist parliamentarian on the Lungotevere in Rome, and rumours of Mussolini's complicity spread within days of the deputy's disappearance. The opposition withdrew from the chamber during what came to be known as the Aventine secession.[6] Any spirit of collaboration between the old political class and the fascist regime disintegrated, so the premier looked to the men in the militia and to the provincials in the movement for support. The ministerial crisis confirmed the impossibility of constitutional consolidation, ushering in a 'second wave' of party extremism.[7] The Palazzo Chigi pact between the corporations and the Confindustria fell apart too, and PNF militants resumed the struggle against entrepreneurial worthies. Although the Duce's speech before parliament on 3 January 1925 spelled the beginnings of political dictatorship, the syndical significance of the authoritarian move had yet to be established. A metalworkers' strike that began at Brescia in March finally forced big business to formalize relations with state bureaucracy. The ensuing labour code eliminated union independence once and for all.

The Course of the 1924 Campaign

The presence of prominent parliamentarians on the fascist ticket in Brescia discomfited local intransigents and reinspired dissension during the electoral campaign. Militiamen and early converts to the movement, who had counted on a purge of the old politicians during the seizure of power, saw slots on the slate fill with orthodox democrats and conservative liberals. More than a month before the February presentation of the list, squad members at Salò complained of the government's 'revisionist stench'.[8] The Duce apparently reeked of the smell as well, since these dissidents instead embraced Gabriele D'Annunzio as their patriarch. Intent on keeping the black syndicates free from centrist contamination, 'national revolutionaries' in the town corporations likewise looked to the poet at Gardone for spiritual leadership.[9] The Comandante, on behalf of all party purists, warned Mussolini of the 'sad and bitter' repercussions the inclusion of

[6] L. Sturzo, *Italy and Fascismo* (London, 1926), pp. 187-95.
[7] A. Lyttelton, 'Fascism in Italy: The Second Wave', in W. Laqueur and G. Mosse (eds.), *International Fascism: 1920–1945* (New York, 1966), pp. 75-100.
[8] *Il Popolo di Brescia*, 15 January 1924.
[9] Ibid., 21 January 1924; see also F. Cordova, *Arditi e legionari dannunziani* (Padua, 1969), pp. 161-70.

'certain obtuse and malicious candidates' would have on the integrity of the provincial federation.[10]

D'Annunzio claimed that ideology lay behind the chronicle of recurrent crises at Brescia. The principles invoked by Mussolini during the selection of the slate had underscored collaboration with bankrupt clienteles and drawn a veil over the forces of social radicalism. Indeed Alfredo Giarratana, a favourite among the PNF's industrial backers, stayed linked to the Edison conglomerate. His friend Marziale Ducos, another candidate on the national ticket, ran as a moderate liberal for conservative agrarian interests. The former mayor of the town, Gerolamo Orefici, billed by the list as 'the legitimate heir to Pì Zanardel', remained a steadfast democrat.[11] Personal rivalry and competition for power, however, certainly played a major part in the controversy. The first and intended casualty of the formal protest to Rome came from within the leadership of the provincial movement. Enrico Bozzi, a lawyer who had wormed his way into the local hierarchy with the help of Carlo Bonardi, figured as the main victim of the complaint from the Vittoriale.[12]

Such habitual and trivial discontents did not endanger Turati's position as a local potentate. In fact, the *ras* himself encouraged D'Annunzio's diatribes to eliminate possible contenders for the provincial leadership. The ploy worked with curious speed in the case of Bozzi. Mussolini revoked the candidature of this party revisionist just hours after receiving the protest.[13] And Antonio Masperi, the choice of the Comandante as a replacement, never appeared as a nominee on the national list. Because the Duce sought to circumscribe the poet's influence, he entrusted Turati with the task of settling the situation. Thus by playing Rome and Gardone off against each other, the Brescia boss managed to subvert one possible challenge to his authority in the zone.[14] Giarratana presented more of a problem. His patrons in Lombard industrial, banking, and agrarian circles held too much sway, and the government never seriously considered removing him from the slate. The growing importance of the engineer, now an ally of Roberto Farinacci, became a constant source of tension within the higher ranks of the movement.

[10] ACS, Carte D'Annunzio, b. 1, n. 28, 17 February 1924.

[11] *Il 'Rompiscatole'*, 4 April 1924; *La Provincia di Brescia*, 5 March 1924.

[12] Bonardi Papers, Turati to Bonardi, 5 February 1924; Marri to Bonardi, 5 February 1924.

[13] Ibid., Bonardi to Turati, 18 February 1924.

[14] ACS, Carte Farinacci, b. 1, fasc. 3 (1924), 23 February 1924.

Turati made the gentlemen on the national list pay penance. In exchange for the predominance of fellow-travellers on the Brescia slate, he convinced Carlo Bonardi to appoint six blackshirts to the governing board of the local liberal club. But even if their president held an important post in the Mussolini ministry, most members of the association felt queasy about the sacrifice of independence that an agreement with any party might entail. To the majority of notables it appeared as though the PNF intended to 'seize' their sacred fraternity at all costs.[15] Bonardi preferred to see the proposed administrative ingress as 'the first step towards pacification', a nominal reshuffling which fussy constitutionalists with narrow popular appeal should accept.[16] His attitude testified to the crass careerism and ideological poverty of cross-over politicians.

Intransigents reacted badly to news of all the electoral double dealing, especially when they learned that the 'flankers' outnumbered the fascists on the national list. Turati tried to resurrect his own radical image to placate these provincials during the campaign. In the past an opening to the party 'left' simply meant renewed vigour in the syndical field alone, since a vague producer ideology formed the basis of the old polemic against parasitic parliamentarians. Therefore detractors, whether they were disappointed unionists or D'Annunzian enthusiasts, could hardly find fault with an aggressive PNF labour front. And so the Brescia corporations endeavoured to get special treatment for members employed at the Togni steelworks.[17] The Duce, at all events, stood by the Chigi accord and sabotaged the initiative. Unable to disturb the calm enforced by government on the shop floor, the *ras* had to make amends outside the factory gates.

Turati pulled the few proletarian clubs still in existence around town into the orbit of the provincial federation. The methods used to bring about this conversion pleased PNF extremists and kept D'Annunzio busy during the electoral campaign. Black unionists, for example, annexed the largest PSI co-operative in just six weeks.[18] The Casa del Popolo, which had served as a recreational centre and shopping facility, lost powers of supervision through charges of fraud, and the fascists tampered with the house books to justify the injunction.

[15] Bonardi Papers, Tarenzi to Bonardi, 23 January 1924.
[16] Ibid., Bonardi to Tarenzi, 2 February 1924.
[17] ACS, Min. Interno, DGPS, AGR 1924, b. 79, cat. D13, fasc. Brescia, 19 February 1924 (Turati to Mussolini).
[18] *La Provincia di Brescia*, 25 January, 18 and 22 March 1924.

After the prefect liquidated the partnership without so much as mock proceedings, D'Annunzio bought the outfit for the metal-workers' corporation at a fraction of its real value.[19] The shady trans-action provoked sharp disapproval from critics in the liberal camp, who fretted more over encroachments by party syndicalists than over disregard for legal procedure.

Their hesitations played into the hands of Turati. He made the generous gesture of dispatching a party hack, as an intermediary for the prefect, to watch over the Casa and to spy on its new keeper. This arrangement in effect made D'Annunzio accountable to both the provincial federation and civilian authority, but what appeared as a concession to the moderates also had its price. While mutual distrust between the local fascists and the government's friends no doubt persisted, Bonardi turned a blind eye to syndicalist enthusiasms during the electoral campaign. The under-secretary also pledged the allegiance of his new veterans' association to the regime, though the group never accepted the formal cachet of the *fascio*.[20] This sort of compromise and contrivance kept the truce among participants on the slate.

The polling gave the ticket 76,255 votes against the 28,221 received by the PPI and the 18,339 cast for the three working-class lists.[21] The provincial results corresponded closely with both the national profile and the two-thirds proviso of the Acerbo law. Government candidates claimed 62 per cent of the ballots at Brescia. They made a clean sweep throughout the basin and the western high ground, since PNF control remained tightest there, but isolated pockets of support for the *popolari* stayed active in the foothills and the mountains. The Catholic constituency had been whittled away by 37 per cent since the 1921 returns, and the combined numbers of the Marxist parties more than halved. Yet the opposition actually increased its mandate in the capital city, where bribery and coercion proved difficult to practise. The abuse of conventional liberties explained some of the plurality enjoyed by the official slate. Despite the intrigues between Turati and Bonardi before the elections, not to mention the wholesale nomination of their

[19] ASB, GP, b. 18, fasc. Casa del Popolo, n. 395/1096, 21 March 1924.
[20] ACS, Min. Interno, DGPS, AGR, Atti Diversi 1903-1949, b. 3, fasc. 22, 24 March 1924; *La Provincia di Brescia*, 25 and 27 March 1924.
[21] All candidates on the *listone* went to parliament, while Longinotti, Bresciani, and Montini represented the PPI in the chamber. Viotto returned as the only PSI deputy from Brescia. See *La Provincia di Brescia*, 8 April 1924; *Il Cittadino di Brescia*, 8 and 9 April 1924.

courtiers to parliament, ideological uncertainties and precarious loyalties tainted the consensus that emerged on 6 April 1924.

Turati had counted on liberal support to see him through municipal elections in the provincial capital and the two surrounding industrial districts. But because of the Matteotti crisis, the alliance with constitutional forces never survived the success of the parliamentary returns. The abduction of the deputy in Rome shook the confidence of established politicians at Brescia, and many retreated from open collaboration with the culprits of the crime.[22] As rumours of pre-meditated murder leaked through the independent press, every shade of opinion outside the fascist party turned against the government. On 22 June 1924 the democrats withdrew from the local PNF slate. The next day the conservative caucus decided to 'defer, for the moment, the untimely question of participation';[23] by July the opposition of moderates to a combined ticket became resolute.[24] A 'subversive' strike in Gardone Val Trompia commemorated the slain victim of squad violence, and 'incidents' broke out in town to condemn the assassination.[25] Even the Catholic right made the unitary socialist into a martyr.[26] The prefect postponed the campaign for the city council indefinitely, for public outrage damaged the coalition strategy beyond repair.

The government crisis heightened the impatience of the party boys. At a public meeting early in July the greatest applause did not erupt during the usual salutations to Mussolini but came after Giuseppe Moretti, personal lieutenant to Roberto Farinacci, delivered an impassioned speech about the squads' second coming. Determined 'to crush all pockets of filth so generously spared following the march on Rome', militants in the local MVSN legion took to the city streets.[27] With liberal collaboration in limbo anyway, Turati also changed course. The reports of Arturo Bocchini, during his later tenure as chief of the fascist police, implicated the Brescia boss as the organizer of other Lombard leaders in an abortive plot to capture the PNF

---

[22] *La Provincia di Brescia*, 13 and 23 June 1924; General Clerici replaced Carlo Bonardi as under-secretary on 1 July 1924.

[23] ASB, GP, b. 21, fasc. crisi comunale-Brescia città, n. 833, 24 June 1924.

[24] Ibid., 3 July 1924.

[25] *Popolo di Brescia*, 12 and 13 June 1924; *Avanti!*, 12 June 1924; *La Provincia di Brescia*, 12-14 June 1924.

[26] *Il Cittadino di Brescia*, 17 June 1924.

[27] ACS, Min. Interno, DGPS, AGR 1924, b. 89, cat. G1, fasc. Brescia, 6 July 1924; *Popolo di Brescia*, 7 July 1924.

during the summer of 1924. Six chieftains in northern manufacturing
zones apparently took part in the scheme, called Buona Causa, to
upstage agrarian interests within the intransigent wing.[28] The cabal
got nowhere. The conspirators failed to halt the national ascendancy
of their neighbour from Cremona, who assumed the secretariat in
February 1925. The appointment of Farinacci stirred the hopes of
provincial extremists, and Turati again sought to assert his own
authority over the proponents of rural paramilitarism.

Politics of the Periphery

The activities of blackshirts concealed little improvisation in agriculture. The PNF pursued a tough line with recalcitrant landlords,
since the Chigi accords left the rural unions untouched. Agrarians
lacked the foresight and leverage of the industrial class, so resistance to
fascist inroads proved seasonal and ineffective long before the 1924 parliamentary campaign. The excesses of the squads never unified farmers,
who preferred to leave their association and ignore the party pact, once
winter had arrived. By February 1924 only 1,200 of the 3,000 employers
in the province remained in the syndicate, and the faithful concentrated
in the basin.[29] Attempts to reconstitute an independent lobby attracted
only a few hundred proprietors in the foothills.[30] Hostile to any hint of
regimentation, over half the propertied interests attempted to profit
from the temporary relaxation of pressure during the general elections.
And village priests encouraged unruliness in the hinterland by offering
to serve as arbitrators between owners and cultivators.[31]

While on their best behaviour during the parliamentary campaign,
the provincials could hardly stand still. Throughout the basin the
peasant following of fascism stayed intact. There, agricultural entrepreneurs seemed resigned to accepting the PNF peasant contract,
even though it reduced seasonal unemployment for wage labour. But
in the hilly green belt, where the intermediate farming categories
predominated, the blackshirts had real cause for concern. The 1923-4
pact never secured better conditions for sharecroppers and small

[28] ACS, Min. Interno, DGPS, Polizia Politica, b. 100, cat. K8, 6 June 1931; Bocchini
also named Nicolato, Ranieri, Capoferri, Ferrari, and Montermatini as later members
of the dissident group.
[29] ASB, GP, b. suppl. 41, n. 215, 11 February and 15 March 1925.
[30] Ibid., 23 March 1924; *Il Cittadino di Brescia*, 16 March 1924.
[31] ASB, GP, b. suppl. 41, n. 215, 12, 15 and 16 March 1924; see also ACS, Min. Interno,
DGPS, AGR 1924, b. 104, cat. K2, fasc. Brescia. sfasc. Don Bignotti (Fiesse), 11 and
12 January 1924.

leaseholders. Subscription among these cultivators depended largely upon the co-operation of landlords, who had promised to engage only members of the rural syndicates.[32] When the fascists failed to ensure special treatment from above, their strength at the grass-roots level began to wane. At this point, however, Turati employed the services of the obliging prefect. Using fines, threats, and friendly persuasion, Marri and his assistants restored the supremacy of the corporations by April.[33] Speedy compliance thus rested upon the party's grip on the local levers of civilian power. Six basin mayors happened to own estates but, entertaining few illusions about the autonomy of public office, they obediently executed the dictates the *ras*. The shrinking role of agrarians in economic disputes coincided with a political decline in municipal affairs.[34] During the May administrative elections at Manerbio, for example, the only votes cast for the opposition came from the humbled employers in the village.[35]

Syndicalists kept a lower profile in rural industry, where militancy in trade disputes receded. The Chigi agreement had tempered PNF organizers in their dealings with employers, but active recruitment continued on another front. The corporations forgot platitudes about class collaboration, as well as threats of strike action, and simply integrated all independent leagues. With chronic troubles flaring on the clothing market early in 1924, many manufacturers did not hesitate to assist in the piecemeal elimination of organized labour, Catholic or otherwise. Cotton exports from the province fell by half, those of wool by two-thirds.[36] Employers intended to slash wages accordingly, and the handful of white unions that managed to resist the trials of 1923 could no longer hold their own.[37] The UCL railed against the growing collusion of textile notables with the PNF, but by February its followers gave way. The Christian social movement, unable to guarantee co-operation from management or benefits to members, lost its old resilience.[38] The blackshirts exploited the reaction of mill owners to absorb the shaken cadres of the competition.

---

[32] ASB, GP, b. suppl. 41, n. 215, 22 March 1924.
[33] Ibid., 1 April 1924; *Popolo di Brescia*, 28 March and 3 April 1924.
[34] ASB, GP, b. suppl. 41, n. 215, 4 April 1924.
[35] Ibid., 25 May 1924; *Popolo di Brescia*, 27 May 1924.
[36] Camera di Commercio e Industria di Brescia, *L'Industria Tessile*, appendix; *L'economia bresciana*, vol. ii, fasc. 2, p. 140.
[37] *La Provincia di Brescia*, 27 January and 5 February 1924.
[38] ACS, Min. Interno, GF, OP, b. 11, fasc. 119, sfasc. 12, Castagna, 4 February 1924; *Il Cittadino di Brescia*, 5, 10, and 11 February 1924.

The April returns in the eastern foothills showed that a monopoly of labour representation did not always ensure victory at the polls. Workers in rural manufacture may have joined the corporations, but many continued to back the Catholic list. Fascist organizers went so far as to stage a strike to avoid embarrassment during the municipal campaign that was approaching. They received help from the Cartiera Maffizzoli, which employed half the electorate in the town of Toscolano. Since the black syndicate had become the company union less than a year before, earnings had dropped by 20 per cent, and the number of jobless peaked.[39] Demoralized by deteriorating conditions, those still on the payroll refused to forsake old loyalties for empty slogans of class collaboration. As in agriculture, the party needed to deliver the goods. When the owner proposed further pay cuts, the *fascio* intervened to protest against the new set-back at the paper mill.[40] About 800 operatives left the shop floor in a partial stoppage calculated to last a few hours. The firm apologized for its 'unfascist comportment' and promised to revoke the 'inappropriate' wage reductions.[41] The weight of management in the speedy settlement bared the shortcomings of PNF action on the shop floor. Turati postponed voting day in the district until he could consolidate a popular base there.[42]

At first PNF prospects looked better in other parts of the back country. Tensions between the leadership and extremists eased after the general elections. With no holds barred on reprisals, anxious provincials let loose on the opposition. The revival of squad warfare served a dual purpose during the spring of 1924. The parish raids and pitched brawls kept disruptive elements within the local movement absorbed in the familiar cult of violence and also warned Catholics to stay away from the polling stations during the municipal campaign. At the village of Nuvolento, for example, a band of blackshirts went looking for a member of the PPI slate; the gunmen clubbed his brother to death instead, when by nightfall the candidate, once mayor, had eluded them. Marziale Ducos expressed concern about the new upsurge of punitive expeditions. Turati, a champion fencer, defended

[39] *Il Cittadino di Brescia*, 10 March 1924.

[40] ACS, Min. Interno, GF, OP, b. 11, fasc. 119, sfasc. 12, 2 June 1924.

[41] *Popolo di Brescia*, 1 and 4 June 1924; *Brescia Nuova*, 26 July 1924 (the local corporations printed the issue).

[42] ASB, GP, b. 14, n. 609, 3 June 1924. The fascist slate won the administrative elections, which the prefect put off until September 1924, but only 32 per cent of the registered voters in Tosoclano cast ballots.

the plebeian troopers not by a bludgeon but with a sword. The fascist deputy challenged his liberal associate in parliament to a proper duel, and won hands down. The party chose to bill this farce as the federation's ultimate triumph over the forces of revisionist infiltration.[43]

Post-electoral bickering represented more than mere theatricals in the outlying areas bordering Bergamo. The alliance with Carlo Bonardi and his autonomous veterans' association gave the government list an overwhelming majority. All opposition seemed to disappear on 6 April 1924, though open polling made deviation difficult in isolated hamlets. Turati finally saw an opportunity to bring the combatants of the area under the official tutelage of the PNF. Soon after the returns came in, he invited the federation's new friends to join the party. Conflict immediately erupted when the recent recruits far outnumbered the old members.[44] One section boasted 380 patrons, 300 of whom signed up in May. At Iseo the movement grew from seventy adherents to almost 300. Many regulars refused to let the former servicemen enter the legions, while three MVSN officers threatened to protect their independence by violence.[45] And when Vittorio Cochard, a beginner in the movement, received the mayoral nomination in the town of Adro, first-hour fascists organized a small revolt. Corrado Ciocia, a squad leader from Capriolo, decided to turn the tables on the provincial leadership and campaign for the PPI candidates.[46] One week before polling day, Turati dissolved six *fasci* in the Franciacorte, and fifty militants in the militia faced formal expulsion. In the northwest foothills too, the prefect adjourned administrative battles on orders from the local boss.

Zealots from the hills exploited the provincial repercussions of the government crisis. They justified the parochial rebellion as intransigent euphoria. One platoon commander in the MVSN got triggerhappy and took pot-shots at the members in the Paderno *fascio* who had voted to replace him as political secretary.[47] The Centurione Ciocia enlisted about 200 disillusioned fascists, 120 of them armed militiamen, to liberate the sections near Lake Iseo from the clutches of combatants. Dissident gangs would roam the hamlets at night yelling

---

[43] *Popolo di Brescia*, 29 April 1924.

[44] ASB, GP, b. 18, n. 1629, 10 April 1924.

[45] Ibid., b. 14, cat. 20, dissidio, 27 June, 20 and 28 July, 12 August 1924.

[46] *Il Cittadino di Brescia*, 15 May 1924; *Popolo di Brescia*, 17 May 1924.

[47] ASB, Corte d'Assise, b. 77, fasc. 9, procedimento penale contro Luigi Francesconi, Giuseppe Mensi, Mario Mensi, Fausto Vivenzi, Pietro Vivenzi, e Giacomo Belleri (see Turati's letter of 30 October 1924); *La Provincia di Brescia*, 30 August 1924.

'Matteotti' or '*assassini*'. Expecting clashes with agitators from the opposition, the former servicemen rushed out and instead got jumped by the roving corps. Twenty-seven veterans were beaten or stabbed during the month of August alone. Turati avoided official recourse to the ministry of the interior and repressed rumours. Private appeals to the neighbouring prefect, however, encouraged intrigue. The Bergamo federation, pleased to underwrite sedition at Brescia, offered asylum by day to the mutineers. Once again, discord between adjacent fiefs amplified domestic feuds.[48]

By autumn 1924 the autonomist movement spread to the Valcamonica, and publicity made enquiries impossible to divert. The independent dailies reported on the escapades of Ciocia, the shopkeeper turned bandit.[49] Turati dispatched a party henchman to restore order, but Ernesto Gulì's attempts at mediation met with disaster. When the dissidents espied former servicemen canvassing for the strike fund of the town corporations, they led an attack of incensed mountaineers to steal the money. Seven newcomers to the *fascio*, all manual labourers for a local cement company, retaliated by confiscating nearly 6,500 lire from a village merchant who no longer belonged to the movement.[50] The Rome authorities finally demanded the facts of the affair, and PNF activity in the Franciacorte came to a standstill.[51]

The brigands in black shirts continued to bait the provincial federation. Despite Gulì's presence in the Franciacorte, the petty mountain warfare evolved into murder and mayhem. Police flooded the region, but the renegades still managed to maim three combatants in November and wound twenty-three others during December. One PNF convert from the ANC died of his injuries. Road-blocks at the Bergamo border proved vain since the Ciocia clan evaded them almost nightly.[52] If civilian officials questioned a victim of assault, they

[48] ASB, GP, b. 14, cat. 20, dissidio, 12 October 1924; on past feuding in the area, see Corte d'Assise, b. 91, fasc. 1, procedimento penale contro Alghisio Piatti, Giovanni Piatti, e Gabriele Santicoli.

[49] *La Provincia di Brescia*, 9, 15, and 22 September 1924; *Avanti!*, 23 September 1924; *La Sentinella Bresciana*, 28 September 1924.

[50] ASB, GP, b. 14, cat. 20, n. 1359, 12 October 1924.

[51] ACS, Min. Interno, DGPS, AGR 1924, b. 85, cat. G1, fasc. Brescia, sfasc. Adro, 10–13 November 1924; ASB, Corte d'Assise, b. 81, fasc. 3, procedimento penale contro Luigi Ghitti, Giuseppe Ghitti, Pietro Ghitti, Pietro Vecchiati, Guido Donna, e Cesare Martinelli; b. 86, fasc. 3, procedimento penale contro Corrado Ciocia; *La Provincia di Brescia*, 8 and 15 November 1924.

[52] ACS, Min. Interno, DGPS, AGR 1924, b. 89, cat. G1, fasc. Brescia, 27 October 1924; ASB, GP, b. 18, n. 1590, 10 and 21 December 1924.

encountered a conspiracy of silence. The new fascists refused to co-operate with state functionaries, and the mayor of Capriolo conspired against three *carabinieri* who attempted to interfere in the vendetta. Only after a bloody battle in an abandoned piazza did the rookies finally wound the infamous rebel, and two veterans got killed in the crossfire.[53] Authorities captured Ciocia during a rooftop escape attempt, and his arrest marked the end of the upland feud.[54] The insurgency that stirred in the hills harked back to animosities of an old sort, and these dissolved in the absence of the gang leader. Fascist dissidence had provided a convenient rubric under which partisan politics could keep the local community insulated from foreign infringement.[55]

Turati scheduled administrative elections in the Franciacorte during April and May. With Ciocia under arrest, former servicemen delivered overwhelming victories to the PNF in all but two dissident strongholds. There, polling day waited until autumn, when the veterans had mobilized 79 per cent of those registered to vote the party ticket.[56] Sixty of the 107 combatants' groups in the province had gone over to the PNF by 1925, and most of these converts came from the lower uplands. Fascism thus obtained the active support of the old ANC sections in zones where perennial mountain feuds obscured modern class alignments. Traditional rivalries assumed new political labels.

Fascist Syndicalism in Industry

The Matteotti murder roused organized industry's distrust of fascism. In September 1924 the Confindustria broke its post-mortem silence and refused to collaborate further with the regime. Syndicalists of the provincial federation delighted in the annulment of the Chigi accords, for they wanted the chance to build up strength through trade disputes. During the stalemate between government and business, the corporations also benefited from the relaxation of pressures on the local party. Although the defunct pact denied official recognition to the free unions, and socialist competition might return as a result of

[53] *La Provincia di Brescia*, 9-11 March 1925.

[54] ACS, Min. Interno, Ufficio Cifra, in arrivo, n. 8471, Valenti to Federzoni, 10 and 13 March 1925; in partenza, n. 5475, Federzoni to prefect of Bergamo, 13 March 1925; *Corriere della Sera*, 10 March 1925.

[55] ACS, DGPS, AGR 1925, b. 88, cat. G1, fasc. Brescia, sfasc. Capriolo, 10 and 19 March 1925.

[56] ASB, GP, b. 18, n. 1449, 27 September and 10 October 1925.

the countermand, Turati too enjoyed new scope for action. He intended to exploit normal channels of arbitration, expecting management to respond with reciprocity. Employers chose to ignore all overtures from this incipient demagogue, who had yet to establish himself among the urban working class.

The revived independence of the Confindustria coincided with renewed economic growth. Improved conditions in the capital goods sector drove down unemployment during the spring of 1924. By August, the number of jobless in provincial iron and steel fell to less than a fifth of the figure registered one year before. Political strains eased in the autumn, and the FIOM began to stake a claim in the restored prosperity for workers. September saw the Lombard steel consortium agree to negotiate wage increases with the socialist federation. Turati countered by presenting his own set of demands, which went for higher hourly rates at the expense of overtime pay and indemnity against dismissal.[57] The Consorzio still refused to recognize the party extremist as a legitimate delegate of any trade association. Business spokesmen offered to discuss the issue with Luigi Razza, who represented the Milan corporations, but would not talk to a local boss of dubious importance. Industry's hostile reception landed the pretender from Brescia in a situation for which he knew only one solution. Turati threatened a strike.[58]

Such stirrings of labour militancy discomfited moderates in the provincial movement. PNF syndicalism could cut short negotiations with the FIOM to the advantage of industry, but the position of intransigents would strengthen in the process. Both Giarratana and Bonardi opposed the manœuvre. Turati went over their heads and took his case straight to Rossoni and Mussolini.[59] Businessmen at Brescia now became cagey and offered corporation members one-third of the hourly increase requested.[60] Fascists rejected the token supplement on the grounds that their main competition remained in the contest. Two days later the Consorzio came around and announced an exclusive agreement with the party unions. Although

---

[57] B. Uva, 'Gli scioperi metallurgici italiani del marzo 1925', in *Storia Contemporanea*, vol. i (1970), pp. 1016-17.

[58] ACS, Presidenza del Consiglio, 1924, fasc. 3.7/2244, Turati, 20 and 25 September 1924; Min. Interno, DGPS, AGR 1924, b. 79, cat. D13, fasc. Brescia, 22 September 1924; *Popolo di Brescia*, 21-23 September 1924.

[59] ACS, Min. Interno, DGPS, AGR 1924, b. 79, cat. D13, fasc. Brescia, 25 and 26 September 1924.

[60] *Popolo di Brescia*, 27 September 1924; *L'Unità*, 29 and 30 September 1924.

Turati failed to secure minimum wage requirements and unemployment insurance, he managed to double the cost-of-living supplements put forth by the rival union. Throughout Lombardy the snubbed socialists protested against the intrusion of new claimants in centralized bargaining, but at Brescia less than half of those engaged in heavy industry participated in the strike.

In November troubles broke out again when the Franchi Gregorini steelworks refused to apply the wage increases, guaranteed by the consortium weeks before, to company operatives. Turati called a partial stoppage to press the issue, but management responded by firing a hundred participants.[61] Prefectural efforts at mediation convinced the firm to reinstall the strikers at standard pay.[62] Membership in the metallurgical syndicate soared to 4,000, but December also witnessed decisive expansion in other sectors. If enrolment fell among transport workers as a whole following two failed labour offensives in trucking, the majority of municipal tramway employees now belonged to the corporation in services. The PNF developed a solid position among men in the building trades.[63] The fascist daily boasted over 20,000 adherents in the textile union.[64] Only in the chemical and food industries of the province did the fascist subscription seem slight.[65]

Mussolini's address to parliament on 3 January 1925, to all appearances, raised the curtain on a PNF militancy broadened in scope. The liberal and Aventine parties acted with fatal indecision, and their inability to meet the prime minister's challenge damned all legal order. The isolation and feebleness of the opposition after the defiant speech, in which Mussolini assumed personal responsibility for blackshirt crime, strengthened the intransigent wing. And the longer central government deferred reconciliation with industry, the more vulnerable moderates in the movement became. Turati kept a watchful eye on estranged members of the federation during those uncertain days, but stayed active on another front. When the working-class discontents nurtured by severe inflation in late 1924 finally surfaced, he turned a routine wage dispute into an historic fascist strike.[66]

---

[61] ACS, Min. Interno, DGPS, AGR 1924, b. 79, cat. D13, fasc. Brescia, 27 and 28 November 1924.

[62] *Popolo di Brescia*, 1 December 1924.

[63] *La Provincia di Brescia*, 5 January 1925.

[64] *Popolo di Brescia*, 18 December 1924.

[65] *L'Inizio e sviluppo del sindacalismo fascista nella provincia di Brescia* (Brescia, 1925), p. 13.

[66] *Popolo di Brescia*, 12 and 30 January 1925; F. Cordova, *Le origini dei sindacati fascisti*, pp. 353-6; B. Uva, *La nascita dello stato corporativo e sindacale fascista* (Assisi, 1975), pp 95-8.

The FIOM had already begun negotiations for pay increases that would compensate for the dramatic drop in purchasing power, but at Brescia some fascist metalworkers drafted their own demands. On 17 February 1925, these operatives at the Officine Meccaniche left the shop floor without their corporation's consent. Management docked the pay of all participants in the two-hour stoppage, and five party militants got the sack. Turati appealed to the Consorzio, which reinstated the strikers but refused to discuss wage scales with a provincial potentate.[67] The organization offered to meet Razza in his capacity as Lombard union chief and declined to pursue arbitration with any other PNF claimant. Turati, offended by 'such contemptuous disrespect', retaliated by promising 'agitation'.[68] A provincial offensive in heavy industry risked revealing the superiority of the FIOM, so the local boss played off divisions within the employers' camp itself to contain grievances and avoid embarrassment. The Franchi Gregorini steelworks, which habitually ignored the directives of the Confindustria, had reneged on earlier concessions and the fascists enjoyed a numerous following at that firm. On the evening of 2 March Turati ordered members there to stay outside the factory gates. The strike aimed to end management's 'insatiable greed and unwarranted indiscipline once and for all'.[69]

The instant success of the labour assault baffled even its organizers. *Popolo di Brescia* reported that some 6,000 workers had participated on the first day of the walk-out, though the prefect counted about 4,000 on the picket line.[70] Turati mobilized the city squads to tame socialist 'blacklegs' and make the stoppage general; forty co-operatives that once belonged to the Camera del Lavoro now rationed food to sustain the PNF protesters.[71] The strike spread to most steel and engineering firms of the zone within forty-eight hours. Some pockets of FIOM resistance held out despite street skirmishes, and fascist white-collar employees wavered in battle.[72] Middle-class support, in any case, was not a *sine qua non*: by 7 March just about 8,000 of the 10,000 metal-

---

[67] ACS, Min. Interno, DGPS, AGR 1925, b. 77, cat. D13, fasc. Brescia, 17 and 19 February 1925.

[68] *Popolo di Brescia*, 26 February 1925.

[69] Ibid., 3 March 1925.

[70] Ibid., 4 March 1925; ACS, Min. Interno, DGPS, AGR 1925, b. 77, cat. D13, fasc. Brescia, 3 March 1925; *La Provincia di Brescia*, 3 and 4 March 1925.

[71] *Popolo di Brescia*, 5-8 March 1925; *La Sentinella Bresciana*, 7 March 1925.

[72] *Corriere della Sera*, 7 and 8 March 1925; A. Lyttelton, *The Seizure of Power*, pp. 315-16.

lurgists in the province had laid down their tools.[73] The mass response astounded all observers.[74] The next day the Lombard consortium agreed to revise pay scales for those employed in Brescia alone.[75] But national publicity intoxicated the local leader, and he would no longer hear of a special settlement. Turati vowed to bring out the syndicates in textiles should the resolution stay limited to his home base.[76]

Turati's boldness wrought havoc among CGL organizers, who declared that the corporations 'had no right to represent the working class.[77] Palmiro Togliatti, future secretary of the communist party, implored comrades to collect 'all information available' on the strike, 'a dispute of the utmost importance even in the international context'.[78] The easy pre-eminence of the black unionists surprised the prime minister as well. When the walk-out's extension to other Lombard manufacturing centres appeared imminent, Mussolini expressed concern about reactivating 'the old pernicious socialist habits against which fascism has waged its best battles'.[79] Rossoni, excited by the sheer number of participants, pledged solidarity with the militant Brescians; he asked members of the consortium to begin serious negotiations lest the agitation assume national proportions.[80] Farinacci gave the PNF's formal approval as the strike spread to Milan, Pavia, and Bergamo on 12 March 1925.[81] The next evening, the competition officially endorsed the labour action, and the FIOM began to call the shots. The stoppage grew overnight to include almost 100,000 metalworkers, four-fifths of them out on orders from the old federation.[82]

The FIOM's entry into negotiations bore out the perplexities of

[73] ACS, Min. Interno, DGPS, AGR 1925, b. 77, cat. D13, fasc. Brescia, 5-7 March 1925; *Corriere della Sera*, 8 March 1925; *La Provincia di Brescia*, 8 and 9 March 1925.

[74] *L'Unità*, 8 and 9 March 1925.

[75] ACS, Min. Interno, DGPS, AGR 1925, b. 77, cat. D13, fasc. Milano, 8 March 1925. Three Brescian firms had already defied the consortium by conceding cost-of-living increases that were twice the amount offered by other industrialists; see Ufficio Cifra, in arrivo, n. 8295, Pugliese to Federzoni, 9 March 1925; *Popolo di Brescia*, 10 March 1925.

[76] ACS, Min. Interno, DGPS, AGR 1925, b. 77, cat. D13, fasc. Brescia, 8 March 1925.

[77] *Avanti!*, 9 and 10 March 1925.

[78] ACS, MRF, Carteggio Serrati, b. 141, cartella 23, n. 10, Ercoli, 17 March 1925; see also *L'Unità*, 12 March 1925.

[79] ACS, Min. Interno, DGPS, AGR 1925, b. 77, cat. D13, fasc. Brescia, 8 March 1925.

[80] Ibid., 10 March 1925.

[81] *Corriere della Sera*, 12 March 1925; F. Cordova, *Le origini dei sindacati fascisti*, pp. 363-5; E. Malusardi, *Elementi di storia del sindacalismo fascista* (Genoa, 1932), p. 117.

[82] *Avanti!*, 14 and 15 March 1925; *L'Unità*, 15 March 1925; B. Uva, *La nascita dello stato corporativo*, pp. 116-27.

fascist syndicalism. When agitation crept into enemy territory, the dispute slipped from party control. Industry could not agree about the better of two evils: some employers preferred to deal with the claimants of the left, though most businessmen seemed reluctant to grant socialists a monopoly of labour representation.[83] The government feared continuation of the *sciopero nero*, which was the greatest strike of any colour during the twenty-one-year history of the regime. Mussolini's attempts to force a hasty settlement on indecisive industry and divided labour exhausted conflict within his own movement, so the issue of local authority versus central direction remained unresolved. But the real drama belonged to the socialists, who watched the tragic irony of PNF trade unionism unfold. Twice during negotiations Turati made contact with Bruno Buozzi through the labour leader's personal secretary, a reluctant Edgardo Falchero.[84]

The agitation which demonstrated the freedom of party unions in action also inspired the elimination of local syndical autonomy. Much to Turati's dismay, the national corporations reached a quick accord with the Confederation of Industry two days after socialists helped make the strike general. The settlement stipulated a wage increase of 2.20 lire a day, 1.30 lire short of the original demand, yet the source of his displeasure went beyond the economic terms of the pact.[85] Centralized bargaining had taken place far from the dominion of the provincial leader. The controversial strike initiated by the Brescian fascist did not find resolution through his own intervention. Instead, the ministry of the interior mediated negotiations from Rome and forced the collective decision on all labour representatives.

Turati threatened to resume agitation should the pay supplements first proposed in February fail to come through.[86] The establishment of governmental controls soon after the March episode eliminated this prospect. The Grand Council met in April to place fascist unions under a regulated corporative order.[87] While the boundaries of syndical control still needed definition, provincial intransigents quietly stepped into line with the directives of the national movement. Having been declared 'acts of war', strikes were no longer instrumen-

---

[83] M. Abrate, *La lotta sindacale*, pp. 417-18.

[84] *La Sentinella Bresciana*, 14-16 March 1925; *Popolo di Brescia*, 13-15 March 1925; B. Uva, *La nascita dello stato corporativo*, pp. 119-22.

[85] ACS, Presidenza del Consiglio, 1925, fasc. 3.3/813, Turati, 15 March 1925; *Corriere della Sera*, 15 and 17 March 1925; *La Stirpe*, April 1925.

[86] ACS, Presidenza del Consiglio, 1925, fasc. 3.3/813, Turati, 15 March 1925.

[87] E. Malusardi, *Elementi di storia del sindacalismo fascista*, pp. 118-21.

tally available to local party activists.[88] The Brescia boss, however, did not lose everything. By May his corporations boasted nearly 9,500 adherents in heavy industry, and over 25,000 in textiles.[90] Perhaps PNF labour militancy was eroded, but conservative centralization at least consolidated organized strength at the expense of free competition.

The agreement signed at the Hotel Corso in Milan fulfilled one of Turati's initial objectives, for the feckless autonomy of local industry came under fire as a result of the trade dispute. The March strike ended a decade of factiousness within the Brescian entrepreneurial community. The Confindustria issued an official statement of censure which 'deplored the behaviour of management' at the Franchi Gregorini company, 'a firm which has shown itself unworthy of membership in any employer association'.[90] The pact of Palazzo Vidoni, concluded on 2 October 1925, took this repudiation of liberal individualism one step further. The accord granted political immunity to big business in Italy. The Confindustria retained margins for manœuvring, but acknowledged the corporations as the exclusive representatives of labour, in return for the abolition of workers' councils on the shop floor. Though the parameters of public and private domains required delineation, the Vidoni provisions did institutionalize collective bargaining under authoritarian auspices.[91]

The October agreement of 1925 and the syndical law drafted by Alfredo Rocco in April 1926 produced little echo in the town where the troubles that prompted Mussolini's reconciliation with industry had begun.[92] If Turati's strike failed to precipitate the desired result in the

[88] ACS, SPCR, b. 26, fasc. 242/R, sfasc. 3, inserto B, 'Sullo Sciopero' (April 1925); Partito Nazionale Fascista, *Il Gran Consiglio nei primi sei anni dell'era fascista* (Rome, 1929), pp. 175-7; L. Rosenstock-Franck, *L'économie corporative fasciste*, pp. 37-8; A. Aquarone, *L'organizzazione dello Stato totalitario* (Turin, 1965), pp. 119-20.

[89] *Popolo di Brescia*, 23 May 1925; see also *L'Inizio e sviluppo del sindacalismo fascista*, pp. 13, 15-16.

[90] *Corriere della Sera*, 16 March 1925. The Confindustria recommended disciplinary action, but the Lombard consortium rescinded the censure on 16 June 1925, after the company appealed against the decision; see ASIG, Società Anonima Franchi Gregorini, Consiglio di Amministrazione, verbale, 30 June 1925.

[91] P. Melograni, *Gli industriali e Mussolini*, pp. 151-3; V. Castronovo, *Giovanni Agnelli* (Turin, 1971), pp. 417-22; C. Maier, *Recasting Bourgeois Europe*, p. 564; F. Cordova, *Le origini dei sindacati fascisti*, pp. 424-34.

[92] The Rocco law widened the Confindustria's sphere of influence over small producers; it gave the employer association new legal authority in the regime and disciplined fascist unions; see F. Guarneri, *Battaglie economiche*, vol. i, pp. 140-1; *La Stirpe*, June 1926; R. De Felice, *Mussolini il fascista. II. L'organizzazione dello Stato fascista 1925-1929* (Turin, 1968), pp. 266-75; P. Ungari, *Alfredo Rocco e l'ideologia giuridica del fascismo* (Brescia, 1963).

capital, the labour offensive served to stabilize his position at home. Brescia fell under firm control, and calm returned to the countryside too. The fascists never managed to break the hold of church tradition, but forced most co-operatives and unions into inactivity.[93] The PPI lost all political strength when Catholic Action sought to take on the lay party's organizing role.[94] Prominent working-class activists went underground.[95] The once uncompromising *ras* could now afford to subdue his radical ebullience.

One year after the metallurgical strike, the leader of Brescian fascism discovered the path to Rome. He became national party chief in April 1926, following the defeat of Roberto Farinacci. Given Turati's record, blemished by two attempts to dethrone the Duce, the nomination at first appeared rather imprudent. The downfall of the Cremona boss, however, represented a defeat for agrarian extremists, since it modified the balance of forces within the regime to the disadvantage of the PNF. Despite recent docility to the government, Turati certainly projected intransigent panache, and his appointment mollified provincial fanatics during the administrative shake-up. The more obvious contenders for the secretariat, such as Bologna's Leandro Arpinati, might menace Mussolini's personal dictatorship.[96]

From the march on Rome in 1922 to the metalworkers' strike of 1925, Augusto Turati had played the *enfant terrible* of fascism. The revisionist directives of the central government and the extremist tendencies of neighbouring fiefs drove him to assert authority in the name of radical intransigence. Struggling against the political insolence of the industrialists and the social indiscipline of the agrarians, he made a bid for the urban working class and posed as the oracle of the proletariat. Legal pressure and illegal coercion buttressed the local chieftain's ability to exploit a situation of genuine economic discontent. Yet precisely because of his syndicalist *élan*, Turati was almost left behind. He stepped into the realm of national debate only after learning the advantages of collaboration and compromise.

[93] ACS, Min. Interno, DGPS, Serie G1, Associazioni 1896-1897 e 1910-1934, b. 8, fasc. Unione del Lavoro, 2 January and 17 December 1925; fasc. circoli cattolici, 20 December 1925.

[94] Ibid., AGR 1926, b. 112, cat. K2, fasc. Brescia, 19 February 1926.

[95] Archivio Partito Comunista, b. 467, 18 and 26 October 1926.

[96] On Turati's secretariat (1926-1930), see R. De Felice, *Mussolini il fascista. II*, pp. 175-200; P. Morgan, 'Augusto Turati', pp. 488-511.

Conclusion

In September 1924, when the crowd at a PNF rally chanted, 'Turati is our god, Mussolini our king', a first-hour enthusiast took offence and reported the incident to the local authorities.[1] The new regime destroyed neither the church nor the monarchy. In the pantheon of provincial politics, only the idols had changed, and the denouncer seemed especially concerned about the precedence. Although the Duce crowed that he had undermined the ideals and structures of liberal Italy, the actual achievements of the dictatorship belied its leader's claims. Perhaps the 'fascist revolution' had occurred, but only within the framework of inherited values and established trends.

Nineteenth-century liberalism aimed to contain the social consequences of industrial growth by reconciling order and tradition within a progressive and unified economy. World War I, however, effaced this vision of a modern, bourgeois utopia when it divided the country into those who embraced an élitist conception of the nation-state and those orientated towards the people. The constitutional right looked to intervention for internal strength and cohesion. Instead, socialist trade unionism emerged the apparent victor. The mobilization in 1915 both stimulated the mass organization of labour and exposed the patchy pattern of development in private enterprise. While the terms of industrial conflict underwent a dramatic transformation, the military effort also strained the fragile institutions of parliamentary democracy. The state assumed a central role in regulating arms production, commercial activity, and politics on the home front. And just as the autarky of the provincial community began to fade away, bureaucracy in Rome started its retreat from civilian life. The old governing class returned to power only to confront a crisis of legitimacy.

If the Great War damaged the prospects of democratic representation in Italy, then the beginning of demobilization in 1918 and the onset of deflation in 1920 eliminated them. At Brescia the Partito Popolare was the obvious heir to the constitutional parties. Despite its ambiguities and limitations, Don Sturzo's movement could mobilize

[1] ASB, GP, b. 18, n. 1264, Gargnano, 21 September 1924.

the mass support that the liberals so desperately lacked. The *popolari* offered a compromise between hierarchy and mobility that sought to preserve the alignments of local tradition. Their programme of class collaboration, however, depended on ministerial stability, economic prosperity, and the absence of social conflict. But inflation followed by recession unsettled labour relations and unhinged government coalitions. Peacetime domestic realities thus condemned the 'Christian coming' to obsolescence. The provincial PPI disintegrated into ecclesiastical, clerical, and radical factions which steered a common course only after their political eclipse. Failing to graduate from the collectivity of the parish to the national arena of interest-group competition, the Catholic lay party could not capture the institutional power proportionate to its inflated popular following.

The CGL gained official recognition as the sole representative of labour at the wartime bargaining table, and its monopoly over the settlement of wage disputes gave affiliated leagues new strength. Collaboration with the economic effort caused membership to swell, but also established the territorial division of reformist and revolutionary strike action. News of insurrection in Russia and promises to peasants by government kindled mass aspirations all over the peninsula, and the PSI lurched to the left. Despite the general climate in Europe and the militancy of the socialist party in Italy, the stalemate between union bureaucrats and maximalist politicians kept proletarian allegiances at Brescia provincial and personalized. Privations during the recession, moreover, engendered petty feuds and fomented doctrinal disputes. The violence of the class struggle intensified while the cohesion of trade unionism deteriorated. Other brokers of power began to bank on fears of a bolshevik rebellion.

Fascism developed as an ill-defined response to this atmosphere of profound social strife and economic dislocation. It promised to revitalize the old parties of order and managed to mobilize the component parts of the right under the banner of antisocialism. As the socialists and Catholics vied for the loyalties of labour, conservative forces overlooked their differences to defend the threatened interests of property. Mussolini's movement merged the grumblings of the upper classes with those of the amorphous 'middling strata'; however, it never unified their aims. By playing on the fissile proclivities of the Italian bourgeoisie, the Duce became prime minister.

A conservative drift during a period of parliamentary decay might lay the foundations for a governing coalition led by the extreme right, but the groundwork for totalitarian rule had yet to be established. Although Mussolini obtained his first mandate from the urban bourgeoisie, the movement went to the hinterland to grasp the local levers of administrative control. This was the real novelty of fascism. It manipulated the loose integration of town and country maintained during the Giolittian period, but which had been displaced after the war. At Brescia, where farmers witnessed the contagious enthusiasms of neighbouring peasant leagues as well as the factory occupations in the capital city, the blackshirts beckoned as a means by which to protect propertied interests. Augusto Turati undertook to restore deference in the rural labour force while leaving the fruits of commercial development untouched, and that he did. But agrarians failed to drive away political change and to regain their former isolation. Employers in agriculture adjusted, albeit reluctantly, to the national homogenization of power.

Fascism fought on many fronts. As rural élites bequeathed the rule of the periphery to the provincial federation, the prime minister slowly made his peace with urban business leaders. Although the reconciliation eventually took the form of producer representation under the authoritarian stamp, corporatism predated the dictatorship. The liberal regime first institutionalized collective bargaining under the patronage of the state during the 1915 mobilization. The bureaucratic machinery constructed over the course of belligerency foreshadowed prominent features of the syndical set-up after 1925. Two important differences, however, distinguish totalitarian corporatism from its military progenitor. General Dallolio's variation brought about an initial prosperity which would buy off organized labour, whereas the Duce's brand put a deflationary damper on the working class. Furthermore, the need to churn out armaments at all costs presented opportunities for small and large firms alike, encouraging the haphazard expansion of local operators such as Attilio Franchi. Industrial concentration took root as a result of wartime policy, but it developed inconsistently. Rationalization, on the other hand, waited until the revaluation crisis for a decisive boost from public policy. Capitalists despaired when Mussolini pegged the lira at 90 against the pound, but big business recovered quickly at the expense of smaller rivals. Government pitched the exchange rate high, in part for reasons of prestige abroad and popularity at home. Despite these political premises, currency stabilization did not deviate dramatically from trends characteristic of the international economy during the late

1920s. In Italy, what market forces alone could not achieve ensued with the exercise of authoritarian control. The centralization of credit facilities in 1926 accelerated the transition to oligopoly and broke Catholic banking networks.[2]

Quota novanta finished the post-war overhaul of the capital goods sector and destroyed local entrepreneurial autonomy. The stabilization of the lira precipitated catastrophic collapses in the province, and during 1927 some sixty-seven firms went bankrupt.[3] Unemployment soared in all categories. The number of jobless metallurgists increased almost sevenfold from the 1926 figure, while 33,713 textile workers got the sack.[4] Cartelization and rationalization stood as the showpieces of Mussolini's drastic monetary reform, for which the proletariat paid. Ostensibly concerned for his home-town constituency, on 2 May 1927 Augusto Turati announced a 10 per cent wage reduction for agricultural labour that brought on pay cuts in most categories throughout the peninsula. Once again the PNF secretary placed the masses at Brescia in the vanguard of the party's national campaign, yet it took the corporation ranks nearly twenty years to recover from this move.[5] When the great depression struck, native manufacture languished further. Attilio Franchi remained a bachelor married to his business in Marone. He had learned to stay away from creditors, and managed to outlast the crisis.[6] The crash took its toll on others. Giulio Togni, the most conspicuous casualty, committed suicide in 1933 amid rumours of financial scandal; the Falck steelworks and the ILVA trust assumed control of his concerns within months of the tragedy. Breda from Milan and FIAT of Turin firmly established themselves in the Bresciano as well during this time of trouble for overextended indigenous industry.

[2] On the 1926-7 revaluation crisis, see P. Grifone, *Il capitale finanziario in Italia* (Turin, 1971) pp. 56-77; G. Toniolo, *L'economia dell'Italia fascista* (Bari, 1980), pp 83-132; R. Sarti, 'Mussolini and the Italian Industrial Leadership in the Battle of the Lira 1925-1927', in *Past and Present*, no. 47 (1970), pp. 97-112.

[3] ASB, Fondo Camera di Commercio, Consiglio Provinciale dell'Economia, 1927; see also ACS, Min. Interno, DGPS, AGR 1927, b. 110, cat. C1, fasc. Brescia, sfasc. disoccupazione, 10 January and 16 February 1927.

[4] Consiglio Provinciale dell'Economia di Brescia, *Svolgimento delle attività produttrici nella provincia di Brescia: Relazione Statistica 1927–1928* (Brescia, 1929), pp. 289, 297-9.

[5] ACS, Presidenza del Consiglio, 1927, fasc. 3.5/762, 2 May 1927; A. Lyttelton, *The Seizure of Power*, pp 344-5. On the regime's attempts at welfare organization, see V. De Grazia, *The culture of consent: Mass organization of leisure in fascist Italy* (Cambridge, 1981).

[6] Banca Credito Agrario Bresciano, *La Banca Credito Agrario Bresciano e un secolo di sviluppo* (Brescia, 1983), p. 364; in 1932 Franchi ventured into felt production in addition to dolomite extraction.

Commercial agriculture on the flatlands survived the deflationary spiral which had begun with monetary reform. Mussolini may have launched 'the battle of wheat' in tandem with 'integral land reclamation' for the benefit of rural folk, but smallholders faced financial ruin as a result of their revalued debts.[7] Again, economic policies from Rome betrayed the interests of *petit-bourgeois* backers in the hills, but the impoverishment of intermediate peasant categories did reverse the post-war trend towards greater dispersion of property.[8] As a result, government measures to buoy wheat prices and induce growers to increase productivity benefited those landed farmers on the plain with easy access to credit. The Brescia wheat commission worked alongside the Cassa di Risparmio in the race against Cremona cultivators. Participants in the programme, such as the Folonari brothers, received insurance against hailstorms, in addition to seeds and fertilizers from the provincial agency.[9] Low rates for wage work and reduced consumer demand figured as the domestic costs of such protection for private enterprise.[10] Development in the basin fields began to keep pace with the growth of other rich estates in the North.

Brescia presents a rather anomalous site on the national landscape. Its striking diversity, with mountains and plains, heavy industry and rural manufacture, capitalist agriculture and subsistence farming, set it apart from the social uniformity and economic specialization of other zones. Still, the class divisions, political struggles, and commercial heterogeneity created a complex picture that illustrates the predicament of Italy as a whole: the fragmented Lombard province seems almost a miniature of the fragmented country. Far from entailing a *petit-bourgeois* revolution of the right, the Brescian experience suggests that fascism represented a conservative reshuffling of the middle and upper classes. The regime brought together transformed élites with a militant populist party; economic modernization advanced under new political controls. By balancing hierarchy and change, Mussolini's dictatorship completed the liberal programme through the instruments of totalitarian rule.

[7] C. T. Schmidt, *The Plough and the Sword: Labor, Land, and Property in Fascist Italy* (New York, 1938), pp. 49-104.

[8] A. Lyttelton, *The Seizure of Power*, p. 352.

[9] ACS, Presidenza del Consiglio, 1929, fasc. 3/1.2, no. 7040.

[10] P. Corner, 'Fascist Agrarian Policy and the Italian Economy in the Inter-war Years', in John Davis (ed.), *Gramsci and Italy's Passive Revolution*, pp. 239-74; E. Fano, 'Problemi e vicende dell'agricoltura italiana tra le due guerre', in *Quaderni Storici*, vol. x (1975), pp. 468-96.

Bibliography

MANUSCRIPT SOURCES

A. *Archivio Centrale dello Stato (Rome)*

Ministero dell'Agricoltura, Inchiesta Parlamentare
Ministero di Armi e Munizioni
Comitato Centrale di Mobilitazione Industriale
Ministero di Grazia e Giustizia, Affari Penali
Ministero dell'Interno
  (All footnotes refer to the original catalogue of the Ministry of the Interior
  files. The Archivio Centrale dello Stato recently renumbered the series
  containing prefectural reports, and is preparing a table of equivalence.)
  Direzione Generale di Pubblica Sicurezza:
    Affari Generali e Riservati
    Atti Diversi 1903-1949
    Serie G1, Associazioni 1896-1897 e 1910-1934
  Gabinetto Bonomi (1921-1922)
  Gabinetto Finzi (1922-1924)
  Ufficio Cifra
  Casellario Politico Centrale
Segreteria Particolare del Duce, Carteggio Riservato
Mostra della Rivoluzione Fascista
Carte D'Annunzio
Carte Farinacci
Presidenza del Consiglio dei Ministri

B. *Archivio di Stato di Brescia*

Gabinetto della Prefettura
Corte d'Assise
Fondo Camera di Commercio

C. *Archivio Storico delle Società Italsider (Genoa)*

D. *Archivio Comunale di Palazzolo sull'Oglio*

E. *Bonardi Papers (Brescia)*

F. *Archivio Rigola (Istituto Feltrinelli, Milan)*

G. *Archivio Partito Comunista 1917–1940 (Istituto Gramsci, Rome)*

H. *Archivio della Camera dei Deputati (Rome)*

I. *Italian Documents Collection, St Antony's College (Oxford)*

NEWSPAPERS AND JOURNALS

A. Fully consulted for the period relevant to this work:
L'Agricoltura Bresciana
L'Azione Civile
Brescia Nuova
Il Cittadino di Brescia
Il Combattente
Commentari dell'Ateneo di Brescia
Il Contadino
Il Contadino Rosso
Fiamma
Popolo di Brescia
La Provincia di Brescia
La Riscossa
La Sentinella Bresciana

B. Consulted on specific issues:
Avanti! (Milan edition)
Bandiera Bianca
Corriere della Sera
Guerra di Classe
Idea Nazionale
Il Monte Orfano
Popolo d'Italia
Il 'Rompiscatole'
Il Sole
La Stirpe
L'Unità
La Voce del Popolo

BOOKS AND ARTICLES

ABRATE, M. *La lotta sindacale nella industralizzazione in Italia 1906–1926* (Turin, 1967).

ALBERTARIO, P. *I salari agricoli nelle zone ad economia capitalistica della Bassa Lombarda nel cinquantennio 1880–1930* (Pavia, 1930).

Almanacco Socialista Italiano (Milan, 1917-25).

AMMINISTRAZIONE PROVINCIALE DI BRESCIA. *L'attività svolta nel quinquennio 1928–1932* (Brescia, 1932).

AQUARONE, A. *L'organizzazione dello Stato totalitario* (Turin, 1965).

— 'La milizia volontaria nello stato fascista', in A. Aquarone and M. Vernassa, *Il regime fascista* (Bologna, 1974).

ARE, G. 'Alla ricerca di una filosofia dell'industrializzazione nella cultura economica e nei programmi politici in Italia dopo l'unità', in G. Mori, *L'industrializzazione in Italia (1861–1900)* (Bologna, 1977).

ARFÉ, G. *Storia del socialismo italiano (1892–1926)* (Turin, 1965).

Atti del Comitato dell'inchiesta industriale (Rome, 1873-4).

Atti della Giunta per l'Inchiesta agraria e sulle condizioni della classe agricola, vol. vi (Rome, 1882).

BACHI, R. *L'economia dell'Italia in guerra* (Rome, 1918).

— *L'economia italiana alla vigilia della guerra* (Rome, 1918).

— *L'Italia economica* (Città del Castello, 1914-22).

BAGLIONI, G. *L'ideologia della borghesia industriale nell'Italia liberale* (Turin, 1974).

BANCA CREDITO AGRARIO BRESCIANO. *La Banca Credito Agrario Bresciano e un secolo di sviluppo* (Brescia, 1983).

BARBADORO, I. *Storia del sindacalismo italiano dalla nascita al fascismo* (Florence, 1973).

BARNI, E. *Per una politica delle acque* (Brescia, 1917).

BEAUCLERK, W. H. *Rural Italy* (London, 1888).

BELL, D. H. 'Working-class culture and Fascism in an Italian industrial town, 1918-22', in *Social History*, ix (1984), 1-24.

BENEDINI, B. *Terra e agricoltori nel circondario di Brescia* (Brescia, 1881).

— 'De'contratti agrari e della condizione dei lavoratori del suolo nel circondario di Brescia', in *Commentari dell'Ateneo di Brescia* (1882).

— 'Industria e commerci', in *Brixia* (Brescia, 1882).

BETTONI, A. 'Condizioni demografico-sanitarie del comune di Brescia in rapporto all'abitato urbano', in *Commentari dell'Ateneo di Brescia* (1911).

BIANCHI, A. *Notizie su alcune delle principali attività della Cattedra Ambulante di Agricoltura per la provincia di Brescia dal 1915 al 1920* (Brescia, 1920).

BIANCHI, G. *Per l'agricoltura a per i contadini nel 'dopo guerra'* (Brescia, 1919).

BINCHY, D. A. *Church and State in Fascist Italy* (Oxford, 1941).

BONARDI, M. *Il ferro bresciano* (Brescia, 1889).

BONATO, C. *L'economia agraria della Lombardia* (Milan, 1952).

BONELLI, F. *La crisi del 1907: Una tappa dello sviluppo industriale in Italia* (Turin, 1971).

— *Lo sviluppo di una grande impresa in Italia: La Terni dal 1884 al 1962* (Turin, 1974).

BOSIO, G. *La grande paura: Settembre 1920* (Rome, 1970).

BOSWORTH, R. *Italy and the Approach of the First World War* (London, 1983).

BRENTANO, D. *La vita di un comune montano* (Brescia, 1934).

BUOZZI, B. *Le condizioni della classe lavoratrice in Italia 1922–1943* (Milan, 1973).

CAFAGNA, L. 'La "rivoluzione agraria" in Lombardia', in *Annali dell'Istituto Giangiacomo Feltrinelli* (Milan, 1959).

CAIZZI, B. *Storia dell'industria italiana dal XVIII secolo ai giorni nostri* (Turin, 1965).

— *L'economia lombarda durante la Restaurazione (1814–1859)* (Milan, 1972).

CAMARDA, A. and PELI, S. *L'altro esercito: La classe operaia durante la prima guerra mondiale* (Milan, 1980).

CAMERA DEI DEPUTATI. *Atti Parlamentari del Regno d'Italia*, Legislatura XXVI (1921-1923), documento XXI (Rome, 1923).

CAMERA DI COMMERCIO ED ARTI DELLA PROVINCIA DI BRESCIA. *Sul progetto di un Consorzio per la tutela degli interessi serici* (Brescia, 1908).

CAMERA DI COMMERCIO E INDUSTRIA DI BRESCIA. *Statistica Industriale al 30 Giugno 1910: Industrie mineralurgiche, metallurgiche e meccaniche* (Brescia, 1910).

— *Statistica Industriale al 30 Gennaio 1911: Industrie varie* (Brescia, 1911).

— *Costituzioni, modificazioni, scioglimenti di società* (Brescia, 1911).

— *Atti* (Brescia, 1915-24).

— *Problemi e possibilità del dopo-guerra nella provincia di Brescia* (Brescia, 1916).

— *Problemi e possibilità del dopo-guerra nella provincia di Brescia. II: Inchiesta sui salari nel 1915 e 1916* (Brescia, 1917).

— *Problemi e possibilità del dopo-guerra nella provincia di Brescia. III: Inchiesta sul capitale e sulla tecnica* (Brescia, 1917).

— *Variazioni nel costo della vita e nei salari a Brescia prima, durante e dopo la guerra* (Brescia, 1920).

— *Variazioni nella produzione industriale della Provincia di Brescia a causa degli scioperi e della diminuzione degli orari di lavoro* (Brescia, 1920).

— *L'Industria Tessile al 1 Gennaio 1923* (Brescia, 1923).

— *Cenni sulla struttura economica della provincia di Brescia* (Brescia, 1924).

— *L'economia bresciana (Struttura economica della provincia di Brescia)* (Brescia, 1927).

CANDELORO, G. *Storia dell'Italia moderna* (Milan, 1956-81).

CARACCIOLO, A. 'La crescita e la trasformazione della grande industria durante la prima guerra mondiale', in G. Fuà, *Lo sviluppo economico in Italia*, vol. iii (Milan, 1975).

— 'La grande industria nella prima guerra mondiale', in A. Caracciolo, *La formazione dell'Italia industriale* (Bari, 1969).

CARDOZA, A. *Agrarian Elites and Italian Fascism: The Province of Bologna, 1901–1926* (Princeton, 1983).

CARLI, F. *La riforma della tariffa doganale e le industrie meccaniche e chimiche* (Brescia, 1915).

— *L'altra guerra* (Milan, 1916).

— *Due anni e mezzo di economia di guerra nella provincia di Brescia* (Brescia, 1916).

— *La partecipazione degli operai alle imprese* (Brescia, 1918).

— *La borghesia fra due rivoluzioni* (Bologna, 1922).

— *Il costo della vita e i salari a Brescia dal 1914 al 1922* (Brescia, 1923).

CAROCCI, G. *Agostino Depretis e la politica interna italiana dal 1876 al 1887* (Turin, 1955).

— *Giolitti e l'età giolittiana* (Turin, 1971).

CASTRONOVO, V. *La stampa italiana dall'unità al fascismo* (Bari, 1970).

— *Giovanni Agnelli* (Turin, 1971).

— 'La storia economica', in *Storia d'Italia*, vol. iv (Turin, 1975).

CATALANO, F. *Potere economico e fascismo: La crisi del dopoguerra, 1919–1921* (Milan, 1964).

CATTEDRA AMBULANTE DI AGRICOLTURA. *Gli agricoltori e la guerra* (Brescia, 1915).

— *Patto colonico per la pianura bresciana* (Brescia, 1912).

CAVALLERI, O. *Il movimento operaio e contadino nel Bresciano (1878–1903)* (Rome, 1973).

Censimenti del Regno 1901, 1911, 1921, and 1931.

CESARESCO, E. M. *Lombard Studies* (New York, 1902).

CHIARINI, R. *Politica e società nella Brescia zanardelliana* (Milan, 1973).

CHIURCO, G. A. *Storia della Rivoluzione fascista* (Florence, 1929).

CIVILTÀ, D. *Il problema idroelettrico in Italia e l'attività delle Imprese Elettriche* (Rome, 1922).

CLARK, M. *Antonio Gramsci and the Revolution that Failed* (New Haven, 1977).

COCCHETTI, C. 'Brescia e sua provincia', in C. Cantù, *Grande illustrazione del Lombardo-Veneto*, vol. iii (Milan, 1858).

COLAPIETRA, R. *Napoli tra dopoguerra e fascismo* (Milan, 1962).

COLARIZI, S. *Dopoguerra e fascismo in Puglia (1919–1926)* (Bari, 1971).

COLETTI, F. *Economia rurale e politica rurale in Italia* (Piacenza, 1926).

COMINAZZI, M. *Cenni sulla fabbrica d'armi di Gardone di Valtrompia* (Brescia, 1861).

COMITATO BRESCIANO DI PREPARAZIONE. *Relazioni* (Brescia, 1916-20).

CONFALONIERI, A. *Banca e industria in Italia 1894–1906* (Milan, 1976).

— *Banca e industria in Italia dalla crisi del 1907 all'agosto 1914* (Milan, 1982).

CONSIGLIO PROVINCIALE DELL'ECONOMIA DI BRESCIA. *Svolgimento delle attività produttrici nella provincia di Brescia: Relazione statistica 1927–1928* (Brescia, 1929).

CONSIGLIO PROVINCIALE DI BRESCIA. *L'attività della Reale Commissione nel 1924* (Brescia, 1925).

CONTI, E. *Dal taccuino di un borghese* (Milan, 1946).

CORBINO, E. *Annali dell'economia italiana* (Città del Castello, 1931-8).

CORDOVA, F. *Arditi e legionari dannunziani* (Padua, 1969).

— *Le origini dei sindacati fascisti 1918–1926* (Bari, 1974).

CORNER, P. *Fascism in Ferrara 1915–1925* (London, 1975).

— 'Fascist Agrarian Policy and the Italian Economy in the Inter-war Years', in J. Davis, *Gramsci and Italy's Passive Revolution* (London, 1979).

Il Cotonificio Vittorio Olcese nelle sue vicende e nella sua attività (Milan, 1939).

CREDITO ITALIANO. *Società Italiane per Azioni: Notizie Statistiche 1914* (Milan, 1915).

— *Società Italiane per Azioni: Notizie Statistiche 1920* (Rome, 1921).

DA COMO, U. *La repubblica bresciana* (Bologna, 1926).

DE BEGNAC, Y. *Palazzo Venezia: storia di un regime* (Rome, 1950).

DE FELICE, R. *Mussolini il rivoluzionario, 1883–1920* (Turin, 1965).

— *Mussolini il fascista. I. La conquista del potere 1921–1925* (Turin, 1966).

— *Mussolini il fascista. II. L'organizzazione dello Stato fascista 1925–1929* (Turin, 1968).

— *Mussolini il Duce. I. Gli anni del consenso 1929–1936* (Turin, 1974).

— 'Primi elementi sul finanziamento del fascismo dalle origini al 1924', in *Rivista Storica del Socialismo*, viii (1964), 223-51.

— *Sindacalismo rivoluzionario e fiumanesimo nel carteggio De Ambris–D'Annunzio 1919–1922* (Brescia, 1966).

DE FELICE, R. and MARIANO, E. *Carteggio D'Annunzio–Mussolini (1919–1938)* (Milan, 1971).

DE GRAND, A. *Italian Fascism: Its Origins and Development* (Lincoln, 1982).

— *The Italian Nationalist Movement and the Rise of Fascism in Italy* (Lincoln, 1978).

DE GRAZIA, V. *The culture of consent: Mass organization of leisure in fascist Italy* (Cambridge, 1981).

DE MADDALENA, A. 'L'economia bresciana nei secoli XIX e XX', in *Storia di Brescia*, vol. iv (Brescia, 1964).

DE ROSA, G. *Storia del movimento cattolico in Italia* (Bari, 1966).

DEL CARRIA, R. *Proletari senza rivoluzione* (Milan, 1970).

DELLA PERUTA, F. *Democrazia e socialismo nel Risorgimento* (Rome, 1965).

DETTI, T. *Serrati e la formazione del Partito Comunista Italiano* (Rome, 1972).

Diario Guida: Brescia e Provincia (Brescia, 1905).

EINAUDI, L. *La condotta economica e gli effetti sociali della guerra italiana* (Bari and New Haven, 1933).

FABBRI, L. G. 'Crescita e natura delle Casse Rurali Cattoliche', in *Quaderni Storici*, xii (1977), pp. 789-803.

FABBRO, M. *Fascismo e lotta politica in Friuli 1920–1926* (Padua, 1974).

FACCHINI, F. *Alle origini di Brescia industriale: Insediamenti produttivi e composizione di classe dall' Unita al 1911* (Brescia, 1980).

FAINI, M. *La marcia su Brescia 1919–1922: Nascita e avvento del fascismo bresciano* (Brescia, 1975).

FANO, E. 'Problemi e vicende dell'agricoltura italiana tra le due guerre', in *Quaderni Storici*, x (1975), pp. 468-96.

FAPPANI, A. *La guerra sull'uscio di casa: Brescia e bresciani nella prima guerra mondiale* (Brescia, 1969).

— *Guido Miglioli e il movimento contadino* (Rome, 1978).

FARINACCI, R. *Squadrismo: Dal mio diario della vigilia 1919–1922* (Rome, 1933).

FERRATA, M. *La Mobilitazione Industriale e il dopo guerra* (Brescia, 1918).

FONZI, F. 'Giuseppe Tovini e i cattolici bresciani del suo tempo', in *Rivista di Storia della Chiesa in Italia*, ix (1955), pp. 233-48.

FORNARI, H. *Mussolini's Gadfly: Roberto Farinacci* (Nashville, 1971).

FOSSATI, A. *Lavoro e produzione in Italia dalla metà del secolo XVIII alla seconda guerra mondiale* (Turin, 1951).

FRIED, R. C. *The Italian Prefects: A Study in Administrative Politics* (New Haven, 1963).

FRUMENTO, A. *Imprese lombarde nella storia della siderurgia italiana: Il contributo dei Falck* (Milan, 1952).

GERMINO, D. L. *The Italian Fascist Party in Power: A Study in Totalitarian Rule* (Minneapolis, 1959).

GERSCHENKRON, A. *Economic Backwardness in Historical Perspective* (Cambridge, Mass., 1966).

GHIDOTTI, F. *Palazzolo 1890: Notizie sull'agricoltura, l'industria e il commercio e sulle condizioni fisiche, morali, intellettuali, economiche della popolazione* (Palazzolo sull'Oglio, 1969).

GIARRATANA, A. *L'industria bresciana ed i suoi uomini negli ultimi 50 anni* (Brescia, 1957).

— 'L'industria nei secoli XIX e XX', in *Storia di Brescia*, vol. iv (Brescia, 1964).

GINO, C. *Problemi sociologici della guerra* (Bologna, 1921).

GIOLITTI, G. *Memoirs of My Life* (New York, 1973).

GIUSTI, U. *Le correnti politiche italiane attraverso due riforme elettorali dal 1909 al 1921* (Florence, 1922).

GNAGNA, A. *La Provincia di Brescia e sua Esposizione, 1904* (Brescia, 1905).

GNOCCHI-VIANI, O. *Dieci Anni di Camere del Lavoro* (Bologna, 1899).

GOLDSMITH, O. *Essays* (London, 1766).

GOLZIO, S. *L'industria dei metalli in Italia* (Turin, 1942).

GRAMSCI, A. *Selections from the Prison Notebooks* (London, 1971).

GRANATA, I. 'Storia nazionale e storia locale: Alcune considerazioni sulla problematica del fascismo delle origini (1919-1922)', in *Storia Contemporanea*, xi (1980), pp. 503-44.

GREENFIELD, K. R. *Economics and Liberalism in the Risorgimento: A Study of Nationalism in Lombardy, 1814–1848* (Baltimore, 1934).

GREGOR, A. J. *Italian Fascism and Developmental Dictatorship* (Princeton, 1979).

GRIFONE, P. *Il capitale finanziario in Italia* (Turin, 1971).

GUARNERI, F. *Battaglie economiche tra le due grandi guerre* (Milan, 1953).

GUERRINI, L. *Organizzazioni e lotte dei ferrovieri italiani* (Florence, 1957).

L'Inizio e sviluppo del sindacalismo fascista nella provincia di Brescia (Brescia, 1925).

ISTITUTO CENTRALE DI STATISTICA. *Comuni e loro popolazione ai censimento dal 1861 al 1951* (Rome, 1960).

ISTITUTO CENTRALE DI STATISTICA E MINISTERO PER LA COSTITUENTE. *Compendio delle statistiche elettorali italiane dal 1848 al 1934* (Rome, 1946).

L'Italia economica nel 1873 (Rome, 1874).

JACINI, S. *La proprietà fondiaria e le popolazioni agricole in Lombardia* (Milan, 1856).

JACINI, S. *Storia del partito popolare italiano* (Milan, 1951).

JEMOLO, A. C. *Chiesa e Stato in Italia negli ultimi cento anni* (Turin, 1948).

KING, B. and OKEY, T. *Italy To-Day* (London, 1901).

LANARO, S. *Nazione e lavoro: Saggio sulla cultura borghese in Italia 1870–1925* (Venice, 1979).

LOTTI, L. *La settimana rossa* (Florence, 1965).

LUMBROSO, G. *La crisi del fascismo* (Florence, 1925).

LUSCIA, G. 'Sulla proposta di una Società Anonima Bresciana per l'industria del ferro in Valtrompia', in *Commentari dell'Ateneo di Brescia* (1865-8).

LUZZATTO, G. *L'economia italiana dal 1861 al 1914* (Milan, 1963).

LYTTELTON, A. 'Fascism in Italy: The Second Wave', in W. Laqueur and G. Mosse, *International Fascism: 1920–1945* (New York, 1966).

— *The Seizure of Power: Fascism in Italy 1919–1929* (London, 1973).

— 'Landlords, Peasants and the Limits of Liberalism', in J. Davis, *Gramsci and Italy's Passive Revolution* (London, 1979).

MACK SMITH, D. *Italy: A Modern History* (Ann Arbor, 1959).

MAESTRI, P. *L'Italia economica nel 1868* (Florence, 1868).

— *L'Italia economica nel 1870* (Florence, 1871).

MAGNI, C. *Il tramonto del feudo lombardo* (Milan, 1937).

MAIER, C. *Recasting Bourgeois Europe: Stabilization in France, Germany, and Italy in the Decade after World War I* (Princeton, 1975).

MAIONE, G. *Il biennio rosso: Autonomia e spontaneità nel 1919–1920* (Bologna, 1975).

MALATESTA, A. *I socialisti italiani durante la guerra* (Milan, 1926).

MALUSARDI, E. *Elementi di storia del sindacalismo fascista* (Genoa, 1932).

MANACORDA, G. *Il movimento operaio italiano attraverso i suoi congressi: Dalle origini alla formazione del Partito Socialista 1853–1892* (Rome, 1952).

MEDA, F. *I cattolici italiani nella prima guerra mondiale* (Verona, 1965).

MEDICI, G. *Rapporti fra proprietà, impresa e mano d'opera nell'agricoltura italiana: Lombardia* (Rome, 1932).

MELCHIORI, A. *Milizia Fascista* (Rome, 1929).

MELOGRANI, P. *Storia politica della grande guerra 1915–1918* (Bari, 1969).

— *Gli industriali e Mussolini: Rapporti tra Confindustria e fascismo dal 1919 al 1929* (Milan, 1972).

MINISTERO DELL'ECONOMICA NAZIONALE, DIREZIONE GENERALE DEL LAVORO E DELLA PREVIDENZA SOCIALE. *I conflitti del lavoro in Italia nel decennio 1914–1923* (Rome, 1924).

MINISTERO DI AGRICOLTURA, INDUSTRIA, E COMMERCIO, DIREZIONE GENERALE DELLA STATISTICA. *Notizie sulle condizioni industriali della provincia di Brescia* (Rome, 1892).

— *Statistica degli scioperi avvenuti nell'industria e nell'agricoltura durante l'anno 1901* (Rome, 1905).

— *Statistica industriale: Riassunto delle notizie sulle condizioni industriali del Regno* (Rome, 1905).

MINISTERO DI AGRICOLTURA, INDUSTRIA E COMMERCIO, UFFICIO DI LAVORO. *Le organizzazioni. I: Le agrarie* (Rome, 1912).

MOORE, BARRINGTON, Jr. *Social Origins of Dictatorship and Democracy: Lord and Peasant in the Making of the Modern World* (Boston, 1966).

MORANDI, R. *Storia della grande industria in Italia* (Bari, 1931).

MORGAN, P. 'Augusto Turati', in F. Cordova, *Uomini e volti del fascismo* (Rome, 1980).

MORI, G. *Studi di storia dell'industria* (Rome, 1967).

— 'Le guerre parallele. L'industria elettrica in Italia nel periodo della grande guerra (1914-1919)', in *Studi Storici*, xiv (1973), pp. 313-35.

MORTARA, G. *Prospettive economiche* (Città del Castello, 1921-7).

MUSSOLINI, B. *Opera Omnia* (Florence, 1951-63).

NEPPI MODONA, G. *Sciopero, potere politico e magistratura 1870/1922* (Bari, 1973).

NEUFELD, M. *Italy: School for Awakening Countries* (Ithaca, 1961).

NOZZOLI, G. *I ras del regime: Gli uomini che disfecero gli italiani* (Milan, 1972).

Le officine metallurgiche Togni in Brescia (Milan, 1912).

ONDEI, E. *Guiseppe Zanardelli e un trentennio di storia italiana* (Brescia, 1954).

ORGANSKI, A. F. K. 'Fascism and Modernization', in S. J. Woolf, *The Nature of Fascism* (New York, 1969).

OSTIANI, L. 'I feudatori e i buli', in *Commentari dell'Ateneo di Brescia* (1887).

PAPA, A. 'Guerra e terra 1915-1918', in *Studi Storici*, x (1969), pp. 29-45.

PARTITO NAZIONALE FASCISTA. *Il Gran Consiglio nei primi sei anni dell'era fascista* (Rome, 1929).

PEPE, A. *Storia della CGdL dalla fondazione alla guerra di Libia* (Bari, 1972).

— *Storia della CGdL alla guerra di Libia all'intervento 1911–1915* (Bari, 1971).

PIVA, F. *Lotte contadine e origini del fascismo* (Venice, 1977).

— 'Mobilitazione agraria e tendenze dell'associazionismo padronale durante la grande guerra', in *Quaderni Storici*, xii (1977), pp. 805-35.

PORTA, F. and ROVETTA, R. *L'occupazione delle fabbriche a Brescia: Settembre 1920* (Brescia, 1971).

POZZI, G. B. *La prima occupazione operaia della fabbrica nelle battaglie di Dalmine* (Bergamo, 1921).

PRATT HOWARD, E. *Il Partito Popolare Italiano* (Florence, 1957).

PRETI, L. *Le lotte agrarie nella valle padana* (Turin, 1955).

PREZZOLINI, G. *Fascism* (New York, 1927).

PROCACCI, G. *La lotta di classe in Italia agli inizi del secolo XX* (Rome, 1972).

RÉPACI, A. *Le marcia su Roma, mito e realtà* (Rome, 1963).

ROBECCHI, G. *L'industria del ferro in Italia e l'officina Glisenti a Carcina* (Milan, 1868).

ROBERTS, D. *The Syndicalist Tradition and Italian Fascism* (Chapel Hill, 1979).

ROMEO, R. *Breve storia della grande industria in Italia 1861–1961* (Rocca San Casciano, 1974).

ROSA, G. *Le condizioni economiche-morali dell'agricoltura bresciana* (Milan, 1878).

ROSENSTOCK-FRANCK, L. *L'économie corporative fasciste en doctrine et en fait: Ses origines et son évolution* (Paris, 1934).

ROSSI, C. *Mussolini com'era* (Rome, 1947).

ROSSI, E. *Padroni del vapore e fascismo* (Bari, 1966).

ROSSI, M. *Le origini del partito cattolico* (Rome, 1977).

SABBATUCCI, G. *I combattenti nel primo dopoguerra* (Bari, 1974).

SALANDRA, A. *Italy and the Great War: From Neutrality to Intervention* (London, 1932).

SALOMONE, A. W. *Italy in the Giollitian Era: Italian Democracy in the Making, 1900–1914* (Philadelphia, 1960).

SALVATORELLI, L. and MIRA, G. *Storia del fascismo: L'Italia dal 1919 al 1945* (Rome, 1952).

SALVEMINI, G. *The Fascist Dictatorship in Italy* (New York, 1967).

— *Under the Axe of Fascism* (London, 1936).

SANTARELLI, E. *Storia del movimento e del regime fascista* (Rome, 1967).

SARTI, R. *Fascism and the Industrial Leadership in Italy, 1919–1940* (Berkeley, 1971).

— 'Fascist Modernization in Italy: Traditional or Revolutionary?', in *American Historical Review*, lxxv (1970), pp. 1029-45.

— 'Mussolini and the Italian Industrial Leadership in the Battle of the Lira 1925-1927', in *Past and Present*, 47 (1970), pp. 97-112.

SAVOLDI, G. 'I primi passi del socialismo e Brescia', in *Brescia Nuova*, 30 August 1952.

SCAGNETTI, G. *La siderurgia in Italia* (Rome, 1923).

SCAPELLI, A. *Dalmine 1919* (Rome, 1973).

SCHMIDT, C. T. *The Plough and the Sword: Labor, Land, and Property in Fascist Italy* (New York, 1938).

SERENI, E. *Capitalismo e mercato nazionale in Italia* (Rome, 1966).

— *Il Capitalismo nelle campagne (1860–1900)* (Rome, 1968).

SERPIERI, A. *La guerra e le classi rurali italiane* (Bari and New Haven, 1930).

— *Studi sui contratti agrari* (Bologna, 1920).

SETON-WATSON, C. *Italy from Liberalism to Fascism: 1870–1925* (London, 1967).

SINDACATO NAZIONALE FASCISTA TECNICI AGRICOLI. *Il frumento* (Rome, 1929).

Le società idroelettriche e la recente legislazione (Brescia, 1917).

SPINI, T. *Niggeler e Kupfer S. p. A.: Filatura e tessitura di cotone 1876–1963* (Bergamo, 1963).

SPRIANO, P. *L'occupazione delle fabbriche* (Turin, 1964).

STURZO, L. *Italy and Fascismo* (London, 1926).

SUSMEL, D. *Carteggio Arnaldo–Benito Mussolini* (Florence, 1954).

TASCA, A. *The Rise of Fascism in Italy 1918–1922* (London, 1938).

TASSINARI, G. *L'influenza dello stato di guerra sulla economica di un comune montano di confine* (Brescia, 1919).

TILLY, L. 'I fatti di Maggio: The Working Class of Milan and the Rebellion of 1898', in R. Bezucha, *Modern European Social History* (Lexington, 1972).

TONIOLO, G. *L'economia dell'Italia fascista* (Bari, 1980).

TRANFAGLIA, N. *Dallo stato liberale al regime fascista: Problemi e ricerche* (Milan, 1975).

Tubi Togni. Condotti forzati 1903-1923 (Milan, 1926).

TURATI, A. *Lo spirito e le mete del fascismo* (Milan, 1926).

— *Una rivoluzione e un capo* (Rome, 1927).

— 'Il partito e i sindacati', in *Dottrina e politica fascista* (Perugia, 1930).

— *Fuori dell'ombra della mia vita: Dieci anni nel solco del fascismo* (Brescia, 1973).

TURATI, A. and BOTTAI, G. *La carta del lavoro* (Rome, 1929).

UNGARI, P. *Alfredo Rocco e l'ideologia giuridica del fascismo* (Brescia, 1963).

UVA, B. *La nascita dello stato corporativo e sindacale fascista* (Assisi, 1975).

— 'Gli scioperi metallurgici italiani del marzo 1925', *Storia Contemporanea*, i (1970), pp. 1016-17.

VAINI, M. *Le origini del fascismo e Mantova* (Rome, 1961).

VECCHIA, P. A. *Storia del fascismo bresciano 1919-1922* (Brescia, 1929).

VEZZOLI, A. *Il Partito Popolare a Brescia visto attraverso 'Il Cittadino di Brescia' 1919-1926* (Brescia, 1966).

VIGEZZI, B. *L'Italia di fronte alla prima guerra mondiale* (Naples, 1966).

VIVARELLI, R. *Il dopoguerra in Italia e l'avvento del fascismo (1918-1922). I. Dalla fine della guerra all'impresa di Fiume* (Naples, 1967).

WEBSTER, R. *Christian Democracy in Italy 1860-1960* (London, 1961).

— *Industrial Imperialism in Italy 1908-1915* (Berkeley, 1975).

YOUNG, A. *Travels in France and Italy During the Years 1787, 1788 and 1789* (London, 1915).

ZANARDELLI, G. *Notizie naturali, industriali ed artistiche della provincia di Brescia (Lettere pubblicate nel 1857 sul Giornale 'Il Crepuscolo')* (Brescia, 1904).

ZANGHERI, R. *Lotte agrarie in Italia: La federazione nazionale dei lavoratori della terra, 1901-1926* (Milan, 1960).

ZANIBELLI, A. *Le leghe 'bianche' nel Cremonese (dal 1900 al 'Lodo Bianchi')* (Rome, 1961).

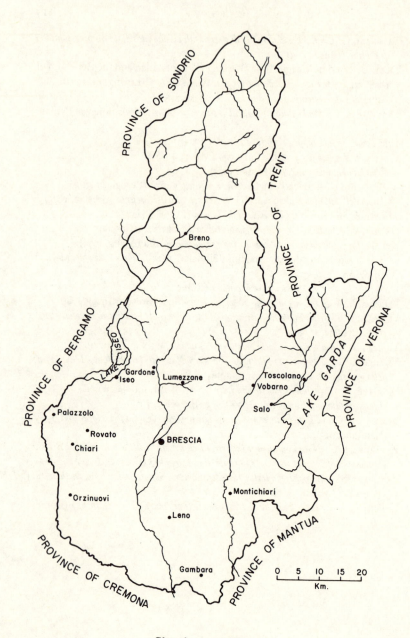

PROVINCE OF SONDRIO

PROVINCE OF TRENT

PROVINCE OF BERGAMO

LAKE ISEO

Breno

Gardone
•Iseo

Lumezzane

Toscolano
•Vobarno

LAKE GARDA

PROVINCE OF VERONA

•Palazzolo

Salo

•Rovato

•Chiari

●BRESCIA

•Orzinuovi

•Montichiari

•Leno

PROVINCE OF MANTUA

PROVINCE OF CREMONA

Gambara

0   5   10   15   20
Km.

1.   Sketch map of Brescia

2. Brescia and the rest of Italy

Index